Endorsements

This book is a joy to read! It offers a pragmatic and accessible analysis of the role of mindfulness, tranquility, and the *brahmavihāra*s in the early discourses of the Buddha. Bhikkhu Anālayo tackles controversial topics: Can insight be practiced during meditative absorption? Are the *brahmavihāra*s liberating? He presents a multitude of relevant ways mindfulness can be understood, inspiring readers to expand their views. His clear and thought-provoking explorations of these questions will help readers explore how the Buddha's teachings lead to liberation; a purpose as relevant for today's world as it was in ancient India.

Shaila Catherine

Early Buddhist Meditation Studies is another example of Bhikkhu Anālayo's keen intellect, far-ranging scholarship, and deep meditation practice illuminating the nuances and controversies of four areas of contemporary Buddhist dialogue. Given the current widespread use of the term *mindfulness,* of particular interest to the general reader will be his careful and systematic elaboration of how this now popular word is being used with different and complementary meanings. And for those interested in delving deeper into the relationship between insight and tranquility, the experience and application of *jhāni*c absorption, and the role of the *brahmavihāra*s on the path of liberation, this wonderful collection will help to clarify and deepen our understanding. This book is a dharma treasure of scholarship and discernment, opening up new possibilities for our own practice and realization.

Joseph Goldstein

Also by Anālayo:

Buddhapada and the Bodhisattva Path
A Comparative Study of the Majjhima-nikāya
Compassion and Emptiness in Early Buddhist Meditation
Dīrgha-āgama Studies
The Dawn of Abhidharma
Ekottarika-āgama Studies
Excursions into the Thought-world of the Pāli Discourses
The Foundation History of the Nuns' Order
The Genesis of the Bodhisattva Ideal
Madhyama-āgama Studies
Mindfully Facing Disease and Death
Perspectives on Satipaṭṭhāna
Saṃyukta-āgama Studies
Satipaṭṭhāna, the Direct Path to Realization
Vinaya Studies

Early Buddhist Meditation Studies

Anālayo

Published by
Barre Center for Buddhist Studies
Barre, Massachusetts
USA

https://www.bcbsdharma.org/

ISBN-13:
978-1540410504

ISBN-10:
1540410501

As an act of Dhammadāna, bhikkhu Anālayo has waved royalty payments for this book.

Cover design by Aldo Di Domenico,
Kanaganahalli, courtesy of Christian Luczanits.

Contents

Foreword

In this book, Bhikkhu Anālayo brings together several papers he has published in an integrated whole that deals with the early Buddhist discourses' accounts of meditation. In particular, it deals with: mindfulness, the gradual path from sense-restraint up to the fourth *jhāna*, the first and second *jhāna*s, the formless states, compassion as found in teaching, and the *brahmavihāra*s.

Throughout, the author's method is a historical-critical one, which compares different versions of the same or related texts, as found in the first four Pāli *Nikāya*s and the Chinese *Āgama*s, along with some Sanskrit survivals and Tibetan texts. While all the extant texts have been to some degree shaped by their process of arrangement, transmission, and sometimes translation, this method has the potential to offer many valuable insights. It produces the nearest we can get to different people's recollections of the same ancient Dharma talk. For a talk given nowadays, there would clearly be variations in people's memories and even notes. But comparing these would enable one to get a richer overview of what was said, along with enabling one to identify certain points that were open to different interpretation by the original audience, and those who transmitted their version.

Anālayo rightly points out that mindfulness in the early texts can have an aspect of evaluation, for example as regards aspects of the body, and feeling as 'worldly' or 'unworldly'. Contemplation of *asubha* or 'not beautiful' aspects of the body's anatomy, though, are intended to counteract sensual attachment and lead to a balanced attitude free of both attachment and aversion. Mindfulness can also involve some application of concepts, used in labeling observed qualities.

Examining the claims of some scholars that tranquillity (*samatha*) and insight (*vipassanā*) were actually competing and incompatible paths, Anālayo adroitly refutes them. He also argues that, while *samatha* and *vipassanā* tended to be assigned to separate stages of the path by the time of the *Visuddhimagga*, in the early texts they are more closely linked as complementary aspects of meditative cultivation.

Anālayo explores how parallel texts vary in what practices and states they include when describing the path from sense-restraint up to the imperturbability of the fourth *jhāna*. He argues that:

> Given that variations are found within a single reciter tradition and even within a single discourse collection, it seems clear that path descriptions were not considered as having to conform to one single model … with complementary perspectives standing side by side, the tendency to latch on to one particular list as the only right way is deprived of a foundation. After all, any description of the gradual path of training is simply a map, whose purpose is to provide guidelines to be put into practice in the particular teaching context within which it evolved. In this way, variations in the gradual-path accounts are like various fingers pointing to the moon. Attention should not be paid to a particular finger, but to the direction in which it points, in order to see the moon for oneself. (p. 89f)

Thus, factors such as sense-restraint, moderation in eating, and wakefulness are cumulative, while those such as seclusion, suspension of the hindrances, the *jhāna* sequence, and imperturbability are sequential. The cumulative factors could be included or omitted according to context and need in a particular *sutta*.

Anālayo explores the similes used for the four *jhāna*s, respectively: working bath powder into a ball of soap, a spring welling up, lotuses pervaded by water, and being covered by a cloth. He brings these alive, with the first three representing

> a progressive deepening of concentration reached at this juncture: from active kneading with water to form a soap ball (illustrative of the joy and happiness of the first absorption), via the welling up of spring water (illustrative of the experience of joy and happiness of the second absorption), to total immersion in water (representing the stable happiness of the third absorption, which is without the mental motion of joy). (p. 77 note 32)

In exploring early description of the *jhāna*s, Anālayo examines how far these envisage whether one in *jhāna* can: have some awareness of the body, practice insight into impermanence, or hear sounds. He argues, plausibly, that there can be some awareness of the body in *jhāna*, such as it being pervaded by joy and happiness, albeit in a state of mental unification in which

> body and mind … become complementary facets of a single mode of experience … [including] a refined sense of the presence of the body, even though this would be … different from ordinary sensory bodily experience. (p. 56)

As he sees *jhāna* as a state of full and continuous mental unification on one object, though, Anālayo sees contemplation of impermanence as requiring a meditator to leave *jhāna*, though he or she may still be in a state of concentration close to it. This is certainly plausible.

As regards whether sounds can be heard in *jhāna*, he argues that this is not possible. I personally think that *some* awareness of sounds may still be possible. This does, though, raise the issue of whether the early texts see '*jhāna*' a) as restricted to moments when the mind is wholly locked onto one object alone, as in the commentaries, or b) as also including states close to this. Anālayo argues for a), but he does allow that

> different understandings of the nature of absorption can arise. In fact the dividing line between absorption and levels of concentration bordering on absorption is not always easily drawn in subjective experience … such a distinction has considerable practical significance, simply because overestimating the absorbed condition of the mind that one has been able to reach could lead to underestimating the potential of going deeper. (p. 146)

Anālayo argues, I think correctly, that the *arūpa* (immaterial, formless) states were not later additions to the descriptions of meditative practice in the early texts, but were seen as states that could make a valuable contribution to the path, albeit falling short, on their own, of its goal. The fact that it is said that the Buddha, after his awakening, first thought of his two teachers of *arūpa* states as ripe for understanding his discovery shows how he valued the states which they taught.

In discussing compassion, Anālayo argues that its typical non-meditative expression in the early texts is teaching the Dharma. In contrast with how compassion came to be seen in the developed Mahāyāna,

> in fact the early discourses do not mark off the Buddha's compassion as something substantially distinct from the compassion of any among his arahant disciples … it also does not even appear to have been considered the result of aeons of intentional cultivation. The *Ariyapariyesanā-sutta* and its *Madhyama-āgama* parallel present the quest of the

> Buddha-to-be for awakening as being motivated entirely in terms of wishing to liberate himself. (p. 181)

Indeed,

> texts that reflect beginning stages in the development of the full-fledged bodhisattva ideal ... give the impression that the compassionate wish to save living beings was not a central factor in the early stages of the arising of the bodhisattva ideal, the main driving force rather being the wish to be equal to the Buddha. The compassionate intent to save all living beings appears to have taken a central role in the conception of the bodhisattva ideal only at a subsequent stage of development.
>
> This development had its appeal not only in the Mahāyāna traditions, but also in the Theravāda tradition, where the aspiration to become a Buddha in the future is well attested in texts and inscriptions. This in turn makes it clear that the term Hīnayāna is not applicable to the Theravāda tradition.
>
> In fact there seems to be no evidence that a Hīnayāna tradition, school, or institution ever existed anywhere throughout the history of Buddhism ... in sum, the arahants depicted in the early Buddhist texts teach out of compassion, just like the Buddha, whose compassionate activity in this respect is not yet seen as the result of an intentional cultivation of compassion over a long series of past lives. (p. 183f)

Just as Anālayo argues that the *arūpa* states were not a *later addition* to the meditative path of the early texts, but a valued *part* of it, he argues that the *brahmavihāra*s were not seen as able to encompass the *whole* path, leading to arahantship on their own, but were also valued *parts* of the path.

Overall, readers will find this a fascinating and thought-provoking book that informs, illuminates, and challenges. It is a rich resource that enables both scholars and meditators to reflect more deeply on issues relating to meditation in early Buddhism and how ideas on this have subsequently evolved.

Peter Harvey

Introduction

The cover of this book shows a detail from a relief that stems from the recently excavated Kanaganahalli *stūpa* complex in Karnataka. The depiction in the relief of acrobats performing together seems to correspond to the acrobat simile found in the *Sedaka-sutta* of the *Saṃyutta-nikāya* and its parallels, a suggestion corroborated by the inscription.[1] The simile describes the need of two acrobats to make sure they protect themselves as well as the other in order to be able to perform well. The conclusion drawn by the Buddha is as follows in the Pāli version:[2]

> Monastics, [thinking] 'I will protect myself', *satipaṭṭhāna* should be practiced. [Thinking] 'I will protect others', *satipaṭṭhāna* should be practiced. Monastics, protecting oneself one protects others, protecting others one protects oneself.
>
> Monastics, how does protecting oneself protect others? It is by developing, cultivating, and making much [of *satipaṭṭhāna*]. Monastics, in this way protecting oneself protects others.
>
> Monastics, how does protecting others protect oneself? It is by patience, harmlessness, and *mettā*. Monastics, in this way protecting others protects oneself.
>
> Monastics, [thinking] 'I will protect myself', *satipaṭṭhāna* should be practiced. [Thinking] 'I will protect others', *sati-*

---

[1] On the identification of the simile see Anālayo 2015e: 318 note 20, based on the inscription published by Nakanishi and von Hinüber 2014: 106: *lakhako m(e)yakathālikā*, an identification with which Oskar von Hinüber in a personal communication agreed.

[2] SN 47.19 at SN V 169,11 to 169,24; for a study of the parallel versions see Anālayo 2015e: 311–332 and for a translation of the relevant portion from SĀ 619 below p. 201f.

> *paṭṭhāna* should be practiced. Monastics, protecting oneself one protects others, protecting others one protects oneself.

The Kanaganahalli relief, which to my knowledge is the only surviving instance in Indian art of a portrayal related to this simile, helps to picture how the two acrobats perform together. Although I do not have the rights to reproduce a photograph of the complete relief, the drawing on the next page shows the most important aspects of the performance by the acrobats, leaving aside spectators and drummers depicted in the rest of the relief.[3]

The acrobat below carries a belt over the shoulder that would have served as padding for the pole. He stands with legs widely apart so as to provide a firm foundation. Another acrobat can be seen climbing up the pole, using his companion as a ladder. The top of the pole has a crosspiece, which would have served for performing the final part of the acrobatic feat. The relief also shows what at first sight appears to be yet another acrobat who seems to be somersaulting on the crosspiece.[4] This might well be the same acrobat as the one who is climbing up, in line with a standard procedure in pictorial depiction to portray successive episodes in a single image.[5] On this interpretation, the relief would show two aspects of the same acrobatic feat: climbing up to the top of the pole and then doing a somersault from there to come back down to earth.

---

[3] Courtesy Monika Zin. A photograph of the entire relief can be found in Poonacha 2011: 392.

[4] Poonacha 2011: 268f suggests that this acrobat has the crosspiece "hooked to his waist girdle" and swings downwards from it. Yet to do so would be impossible, as the pole stands on the shoulder of the acrobat below. It would immediately tip over if it were to carry weight on one side only.

[5] On this tendency see Schlingloff 1981; in fact the textual sources speak of two acrobats only, not of three.

The theme of balance, central to the textual descriptions, relates to the combined need of the acrobats to perform in harmony and maintain the pole in balance. For one acrobat to climb up and be standing on the shoulders of the other already requires a well-timed cooperation of both. During actual performance, for each of the two to know when exactly the next actions will take place, music might take the role of setting a rhythm for the different steps to be executed. This would explain the role of the drummers shown in the complete relief.

Although musicians are not mentioned in the texts, this could simply be because the issue at stake is the cooperation of the two acrobats. In fact, even spectators are not explicitly mentioned, yet these must be present, otherwise it would not make sense for the two acrobats to be discussing how best to perform so as to gain wealth.

Throughout the performance, the lower acrobat who carries the pole on his shoulders needs to keep adjusting his position in line with whatever minor movements the other acrobat makes while up on the pole. The upper acrobat needs to be very careful not to make any move that will upset the precarious balance of the pole on the shoulder of his companion. Clearly, both acrobats have to keep their own balance, and with equal clarity both have to take care of the other in order to perform well.

Their successfully undertaken acrobatic feat well illustrates the intrinsic balance of early Buddhist meditation in the way this is described in the Pāli discourses and their *Āgama* parallels.

These early discourses, which according to tradition were spoken by the Buddha and his disciples, have come down to us as part of the scriptural collections of various Buddhist schools. Although this material has been transmitted by reciter lineages that eventually came to be part of different schools, such as the Theravāda tradition, its origins are much earlier than the formation of schools. Therefore comparative study of parallel versions, preserved in a variety of languages such as Chinese, Pāli, Sanskrit, and Tibetan, offers a window on the earliest stages in the development of Buddhist teachings on meditation, inasmuch as these have left their traces in texts.

In other monograph studies, I have employed this type of source material to explore the topics of *satipaṭṭhāna*,[6] compassion and emptiness,[7] how to face disease and death,[8] and recollection of the Buddha.[9] By way of complementing these studies, in the present book I have put together revised shorter or longer extracts from previously published articles that in one way or another are relevant to the topics of mindfulness, the path to awakening, the nature of absorption attainment, and the *brahmavihāra*s.[10] The overall trajectory from mindfulness to *brahmavihāra* in these four topics is intended to reflect these two central qualities in the Buddha's advice after delivering the simile of the acrobats, where mindfulness features in the form of the four *satipaṭṭhāna*s and the *brahmavihāra*s underlie the qualities of patience, harmlessness, and *mettā*. The theme of balance conveyed by this simile is also of relevance to my exploration, since starting with the second chapter I argue that in early Buddhist thought tranquillity and insight are not two distinct and competing paths or techniques of meditative culture, but rather two qualities to be brought into balance and cultivated in conjunction in order to proceed to awakening.

---

[6] Anālayo 2013b and 2014d; on the same topic from the viewpoint of the Pāli version see Anālayo 2003 and 2015g.

[7] Anālayo 2015c.

[8] Anālayo 2016f.

[9] Anālayo 2017c.

[10] The relevant publications are Anālayo 2013a, 2014b, 2014e, 2014g, 2015a, 2015d, 2015f, 2016a, 2016b, 2016d, 2016g, and 2016h.

In order to clarify my position in this respect, I need to survey relevant publications in some detail and point out what I perceive as their respective shortcomings. Such discussions might at times be of less attraction to readers who come to this book with a keen interest in actual practice, catering for which is a central concern of mine in the following pages. Nevertheless, I hope that even from a practice-oriented viewpoint it would be of value to follow such discussions, as they can bring home the need to adopt the proper methodology when interpreting the early discourses as guides for one's own meditation practice.

Instead of approaching this material with preconceived ideas and then somewhat arbitrarily deciding that whatever corresponds to these ideas must be early and what conflicts with them must be late, a relative chronology of passages among the early discourses is best based on a comparative study of the parallel versions. Here a basic principle is that agreement between parallels points to probable earliness,[11] and disagreement between them requires contextualization in order to be able to decide which might be earlier. Such a procedure can help to minimize the impact of subjective bias when evaluating the teachings found in the early discourses.

By way of concluding this introduction, I wish to express my gratitude to all those who commented on the various papers that form the basis of this book and, for permission to reprint, to the editors responsible for articles reproduced in full in this publication.

---

[11] The principle that parallelisms point to a common early core has been questioned by Schopen 1985; for a critical reply see Anālayo 2012b.

Mindfulness

Introduction

In the present chapter I explore aspects of the early Buddhist conception of mindfulness. I begin by taking up the need to give due recognition to the fact that there are different conceptions of mindfulness in various Buddhist traditions as well as in modern clinical usage, and then briefly delineate key features of the early Buddhist notion of mindfulness. Then I turn to the relation of mindfulness to memory. After that I take up the practice of mindfulness of breathing, in particular in relation to the need to maintain mindfulness during everyday activities, and mindfulness of the body. The final topic I examine in this chapter is the early Buddhist attitude toward the body.

Defining Mindfulness

A survey of research on meditation, prepared for the U.S. Department of Health and Human Services in 2007, came to the rather disconcerting conclusion that

> scientific research on meditation practices does not appear to have a common theoretical perspective and is characterized by poor methodological quality. Firm conclusions on the effects of meditation practices in healthcare cannot be drawn based on the available evidence. Future research on meditation practices must be more rigorous in the design and execution of studies …
>
> [In particular] specific attention must be paid to developing definitions for these [meditation] techniques that are both conceptually and operationally useful. Such definitions are a prerequisite for scientific research …

> [In the case of mindfulness practices] general descriptions of mindfulness vary from investigator to investigator and there is no consensus on the defining components or processes.[1]

This finding points to a need to invest more time in clarifying the conceptual models that underpin research into the effects of mindfulness practice.[2] Although there are excellent operational definitions of mindfulness that capture the modern-day clinical perspective on this particular mental quality,[3] understandings of mindfulness, and even more so of its practice in the various Buddhist meditation traditions, are best based on clearly acknowledging that there is a plurality of conceptions of mindfulness.

The theoretical construct of mindfulness and the practices informed by this notion have gone through considerable development during nearly 2,500 years in the history of Buddhist thought, making it practically impossible to speak of "Buddhist mindfulness" as if this were a monolithic concept.

Moreover, a proper assessment of any specific form of mindfulness needs to be based on a study that takes into account all extant traditions pertaining to a particular historical period, instead of uncritically relying on a certain school or line of textual transmission just because that happens to be the

---

[1] Ospina et al. 2007: v, 209, and 32.

[2] Baer 2011: 245 notes that a basis for measuring the effects of mindfulness "is to develop a detailed description of the variable to be measured … this step is uniquely challenging in the case of mindfulness … [as] numerous definitions and descriptions of mindfulness are available." Schmidt 2011: 24 comments that "what we see today is that the meaning of mindfulness is more and more diluted the more popular mindfulness becomes."

[3] See, e.g., Bishop et al. 2004.

one with which one is personally familiar or in which one has received instructions.

Hence, as a contribution to deepening our understanding of the theoretical foundations of the multiple "mindfulnesses" (plural), found in the Buddhist traditions, in the present chapter I take up the notion of mindfulness as reflected in the historically earliest stages of Buddhist thought that is accessible to us through textual records.

Examining what the early Buddhist discourses found in the Pāli *Nikāya*s and their *Āgama* parallels have to say on mindfulness enables one to ascertain continuities as well as discontinuities vis-à-vis the notion of mindfulness one is accustomed to from personal practice or research. Such examination might even open up new avenues for research into the significance and effects of its clinical usage as well as its cultivation in actual meditation practice.

Regarding the early Buddhist conception of mindfulness, a point worthy of note is that the instructions for *satipaṭṭhāna* meditation make use of conceptual labels to facilitate recognition. The actual instructions for contemplation of feelings or of states of mind, for example, use direct speech to formulate the conceptual labels to be used when practicing.[4] In the case of a mind with anger, for instance, the task is to know a mind with anger as being "a mind with anger".[5] This unmistakably envisions that *satipaṭṭhāna* meditation involves the use of concepts. A practice like the labeling technique employed in the Mahāsi tradition does in this respect seem to reflect quite well what the early discourses suggest actual practice to have been about.

[4] See the discussion in Ñāṇaponika 1968/1986: 13.

[5] For a translation of the instructions in the *Satipaṭṭhāna-sutta* and its discourse parallels see Anālayo 2013b: 142f.

This in turn implies that a notion of mindfulness as requiring a non-conceptual state of mind, found in some other Buddhist traditions, involves a different conception of the nature of mindfulness.[6] The same holds for the notion of mindfulness as a non-dual mental quality.[7]

Now early Buddhist thought does seem to recognize the possibility of non-dual forms of mindfulness. This would be the case during the experience of meditative absorption, where mindfulness manifests in a particularly pure form in the fourth absorption.[8] Yet the meditative practice of being mindful of feelings or a mental state of anger, mentioned above, does not involve a non-dual form of awareness. This in turn implies that, although there is a place for non-dual forms of mindfulness in the context of deepening absorption, such a form of mindfulness is only one aspect of the types of mindful meditation practices required to progress to liberation.

The early Buddhist conception of mindfulness also differs from its Theravāda counterpart. Mindfulness constructs in this tradition are often based on a theory of mind-moments and a definition of mindfulness as invariably wholesome.[9] As a result

---

[6] Bodhi 2011: 28 points out that, from the viewpoint of the early discourses, "it is … hard to see how mindfulness can be essentially non-conceptual and non-discursive."

[7] For a discussion of non-dual mindfulness see Dunne 2011.

[8] According to the standard description of the fourth absorption, this state of mind is characterized by purity of mindfulness together with equanimity; see, e.g., MN 19 at MN I 117,16 and its parallel MĀ 102 at T I 589c14. For a survey of the closely similar descriptions of this state in various texts see Meisig 1990: 547.

[9] Olendski 2011: 61 explains that, from the perspective of later Theravāda tradition, "as a universal wholesome factor, mindfulness is exclusive of restlessness, delusion and all other unwholesome states, and cannot co-arise with these in the same moment."

of this doctrinal setting, mindfulness is held to be incapable of coexisting with the presence of a defilement in the same state of mind.[10]

The perspective afforded by the early discourses gives a different impression, as these clearly distinguish between right and wrong forms of mindfulness. Mindfulness can be classified as "right" when it operates from within the perspective of the four noble truths, a perspective that can fulfill the role of right view as a precursor to the noble eightfold path. In other words, mindfulness needs to be part of a mode of behavior or form of practice that leads to diminishing the cause of *dukkha* in oneself and others in order to be directed 'rightly'.

In contrast, when mindfulness comes in conjunction with unwholesome actions and intentions, it will have to be qualified as going in the 'wrong' direction, as it lacks the fundamental insight that each of us builds his or her own affliction and that continuing to do so is bound to lead to an increase of *dukkha* for ourselves and others.

Besides allowing for forms of mindfulness that are "wrong" and thus unwholesome, the early Buddhist discourses also point to a possible coexistence of mindfulness and unwholesome mental qualities. This becomes evident in the instructions given for contemplation of the hindrances as a *satipaṭṭhāna* practice, for instance, which clearly speak of being aware of the presence of a hindrance like sensual desire or anger within one's own mind in the present moment.[11] The

---

[10] Olendski 2011: 64 notes that according to the Theravāda model "one cannot be angry and mindful at the same moment, so at whatever point true mindfulness arises the actual anger is already banished."

[11] This holds for MN 10 at MN I 60,11 and its counterpart in MĀ 98 at T I 584a24. The instructions in EĀ 12.1 just mention the hindrances; for a discussion of this difference see Analayo 2013b:

task here is to know whether sensual desire or anger are present or absent right now, and also to know how they arise and how they are overcome.

These instructions give the impression that, from an early Buddhist perspective, mindfulness of defiled states of mind was not envisaged as merely retrospective. Instead, mindfulness appears to be seen as coexisting with an unwholesome mental state like sensual desire or anger. In fact the presence of mindfulness, in spite of its indubitable advantages, is not seen as the self-sufficient solution to a condition of anger, for example, which requires the additional cultivation of insight as well as of the appropriate remedy to arisen anger: *mettā*.[12]

Another point worth noting is that, by describing the use of conceptual labels to facilitate recognition, the instructions on *satipaṭṭhāna* implicitly show that the presence of mindfulness can coexist with an element of deliberate evaluation.[13]

168f and 174f. The agreement between MN 10 and MĀ 98 also holds for instructions on contemplation of the hindrances in the *Dharmaskandha*, T 1537 at T XXVI 478b27, the *Jñānaprasthāna*, T 1544 at T XXVI 1023b29, the **Śāriputrābhidharma*, T 1548 at T XXVIII 616a20, and the *Śrāvakabhūmi*, Shukla 1973: 298,12.

[12] SN 10.4 at SN I 208,13; see also the discussion in Anālayo 2003: 52. Although the formulations in the parallel versions differ, they similarly highlight the importance of *mettā* to counter anger, see SĀ 1319 at T II 362a25 and SĀ² 318 at T II 480b15. From the perspective of the developed Theravāda theory that often underpins conceptions of mindfulness in the *vipassanā* traditions, however, the presence of mindfulness itself suffices to overcome a state of anger; see, e.g., Olendski 2011: 65f: "if the wholesome attention can be sustained moment after moment, the entire stream of consciousness becomes purified … mindfulness … is transformative precisely because the unwholesome quality … has been replaced with a wholesome attitude."

[13] I come back to this topic below p. 48.

This does not mean, however, that there is no place at all for "bare awareness" in the *Satipaṭṭhāna-sutta*.[14] Of relevance here is a part of the discourse that I have dubbed the "refrain", which shows considerable variations in the parallel versions. In what follows I focus on the Pāli discourse, on the understanding that the suggestions made in this part of my exploration do not hold in the same way for the parallel versions.[15]

In the Pāli version of the *Satipaṭṭhāna-sutta*, this refrain describes three alternative modes of practice (qualified with the conjunction *vā*, "or") and one aspect that appears to be relevant to any *satipaṭṭhāna* meditation (introduced with the conjunction *ca*, "and"), which is the need to dwell independently without clinging to anything. The first of the three apparently alternative modes of contemplation requires contemplation to be undertaken internally or externally (or both). The second speaks of contemplating arising or passing away (or both).

The third is the one germane to my present argument. It speaks of being mindful just for the sake of continuous knowing and awareness. This suggests that there is a place for bare awareness. However, this falls into place *after* an understand-

---

[14] Bodhi 2011: 27 rightly points out that "it is hard to see 'bare attention' as a valid *theoretical* description of mindfulness applicable to all its modalities." Ṭhānissaro 2012: 61 goes considerably further, arguing that "there is no role for bare attention or bare awareness on the path." His position appears to be based on considering bare awareness to be necessarily an unconditioned form of awareness; see, e.g., Ṭhānissaro 2012: 53. This need not be the case. The type of bare awareness required for progress on the path is of course a conditioned mental quality. But if one remains with such bare awareness, the conditioning of one's mind will not automatically lead to habitual reactions, which only too often are of the unwholesome type. Such bare awareness can make its contribution to liberating the mind.

[15] See the survey in Anālayo 2013b: 15–19.

ing of impermanence has been established. Once this foundational insight is in place, as far as I can see "bare awareness" can become part of a form of practice that follows the instructions given in the Pāli version of the *Satipaṭṭhāna-sutta*.

Returning to the comparative study of the early Buddhist conception of mindfulness, the discussion so far would have shown that this conception differs from how mindfulness is understood in later Buddhist traditions and also from the way it is defined in modern-day clinical usage. Needless to say, each of the existing definitions has its rationale and significance within its particular context, hence distinguishing different types of mindfulness is not meant to imply a value judgment of any kind. Drawing such distinctions is only an attempt to sharpen understanding and to clarify what type of mindfulness is being practiced or researched in a particular case. Here it would be helpful to define precisely what type of mindfulness is meant, which could be, for example, "MBSR mindfulness", or "early Buddhist mindfulness", or "*vipassanā* mindfulness", or "*rdzogs chen* mindfulness". Each of these has its own value and specific features, which in turn will influence the type of practice undertaken or the effects being researched.

Mindfulness and Memory

The standard definition of mindfulness in the early discourses describes someone who is mindful and able to recollect and remember what has been done or said long ago.[16] Although this definition establishes a relationship between mindfulness

[16] See, e.g., AN 7.63 at AN IV 111,1: *satimā hoti paramena satinepakkhena samannāgato cirakataṃ pi cirabhāsitam pi saritā anussaritā*, and its parallel MĀ 3 at T I 423a29: 常行於念, 成就正念, 久所曾習, 久所曾聞, 恒憶不忘 (not mentioned in another parallel, EĀ 39.4).

and memory, it needs to be noted right away that it does not just equate the two.

In order to contextualize this definition, I think it is helpful to turn to another recurrent distinction drawn in the early discourses, namely the difference between being with or without mindfulness. From a practical perspective this distinction is more than obvious. Having had even a brief exposure to meditation practice, one will easily appreciate that there are times when one has been mindful and others when such mindfulness was lost and one was carried away by some fantasy or other distraction.

In line with such practical experience, the distinction drawn in this way implies that, from an early Buddhist perspective, mindfulness should be considered something one has to bring into being, something that needs to be established, instead of being a quality that is a natural given of any experience.[17] This in turn implies that mindfulness cannot be identified with a mental quality that is continuously present during the normal waking life of a human being.

For example, mindfulness could not be equivalent to consciousness. Consciousness is one of the five aggregates recognized in early Buddhist thought as the main aspects of experience with which one tends to identify. Here the body furnishes the material and spatial location "where" I am, feelings provide the affective or hedonic tone of "how" I am (in terms of feeling pleasant, unpleasant, or neutral), perceptions supply the conceptual appraisal of "what" I am experiencing, formations are responsible for "why" I react to anything that happens (in the way I actually do), and consciousness is that "whereby" I experience.

---

[17] See also Anālayo 2013b: 31.

Consciousness in early Buddhist thought is not considered to be permanent, but rather stands for a flow of moments of being conscious. Nevertheless, it does stand for something that is experienced as being continuously present during the waking life of an individual. Consciousness is not something that at one moment of one's meditation session one intentionally brings into being, to stay with my earlier example, and which is then lost again at a later moment. Whether one is mindful of the present moment or caught up in day-dreaming, both experiences involve consciousness. The same applies to the other mental aggregates, such as perception. Whether one is perceptive of the object of one's meditation practice or lost in some distraction or the other, some form of perception is present.

Now in the early Buddhist analysis of experience perception stands for matching information derived through the senses (including the mind as a sixth sense) with mental concepts. This relies on having earlier learned those concepts.

My ability at this moment of writing to articulate my thinking in English and the ability of my readers to understand these thoughts rely on both of us having learned the English language at an earlier time. We need not remember now exactly when and from whom we learned the language. The skill we acquired in the past simply informs our present ability to formulate and comprehend English words and sentences. In early Buddhist thought, this type of semantic memory appears to be closely related to the functions of perception, the third of the aggregates.[18]

The circumstance that mindfulness cannot just be equated with perception is relevant for appreciating the relationship of

---

[18] Ñāṇaponika 1949/1985: 69 explains that "we can assume that ancient Buddhist psychology ascribed the main share in the process of recollecting to perception (*saññā*)."

mindfulness to memory. It puts into perspective a position taken at times, according to which mindfulness is an act of memory, in the sense of bringing memories from the past to bear on the present.[19] This proposal seems to conflate the functions of perception and mindfulness and would not work as a way of understanding the early Buddhist notion of mindfulness.

In fact the standard definition of mindfulness mentioned above does not seem to be concerned with the ability to recognize things as such, but more with what we would nowadays call episodic memory, since it speaks of being able to recollect and remember what has been done or said long ago.

A link between mindfulness and episodic memory can be seen in a supernormal ability recognized in early Buddhist thought as possible for those who have trained themselves in meditative cultivation of the mind, referred to as recollection of past lives. The standard description of the exercise of this ability in the early discourses depicts how someone comes to remember various details from several past lives, such as one's former name and appearance, the food one ate and the pleasure and pain one experienced, etc.[20] Such recollection of past lives requires the previously developed ability of attaining the fourth absorption, wherefore it relies on having acquired a

[19] This position has been taken by Ṭhānissaro 2012: 21, who proposes that "mindfulness – whether right or wrong – is a factor present in any experience where memories from the past are brought to bear on what is happening within that experience." Ṭhānissaro 2012: 76 and 150 sums up that, according to his understanding, the "establishing of mindfulness is clearly a process of bringing memory to bear on the present moment", in other words, "mindfulness is an act of memory."

[20] An example of such a description can be found in MN 4 at MN I 22,9 and its parallel EĀ 31.1 at T II 666b22; for a translation and study of EĀ 31.1 see Anālayo 2016c: 9–30.

fairly high degree of proficiency in mindfulness as well as in concentration.

However, such intentional recollection of one's own past is only one form of episodic memory. Past events of one's present life can also intrude into the mind at a time when one had rather decided to focus on another matter at hand. Succumbing to such unintentionally arisen episodic memory from the past meets with criticism in a set of verses, which recommend that one should not run after the past, but should rather try to remain in the present moment.[21]

A more specific relation to the four *satipaṭṭhāna*s can be seen in another passage that explicitly mentions memory. The passage notes that for one who has gone forth as a monastic the four *satipaṭṭhāna*s can fulfill the purpose of overcoming memories and intentions related to one's former life as a householder.[22]

These passages flesh out the observation made above regarding even a short exposure to meditation practice, where one soon enough finds out that there is quite difference between being mindful of the object of one's meditation practice and being carried away by a fantasy or distraction. Such fantasies or distractions can at times be triggered by a memory of something that happened in the past. To be engaging in such episodic memory of the past is the exact opposite of what one intended to do, namely remain mindful of the present moment.[23]

---

[21] The verse is found in MN 132 at MN III 190,20 and its parallel MĀ 167 at T I 700a15; for a comparative study of this discourse see Anālayo 2011: 755–759.

[22] MN 125 at MN III 136,15 and its parallel MĀ 198 at T I 758b11; for a translation and study of MĀ 198 see Anālayo 2012c: 395–419.

[23] Harvey 2015: 128 explains that, when "mindfulness slips … the mind becomes distracted … if one then becomes involved in a long wandering thought, there may be concentration on *this*, but no mindfulness."

In this way, although the canonical definition of mindfulness points to a relationship to episodic memory, the two cannot just be equated with each other. This would not work, as some types of episodic memory can take the form of unintentionally being caught up in memories of the past and related fantasies, which is the very opposite of being mindful.

Another approach to explaining the memory dimension of mindfulness could be to assume that the point is to remember to remain in the present moment.[24] From a practical viewpoint this is indeed what one needs to do so as to stay mindful. However, this does not help explain the standard definition of mindfulness mentioned above, since the passage in question speaks of remembering what was done or said "long ago". This description is not about the mental ability to continue doing what one just now had decided to do, corresponding to the type of remembering that is related to working memory. Instead, it rather describes remembering something that has happened a long time ago.

In fact in relation to working memory the same problem would arise as with episodic or semantic memory. None of these different types of memory can be equated with mindfulness, as each can take place when one has become distracted and mindfulness is lost. A distraction during meditation practice, although involving quite clearly a loss of mindfulness, can involve working memory just as much as it can involve episodic or semantic memory.

In this way, the idea of conceptualizing the relationship between mindfulness and memory in terms of ensuring a conti-

---

[24] In relation to mindfulness of breathing, for example, Gethin 2011: 270 formulates the main task as follows: "one has to remember that what it is one should be doing is remembering the breath."

nuity of practice by "remembering" to stay in the present, although certainly meaningful from a practical perspective, does not yet provide a solution for appreciating the significance of the standard definition of mindfulness in the early discourses.

In view of the problems with the other interpretations discussed so far, it seems to me that a preferable way of conceptualizing the relationship between mindfulness and memory, evident in early Buddhist discourse, would be in the sense that mindfulness strengthens and enhances memory, as the presence of mindfulness makes it easier to remember.[25] Such an approach avoids proposing in some way an equivalence between mindfulness and memory, which is clearly problematic. At the same time it allows for the two to be closely related to each other.

The suggestion that being mindful will make one remember better is in fact quite intuitive. This would hold for working, semantic, as well as episodic types of memory. When one is mindful in the present moment, more data related to that moment can be taken in by the mind. This provides a good foundation for later recalling that moment and its various details. In contrast, if one is absent-minded it can safely be expected that fairly little will be stored in memory. When a particular daily chore is done in autopilot mode, this can lead to being so absent-minded that later one is not even sure of having actually done it. But if such a chore is performed with mindfulness, there will be no need to check later whether one has really done it, as one remembers that one has already taken care of it.

---

[25] I briefly argued this position in Anālayo 2003: 47f, 2006a: 229, and 2013b: 30–38. Cox 1992/1993: 67 speaks of an "underlying unity and interaction between models of memory and religious praxis … [where] the contexts for the operation of *smṛti* suggested by the term *mindfulness* actually encompass the psychological functions of memory as they were understood within Indian Buddhism."

Research in cognitive psychology has confirmed that mindfulness training does enhance working memory.[26] The same also holds for episodic memory.[27] In fact mindfulness training even facilitates recalling associations experienced in the past in relation to a perceptual event.[28]

The support mindfulness can provide for episodic memory concords with the canonical description, according to which being mindful one will be able to recall what has happened or was said long ago. In this way, findings of cognitive psychology would support an interpretation of this definition as implying that mindfulness enhances the ability to remember.

The quality of mindfulness would also be of use at the moment of remembering itself, in line with the importance of attention employment in memory retrieval.[29] Due to the type of open and receptive attitude that can be cultivated with the help of mindfulness, it naturally becomes easier to access data that has been stored in one's memory on a previous occasion. This is particularly relevant at times when attempting to recover a specific piece of information by concentrating on it remains unsuccessful. Instead of trying to force one's way through to the mental record of what happened, simply remaining with an open and mindful attitude can often be the best way to allow the needed details to come to mind naturally.

In this way mindfulness can be of help both when receiving information for storage in one's personal memory bank, and when accessing such information on a later occasion. This potential would help to make sense of the relationship between mindfulness and memory established in early Buddhist dis-

---

[26] Van Vugt 2015: 197–199.

[27] Brown et al. 2016.

[28] Rosenstreich 2016.

[29] Dudukovic et al. 2009.

course, a recurrent topic to such an extent that at times the word *sati* can stand in place of remembering. From the viewpoint of the explanation I have proposed here, this would be a way of speaking about remembering by referring to the appropriate mental condition for recollection.

Besides explaining such usage, the suggested solution to the conundrum of the relationship between mindfulness and memory also helps to preserve the emphasis on being in the present moment that is so crucial for undertaking *satipaṭṭhāna* meditation. This aspect can easily be lost sight of if the relationship between mindfulness and memory is taken to imply an exact equivalence of the two and the practice of mindfulness is then conceptualized as a form of remembering of what happened earlier.

Based on having briefly explored some key features of the early Buddhist conception of mindfulness and its relation to memory, in the remainder of this chapter I turn to its actual practice in relation to the breath and the body in particular.

Mindfulness of Breathing

Instructions on the practice of mindfulness of breathing can be found in the *Ānāpānasati-sutta*, which has parallels in the *Saṃyukta-āgama* and in the Mahāsāṅghika, Mūlasarvāstivāda, and Sarvāstivāda *Vinayas*.[30] The parallel versions describe how

[30] MN 118 at MN III 82,24 to 83,19, SĀ 803 at T II 206a27 to 206b11, T 1425 at T XXII 254c14 to 255a4, T 1448 at T XXIV 32c7 to 32c21 (the instructions in the Tibetan counterpart, D 1 *kha* 62b6 or Q 1030 *ge* 58a6, are abbreviated), and T 1435 at T XXIII 8a17 to 8b2; for translations of the Chinese versions see Anālayo 2013b: 228–230 and 2016f: 245–249 (the instructions in T 1435 have already been translated by Dhammajoti 2008: 264). For variations in the sixteen-fold scheme in other texts preserved in Chinese see also

awareness of the breath can proceed through sixteen steps of practice. Regarding individual steps, they show some differences in formulation, which involve variations on which steps should be considered as involving a form of training, using expressions for the third step that at times point quite clearly to the whole body as the aim of practice, and varying on the three insight contemplations that should build on appreciation of impermanence in the last set of four steps, the last tetrad.[31]

Each of these four tetrads of practice corresponds to one *satipaṭṭhāna*.[32] The rationale given in a discourse in the *Saṃyukta-āgama* for correlating these four tetrads of mindfulness of breathing with the four ways of establishing mindfulness appears quite straightforward,[33] in that with each of these tetrads the object of contemplation is the body, feelings, the mind, and dharmas respectively. Therefore they are indeed instances of cultivating each of the four *satipaṭṭhāna*s. In this way, all of the four *satipaṭṭhāna*s can be developed with the single object of the breath, which itself is a bodily phenomenon.

Deleanu 1992: 51–52 and for a practice-related survey of the sixteen steps see Anālayo 2015h and 2016f: 229–236.

[31] For a more detailed discussion see Anālayo 2013b: 231–233 and 2016f: 242f.

[32] The suggestion by Hartranft 2011: 7 that the correlation between the four ways of establishing mindfulness and the four tetrads of mindfulness of breathing is a "later scholastic" presentation "without much personal grounding in practice" is not supported by a comparative study, as the main elements of this correlation are found similarly in the parallel version; in fact this correlation seems to me to be very much grounded in actual practice.

[33] SĀ 810 at T II 208a29, translated in Anālayo 2015e: 334–341; for a more detailed discussion of the way the Pāli version explains these correlations, which in comparison seems considerably less straightforward, see Anālayo 2013b: 234f.

To put this into practice, however, would not simply be a by-product of just being aware of the breath. Rather, to implement the sixteenfold scheme appears to require a conscious effort at broadening one's awareness which, based on having established mindfulness of the breath, proceeds to awareness of the whole physical body, of feelings, of the condition of the mind, and of impermanence, etc.

Such a mode of practice would begin by contemplating the breath and its relation to the body as a bodily phenomenon. Becoming aware of joy and happiness as effects of the calmness generated through mindfulness of breathing then becomes an instance of contemplation of feelings, which in turn leads over to awareness of the mind, gladdening, concentrating, and freeing it as a form of contemplation of the mind. Contemplation of dharmas then requires giving attention to impermanence and other related insight-perspectives.

In addition to showing general agreement in regard to the scheme of sixteen steps, the presentations in the parallel versions also make a noteworthy indication regarding the practical implementation of the entire scheme. The Mahāsāṅghika and Sarvāstivāda *Vinaya*s describe in detail how a monastic retires into seclusion to sit down and then engages in the sixteen steps of mindfulness of breathing.[34] The association with seclusion is even stronger in the Mūlasarvāstivāda *Vinaya*, as here mindfulness of breathing in sixteen steps is what the Buddha undertook during a period of two or even three months of solitary retreat.[35] The need to withdraw into seclusion is also part of the

---

[34] T 1425 at T XXII 254c12 and T 1435 at T XXIII 8a19.

[35] According to T 1448 at T XXIV 32c7 and SĀ 807 at T II 207a11, the Buddha had gone on a retreat for two months; according to SN 54.11 at SN V 326,1 and D 1 *kha* 62b3 or Q 1030 *ge* 58a3 he had done so for three months.

instructions for mindfulness of breathing in the *Ānāpānasati-sutta*, as well as in discourses in the *Saṃyukta-āgama* and the *Ekottarika-āgama*.[36] Clearly the scheme of sixteen steps for mindfulness of breathing was considered a form of meditation best undertaken in the sitting posture and in a secluded setting. This is significant insofar as the same does not hold for the four *satipaṭṭhāna*s.

Although the Pāli version of the *Satipaṭṭhāna-sutta* begins its exposition with the first tetrad of mindfulness of breathing, this is not the case for its *Madhyama-āgama* parallel and a parallel in the *Ekottarika-āgama* does not have mindfulness of breathing at all.[37] In the Pāli version of the *Satipaṭṭhāna-sutta* the practice of the first tetrad of mindfulness of breathing leads on to awareness of postures and clear comprehension of bodily activities. The postures include walking and the description of the bodily activities explicitly mentions wearing one's robes and carrying one's bowl, a wording that obviously reflects the need for a monastic to be mindful when going out to beg for food.[38] This in turn makes it clear that the introductory phrase for the practice of mindfulness of breathing as being done in the sitting posture and in seclusion does not apply to the remainder of the exposition in the *Satipaṭṭhāna-sutta*.[39]

---

[36] MN 118 at MN III 82,24, SĀ 803 at T II 206a22, and EĀ 17.1 at T II 582a13; see also SĀ 801 at T II 206a5, according to which a secluded location is greatly beneficial for the practice of mindfulness of breathing. Ps I 248,3 notes that it is not easy to develop mindfulness of breathing in the presence of noise and distraction.

[37] See the discussion in Anālayo 2013b: 45–50.

[38] MN 10 at MN I 57,7 and MĀ 98 at T I 582b26 (not mentioned in EĀ 12.1); for a translation of both passages in juxtaposition see Anālayo 2013b: 51.

[39] *Pace* Ditrich 2016: 136f, who assumes that the reference to seclusion at the outset of the instructions for mindfulness of breathing in

Although meditation in seclusion is indeed an important aspect of the practice of a monastic in general, the fact that such monastic practitioners were part of a mendicant tradition makes daily contacts with the outer world inevitable even for someone who otherwise lives in the most withdrawn manner possible.[40] It is precisely at the time of coming out of retreat and having to move into the world that mindfulness is most strongly required.

In relation to this requirement, the descriptions of mindfulness of breathing in the Mahāsāṅghika and Sarvāstivāda *Vinayas* offer another helpful indication. This comes as part of their depiction of how a monastic goes begging before retiring to a secluded spot to sit and practice mindfulness of breathing in sixteen steps. Although both versions give much space to describing the monastic's practice of sense-restraint and setting up of mindfulness, they do not refer to mindfulness of breathing at all in this context. Only when engaging in formal sitting meditation does the meditating monastic's attention turn to the breath.[41] This gives the impression that previously the monastic did not pay specific attention to the breath, and it is at this particular juncture of practice, when engaging in formal sitting meditation, that attention is to be directed to one's inhalations and exhalations.

---

the *Satipaṭṭhāna-sutta* implies that contemplation of feelings or mental states in the "external" (*bahiddhā*) mode could not be concerned with others, as due to the practitioner being in seclusion "there would be no other people to observe." A detailed discussion of internal and external mindfulness can be found in Schmithausen 2012.

[40] As far as the sources allow us to judge, a substantial number of the early Buddhist monks were living in monastic communities; in fact the nuns were required to do so by monastic law. In such a setting the practice of seclusion could only take the form of temporary withdrawal during the times appropriate for formal meditative practice, not a lifestyle of continuous and complete solitude.

[41] T 1425 at T XXII 254c14 and T 1435 at T XXIII 8a23.

The Mahāsāṅghika *Vinaya* explicitly clarifies that the form of mindfulness practice the monastic engages in when going into town is "mindfulness of the body".[42] In principle, "mindfulness of the body" could refer to any type of mindfulness practice that has some relation to the body, even mindfulness of breathing. However, given that the instructions for mindfulness of breathing explicitly mention the sitting posture, it seems fair to conclude that this is not the type of mindfulness of the body that the Mahāsāṅghika *Vinaya* has in mind.

Instead, out of the different types of body-related meditation exercises found under the heading of mindfulness of the body in the *Kāyagatāsati-sutta* and its *Madhyama-āgama* parallel, those that bear a direct relation to the situation of a monastic going begging with mindfulness concern the activities of walking and standing as part of the instructions for awareness of postures, as well as wearing one's robes and carrying one's bowl as part of the instructions for clear comprehension.[43]

These two exercises are in fact interrelated. Mindfulness established by being aware of the posture of the body naturally leads to centered and even dignified behavior when engaging in various bodily activities, to doing these with clear comprehension, which is precisely the appropriate conduct to be adopted by a monastic who goes begging. This brings me to the topic of mindfulness of the body and its relation to everyday practice.

Mindfulness of the Body

In what follows I first explore mindfulness of the body from a practical perspective and then contextualize this with other at-

---

[42] T 1425 at T XXII 254c10: 身念.

[43] MN 119 at MN III 89,25 and 90,3 and its parallel MĀ 81 at T I 555a12 and 555a19.

titudes toward the human body evident in descriptions of early Buddhist meditation.

The *Mahātaṇhāsaṅkhaya-sutta* and its parallel describe a practitioner able to handle sense-experience without reacting with likes and dislikes. The title of the Pāli version rendered in English would be the "Great Discourse on the Destruction of Craving", conveying that its subject matter is precisely about how to overcome craving, recognized in the early Buddhist analysis of existence as the chief culprit for all types of mental bondage. The parallel versions of this discourse describe a practitioner who does not react to anything experienced at the six sense-doors with desire or aversion and who dwells with "a boundless mind". In addition, and from a practical perspective this is a significant indication, the one who has such a boundless mind and is free from reacting with longing and rejecting has established "mindfulness of the body".[44]

The way to establish mindfulness envisaged in this passage stands in relation to breadth of mind, thereby conveying what I would consider a central aspect of mindfulness, namely a sense of open-mindedness. Moreover, such open-mindedness ap-

---

[44] MN 38 at MN I 270,25: *upaṭṭhitakāyasati ca viharati appamāṇa-cetaso* and its parallel MĀ 201 at T I 769c16: 立身念無量心. Polak 2011: 49 argues that this passage in MN 38 describes what happens while still being in the afore-mentioned absorption attainment. Yet, earlier MN 38 at MN I 269,2 describes a comparable situation of experience through the six sense-doors without any relation to absorption. This makes it more convincing to interpret MN 38 as implying that sensory input is experienced before or after absorption, not concomitant with it. Moreover, comparative study of MN 38 gives the impression that precisely this part of the Pāli version suffered from an error in transmission. The parallel MĀ 201 does not mention the absorptions, which appear to have made their way into MN 38 as part of an expansion of the gradual-path account; see Anālayo 2011: 255f.

pears to be based on what could be called an embodied form of mindfulness.

In other words, I suggest taking the description in the *Mahā-taṇhāsaṅkhaya-sutta* and its Chinese parallel to imply that by way of resting in embodied mindfulness one becomes able to maintain a widely open, even boundless mental attitude that remains aloof from reacting with desire and aversion to whatever is experienced via the six senses.

Needless to say, the fact that such descriptions refer to the six senses does not mean that the reference to the body, *kāya*, should be construed as having a meaning that differs from the physical body.[45] Instead, cultivation of an embodied form of mindfulness requires simply that one allow the felt sense of the body's presence to be an intentionally noticed part of the present moment's experience related to any sense-door.

This felt sense of the body's presence corresponds to what clinical psychology refers to as proprioceptive awareness. Here

[45] This has been assumed by Kuan 2008: 100, who proposes that in descriptions of six-sense-door experience the term *kāya* in *kāyasati* refers to "an individual who experiences through the six senses"; see also Kuan 2015: 271. Such passages are indeed about an individual who experiences through the six senses, and not just about a physical body bereft of the ability to experience. But being mindful of the body in the present or similar passages concerns rooting mindfulness in the physical body in order to be able to handle properly experience through any of the six sense-doors. This can be seen particularly well in a simile that compares mindfulness of the body to a strong post to which six animals are bound; see Anālayo 2013b: 55f. However much the six animals struggle to escape in this or that direction, eventually they have to lie down beside the post to which they are strongly bound. The strong post in this simile must stand for the physical body as the type of anchor for embodied mindfulness that enables handling well whatever happens at any sense-door.

the term proprioception stands for the ability to sense the positioning of one's own body and its movements without even needing to open one's eyes. It is a felt physical presence often hardly noticed.

Even right now while reading these words, some degree of proprioceptive awareness is there. If there should be a sudden event like an earthquake or if one's seat should collapse or be tipped over for some reason, this felt sense for one's bodily position would immediately come to the forefront of attention.

Properly cultivated embodied mindfulness then results in the felt sense of bodily presence being no longer overlooked, as is usual, nor being made the object of an all-out focus at the expense of everything else, such as when one suddenly loses balance. Such an embodied form of mindfulness can coexist with other tasks to be done or with cultivating practices related to meditation. It not only can coexist with them, but it can even offer substantial support to them by way of establishing a somatic anchor in the here and now that counters the tendency to distraction, a dimension of embodied mindfulness practice that has been confirmed in recent research.[46]

In order to contextualize the importance given to being "in the body" through mindfulness, in what follows I survey different perspectives on the body. I begin with negative perspectives on embodiment in early Buddhist meditation practice, exemplified in the contemplation of the anatomical parts of the body. Then I turn to neutral perspectives on the body as evident in the development of mindfulness of the body, and finally take up positive perspectives on the embodied mind experienced during progress through the meditative absorptions, where the whole body is described as filled with intense joy

---

[46] See Kerr et al. 2013.

and happiness. My purpose in what follows is to show that, from the viewpoint of actual meditation practice, these three aspects stand in a meaningful relationship to each other.

The Body in Early Buddhist Meditation

The attitude toward the body in the early Buddhist tradition has in the past often been seen as a predominantly negative one. An example of such an assessment stemming from the end of the nineteenth century would be Monier-Williams (1889/1995: 560), who contrasts the Buddhist view of the body to what he sees as a more balanced attitude toward the body in Christianity, concluding that "according to Buddhism, the body … can never be the abode of anything but evil." Hence Buddhists

> look to final deliverance from all bodily life, present and to come, as the greatest of all blessings, highest of all boons, and loftiest of all aims.

In an entry on the topic of the body in Buddhism, compiled for the *Encyclopædia of Religion and Ethics*, Bateson (1909: 759) quotes Monier-Williams and then concludes that

> emancipation from bodily form is therefore the *summum bonum* of Buddhism … the constant endeavour and ultimate hope of the Buddhist is to escape from corporeal existence.

Some sixty years later an entry written for the *Encyclopaedia of Buddhism* by Kajiyama (1972: 257), based on Bateson, again affirms that in the Buddhist tradition "the body is regarded as the origin of disgust, pain and evil, and emancipation from the body is the ideal."

In a study of the Buddhist attitude toward sexuality, Faure (1998: 32) concludes that "Buddhist deprecations of the body … aim at provoking a holy horror of sensual desire."

Recent studies of the attitude toward the body in early Buddhism have been able to show, however, that a closer inspection of the texts does not corroborate the impression of a monolithic negative evaluation of the body.

In a paper on the body in Buddhist monasticism, Collins (1997: 199) highlights that besides "the *deconstruction* and rejection of the body in meditative analysis" there is also "the *construction* of it in social behaviour as a unified and valued public object."

In other words, alongside a negative evaluation in some forms of meditation practice, a positive attitude comes to the fore when the public appearance of monastics is described, whose bodily appearance should ideally be such that it inspires those who meet them.[47]

In a monograph dedicated to the body as a physical manifestation of virtue in Buddhist texts, Mrozik (2007: 86) points out that negative evaluations of the body have their counterpart in a positive evaluation of the body as an embodiment of virtue, concluding that "there is more than one kind of body discourse in Buddhist literature."[48] An obvious example of the embodiment of virtue would in fact be the Buddha himself,[49]

---

[47] Powers 2009: 121 explains that "Buddhist monks are expected to develop a calm demeanor and to walk slowly and thoughtfully and in full understanding of their actions, looking at the ground about three feet ahead. Their dignified bearing proclaims their inner virtues."

[48] Harris 2012: 107 points out that, in the case of the Theravāda tradition in particular, "to stereotype Theravāda Buddhism as having a negative attitude to the body is to distort it. Representations of the body in Theravāda text and tradition are plural."

[49] Already Wüst 1928: 83 highlighted what he felt to be a stark contrast between the evaluation of the average body and the glorification of the body of the Buddha, "die Verherrlichung des Buddha-

who according to tradition was endowed with thirty-two bodily marks that exemplified his virtue and accomplishments.[50]

Inasmuch as early Buddhist meditation practice is concerned, however, the general opinion appears to be still along the lines of what Conze (1956: 30f) describes in a monograph dedicated to meditation in Buddhism, where he concludes that

> it is a fundamental conviction for the majority of Buddhists that the body is an unclean thing, and that it is humiliating to have one.

In what follows, I will argue that more than one kind of body discourse can be discovered in early Buddhist literature in general. Moreover, even within the very texts that deal with early Buddhist meditation practice the negative perspective is not the only one that can be discovered. In addition to this, closer inspection shows that instances of a negative evaluation have a clear purpose that has quite positive results experienced on the level of the body itself.

---

leibes, welche, in genau reziprokem Verhältnis, an Gloriole und Schmuckrede zunimmt, wie der Leib des gewöhnlichen Sterblichen zynisch herabgesetzt wird."

[50] On the thirty-two marks or some of them see, e.g., Burnouf 1852/1925, Senart 1882: 124–149, Waddell 1914/1915, Foucher 1918: 280–312, Coomaraswamy 1928, Stutterheim 1929, Banerjea 1930, Waldschmidt 1930: 270–273, Banerjea 1931a and 1931b, Kramrisch 1935, Sastri 1940: 311–314, Krishan 1966, Skilling 1992, Weber 1994: 41–44, Wimalaratana 1994, van Lohuizen-de Leeuw 1995: 163–168, Skilling 1996, Regnier 1997, Quagliotti 1998, Yamabe 1999: 216–262, Strong 2001: 41–43, Egge 2003, Zin 2003, Bollée 2005, Guang Xing 2005: 14, Dietz 2006, Nitta 2008, Sferra 2008, Anālayo 2011: 528–539, Cicuzza 2011, and Anālayo 2017a; for a survey of similar marks associated with the Jain leader Mahāvīra see Shah 1987: 95f.

A prominent and often quoted instance of a negative attitude toward the body in early Buddhism is the contemplation of its anatomical constitution as part of the practice of mindfulness of the body, such as described in the *Kāyagatāsati-sutta* and its *Madhyama-āgama* parallel.

The instructions are to review the different parts of the body in the same way as one would look at various grains. The *Kāyagatāsati-sutta* indicates that the container of the grains, mentioned in the simile, is a bag with openings at both ends.[51]

Such a bag appears to have been in use in ancient Indian agriculture for sowing, with an upper opening for receiving the seeds and a lower opening that is used as on outlet for the grains during the actual sowing in the field.[52] The idea of employing such a sowing utensil to illustrate the nature of the body might have suggested itself because of the somewhat similar nature of the body, which has an upper opening for the intake of food and a lower opening for discharging the remains after digestion.

Another term that requires further discussion is the qualification of the body as "impure", *asuci*, in the actual instructions. The usage of this term also needs to be understood within its ancient Indian context, where impurity was a term much more naturally associated with the human body than would be the case in a modern-day living situation in the West. Olivelle (2002: 190) explains that in the ancient Indian setting in general "ascetic discourse presents the body as impure in its very essence."

---

[51] MN 119 at MN III 90,19: *ubhato mukhā mūtoḷī* (B^e: *putoḷī*, S^e: *mūtolī*); for the parallel see MĀ 81 at T I 556a16.

[52] Schlingloff 1964: 33 note 10. The same simile recurs in the *Śikṣāsamuccaya*, Bendall 1902/1970: 210,8; see also the *Arthaviniścaya-sūtra*, Samtani 1971: 24,4.

Although the usage of this term appears to be in line with a general attitude to the body among ancient Indian practitioners,[53] here it is of further interest to turn to the standard recollection a monastic should undertake in relation to requisites. This recollection draws attention to how contact with one's own body dirties one's requisites.[54]

On reflection, I think, one would have to admit that this is indeed the case, as one's clothes and bedding do become dirty through use and the source of the dirt is for a great part one's own body. In other words, the idea of the body being "impure" in the sense of "unclean" is after all perhaps not just an ancient Indian cultural construct to be dismissed entirely.

Moreover, besides speaking of the body as impure, the early Buddhist discourses at times use an alternative qualification of the body as "unattractive", *asubha*, when introducing the standard description of its anatomical parts.[55] The Chinese counter-

---

[53] Hamilton 1995: 55 comments: "I suspect that 'impure', when used in connection with the body and its functions, is present in the [Buddhist] canon as the result of the Brahmanical background."

[54] See Ānandajoti 2016. This serves to contextualize the impression, as noted by Shulman 2010: 402, that the "seeing of the body as unclean … this vision of the body is strikingly negative."

[55] E.g. AN 10.60 at AN V 109,18 introduces the listing of anatomical parts as a "perception of unattractiveness" *asubhasaññā*, but then the listing itself begins with the standard phrase on reviewing impurity, *asuci*. The corresponding passage in a parallel to this discourse, preserved in Tibetan, D 38 *ka* 277a1 or Q 754 *tsi* 293b5 (translated from a Pāli original, see Skilling 1993), however, speaks in both instances of impurity, *mi gtsang ba*; for a translation see Analayo 2016f: 111. As noted by Greene 2006: 34, the qualification "impure" is not employed when the anatomical parts occur in the context of contemplation of the four elements; see, e.g., MN 28 at MN I 185,16 and its parallel MĀ 30 at T I 464c7.

part in descriptions of the body is 不淨, which is ambivalent as, even though its primary sense would be "impure", the same term can equally well render *asubha*, "unattractive".[56]

When considered within its context, the nuances conveyed by the simile of looking at various grains point to removing sensual attachment as a central thrust of the exercise. Seeing grains would not naturally call up associations of beauty, especially in the sense of being sexually attractive. Nor does the notion of purity seem particularly relevant. After all, these are just grains to be used for sowing. In this way, from the viewpoint of the simile an undertaking of this exercise to counter sensual attachment, by way of a balanced observation that is free from attraction or repulsion, fits the context well.

Independent of whether the qualification "impure" or "not beautiful" is employed for such contemplation, however, there can be little doubt that carrying out the instruction involves a purposive element of evaluation.[57] Here it is of further interest that the actual instructions do not involve the term mindfulness at all. The task is that one should "examine" the anatomical constitution of the body, the Pāli term being *paccavekkhati*. Although such examination of the anatomical parts requires evaluation and also some degree of recollection of the different parts

---

[56] Hirakawa 1997: 54 s.v. 不淨 lists *aśubha* alongside *aśuddhi* and *aśuci* as possible Sanskrit equivalents.

[57] As already pointed out by Bodhi 2011: 26 in regard to "the common interpretation of mindfulness as a type of awareness intrinsically devoid of discrimination, evaluation, and judgment", this "does not square well with the canonical texts". In fact Kabat-Zinn 2011: 291 explains that to speak of mindfulness practice as "non-judgmental does not mean … that there is some ideal state in which judgments no longer arise." The point is only to avoid habitual judgmental reactions to what is experienced.

of the body listed in the exercise, notably such evaluation and recollection is not designated as a form of mindfulness.

The underlying point could well be that through cultivating a proper understanding of the true nature of the body, mindfulness can become ever better established. "Examining" one's own body as made up of various anatomical parts that are not in themselves particularly beautiful undermines the ingrained tendency of the mind to evaluate bodies, be this one's own or those of others, in terms of their possession or lack of sexual attractiveness. This in turn makes it easier just to be "mindful" of bodies, without immediately reacting with evaluations and the type of desire and aversion that usually follow. Such an understanding conforms to the nuances of a balanced observation conveyed by the simile of the grains.

Not only the simile, but even the listing of anatomical parts itself does not consistently evoke associations of impurity. Parts like teeth, skin, and hair, which in themselves do not necessarily carry any negative associations, are mentioned alongside mucus, pus, and urine. In this way the listing appears to balance what are generally seen as aspects of bodily beauty with what is usually perceived as repulsive, driving home the fact that in the end all of these bodily parts are of the same basic nature.[58] This is quite evident in the *Madhyama-āgama* parallel to the *Kāyagatāsati-sutta*, which introduces the listing of anatomical parts with the indication that the body should be

---

[58] Hamilton 1995: 58 points out that the listing "clearly illustrates the extent to which each and every part is to be observed in the same objective light as part of the analytical meditation exercise. This is regardless of whether it is, say, a tooth or mucus or pus." For various listings of anatomical parts see the survey in Dhammajoti 2009: 250–252; on contemplation of *aśubha* see also Hayashima 1958 and Giustarini 2011.

contemplated "according to its attractive and repulsive [qualities]".[59]

Now the purpose of contemplating the anatomical constitution of the body is clearly to deconstruct the notion of bodily beauty as something sexually attractive.[60] This does not mean, however, that such contemplation has the purpose of leading to an attitude of disgust and aversion toward the body. Wilson (2004: 64) points out that, "one should not assume that Buddhists are phobic about the body", since "ultimately the outlook meditators seek is neither attraction nor revulsion but indifference." Hamilton (1995: 60f) explains that "it is nonsensical in a Buddhist context to cultivate antipathy towards the body or anything else"; instead, "what the monk is aiming for is indifference." Therefore "the earliest Buddhist attitude toward the body is neither positive nor negative; it is analytical."[61]

In this way, the deconstruction of the notion of bodily beauty by contemplating the anatomical parts needs to be evaluated

---

[59] MĀ 81 at T I 556a12: 隨其好惡. For a study of the tale of monks committing suicide after excessive contemplation of the unattractive nature of their bodies see Anālayo 2014f.

[60] This is succinctly expressed in Sn 199, which after a survey of the body in various modes concludes that "a fool, overwhelmed with ignorance, conceives it to be beautiful", *subhato naṃ maññati* (C^e and E^e: *maññatī), bālo avijjāya purakkhato.*

[61] Khantipālo 1980: 2 explains that "some of the material, concerned with bodily unattractiveness, is like a medicine which need only be taken while the disease of greed-lust is active, and afterwards may be discontinued. It is important to understand this, and not to form the mistaken impression that the Buddha advocated viewing all beauty as loathsome." Based on a study of the *Dhammapada*, Dissanayake 1993: 142 similarly comes to the conclusion that "what we see is not … the outright rejection of the body, but rather, a higher synthesis born of the possibilities as well as the limitations of the body."

within the context of actual meditation practice, where it serves as a tool especially for those who have decided to live a life of celibacy, enabling them to overcome the attraction of sensuality.

In fact the early Buddhists do not seem to have been afraid of sexuality or to have had a horror of anything sensual. A telling passage depicts a celestial bard who has the task of drawing the attention of the meditating Buddha to the fact that there are visitors from heaven who like to see him. The bard executes this task by playing his stringed instrument to accompany a song in which he compares the saints of Buddhism to the physical beauties of his beloved, which he describes with sensually alluring details. The Buddha comes out of his meditation and applauds the bard for the harmonious way he has performed.[62]

This little episode exemplifies the attitude of a fully awakened one toward sexuality. Whereas according to early Buddhism an arahant is by nature incapable of engaging in any form of sexual intercourse,[63] an arahant is similarly incapable of reacting to anything with anger or irritation. Even though the Buddha would have had little interest in the detailed description of the beauty of the woman with which the bard had fallen in love, he is clearly shown to be not at all repelled by this description, instead being able to express his appreciation of the musical performance. The balanced attitude exemplified in this episode finds its expression also elsewhere in early Buddhist texts, an example in case being their report that the

---

[62] Three versions continue with an explicit indication that the performance was related to sensual desire; see DN 21 at DN II 267,19: *imā gāthā … kāmūpasaṃhitā* (B^e and S^e: *kāmūpasañhitā*), DĀ 14 at T I 63a19: 說欲縛, and MĀ 134 at T I 633b25: 此欲相應偈.

[63] DN 29 at DN III 133,16, fragment 285v6, DiSimone 2016: 93, and DĀ 17 at T I 75b17.

Buddha had no qualms about accepting an invitation to a meal from a famous and very beautiful courtesan.[64]

Nor is the Buddha depicted as being in principle against the notion of beauty. The *Mahādukkhakkhandha-sutta* and its parallels report that the Buddha described in detail in what way a young girl can be considered to be at the height of her beauty. The undeniable gratification (*assāda*) that comes from seeing her, however, should be counterbalanced by giving attention to the inherent disadvantage (*ādīnava*), more literally the "danger", which becomes evident when the pretty girl becomes old and passes away, a time when her physical appearance will no longer be experienced as gratifying.[65]

In fact in a Pāli discourse without parallels the Buddha even eulogizes the physical beauty of a monk he sees with a string of epithets.[66]

Lack of fear of anything sensual can also be seen in the fact that, in ancient Indian art,[67] sacred Buddhist places were from

---

[64] DN 16 at DN II 95,31 and its parallels DĀ 2 at T I 13c1, T 5 at T I 163c26, T 6 at T I 179b5, and a Tibetan parallel in Waldschmidt 1951: 179,9; see also Sanskrit fragment S 360 folio 168 V1, Waldschmidt 1950: 16, which has preserved her invitation. Pitzer-Reyl 1984: 80 comments that the Buddha's attitude is remarkable in view of the general fear that ascetics have of courtesans, "wenn man die Angst der Asketen vor Kurtisanen bedenkt, so sieht man mit Erstaunen, wie frei und selbstverständlich der Buddha mit ihnen umging."

[65] MN 13 at MN I 88,28 and its parallels MĀ 99 at T I 585c27, T 53 at T I 847c25, EĀ 21.9 at T II 605c7, and T 737 at T XVII 540b14; see also T 1545 at T XXVII 117a16.

[66] SN 21.5 at SN II 279,1: *abhirūpo dassanīyo pāsādiko paramāya vaṇṇapokkharatāya samannāgato*; translated by Bodhi 2000: 717 as "handsome, good-looking, pleasing to behold, possessing supreme beauty of complexion". This forms the physical counterpart to the mental beauty of this monk, who was an arahant.

the earliest times adorned with depictions of sensually aroused women that embrace trees (*sālabhañjikā*).[68] In continuity of this tendency, a cave painting portrays amorous couples just below a row of seven Buddhas together with Maitreya.[69] Those responsible for early Buddhist art evidently did not have "a holy horror of sensual desire".

In sum, early Buddhist meditation on the anatomical constitution of the body is clearly aimed at deconstructing the notion of bodily beauty as something sexually attractive, in order to enable one to overcome sensual desire and be able to progress on the path to total liberation from desire and aversion. This does not in itself imply a total rejection of the body in early Buddhist meditative discourse, however, nor does it necessarily come accompanied by an attitude of disgusted horror toward anything sensual.

In fact a neutral attitude toward the body comes to the fore with mindfulness of the body in action, exemplified by the four postures of walking, standing, sitting, and reclining. This way of developing mindfulness in regard to the body provides a mode of ensuring continuity of meditation practice outside of the formal sitting posture. As mentioned above, an actual undertaking of this exercise can involve a form of proprioceptive awareness, whereby one is aware of the whole body in its various postures. Needless to say, such an embodied form of mind-

---

[67] Olivelle 2002: 197 sums up that "India may be the land of ascetics, but it is also home to some of the best and most explicit erotic sculpture, art, and literature the world has known."

[68] See, e.g., plates 146 to 150, etc., in Agrawala 1983 and the discussion in Bautze-Picron 2010: 205ff; see also Fischer 1980.

[69] Plate 3.4 in Anālayo 2010: 126. Plate 23 in Fischer 1979: 45 shows a third-century *stūpa* that even places an amorous couple about to undress each other above a standing Buddha.

fulness has nothing to do with aversion or disgust toward the body; in fact an attitude of repulsion toward the body would only make it difficult to undertake this exercise.

In this way, the fairly neutral nuances conveyed by this mode of practice already serve to show that the meditative attitude toward the body in early Buddhism is not consistently a negative one and that it would not be accurate to assume that early Buddhist contemplatives necessarily regarded the body as the origin of evil.

The same is all the more the case when others see someone engaging in this type of mindful contemplation. Properly undertaken practice of this exercise leaves on the external observer an impression of gracefulness and serenity in the way the practitioner executes his or her bodily movements.[70] A full undertaking of this exercise requires an accompanying of the body with awareness in as continuous a manner as possible. This is the precise opposite of an attempt to escape from corporeal existence. Instead of escaping, the practitioner's awareness is firmly grounded in his or her corporeal existence.

With the attainment of meditative absorption, a positive perspective emerges. The early discourses describe four such absorptions, which are experiences reached based on having earlier overcome any type of sensual distraction.

Judging from the canonical descriptions, the actual experience of these absorptions nevertheless involves the body, in the sense that the bodily dimension of experience need not be left behind completely in order to be able to enter absorption.[71]

---

[70] Mrozik 2002: 18 comments that "mindfulness and awareness … their practice is explicitly described in the text as graceful movements, pleasant tones of voice, or the absence of undue fidgeting."

[71] As already pointed out by Shankman 2008: 80, "the Kāyagatāsati (Mindfulness of the Body) Sutta … states unambiguously that

This conclusion would also correspond to Buddhist cosmology, according to which mastery of the four absorptions leads to rebirth in the fine material realms,[72] but rebirth in the immaterial realms requires mastery of the immaterial spheres.[73]

This indication regarding realms of rebirth at the same time conveys the impression that the experience of the body can have different dimensions, ranging from coarse modes in the sensual realms to considerably more refined modes in the fine material realms. This in turn suggests that, in the case of absorption attainment, the way the presence of the body is sensed would be much more refined and of an altogether different type compared to how the body is experienced as a sense-door during normal everyday life.[74] This would explain, for example, why an adept can sit for long periods of time without feeling pain.[75]

---

through attaining jhāna one develops mindfulness of the body … the sutta states explicitly that body awareness is present in jhāna."

[72] For a correlation of the four *jhāna*s with rebirth in the respective fine material realms see, e.g., AN 4.123 at AN II 126,16 and its parallel MĀ 168 at T I 700c2.

[73] On rebirth in these three realms being related to involvement with *kāma*, *rūpa*, and *arūpa* respectively see AN 3.76 at AN I 223,26, which has a parallel in EĀ² 42 at T II 881c12. Now *rūpa* could in principle just be a visual object. Given that absorption attainment is not invariably based on a visual object (e.g. in the case of the *brahmavihāra*s), however, the responsible factor for absorption in general to correspond to the *rūpa-loka* would appear to be that the bodily dimension of experience has not yet been left behind with absorption, which only seems to happen definitely with the attainment of the immaterial spheres.

[74] Shankman 2008: 81 reasons that "perhaps the suttas are referring to a subtler type of body awareness, not accessible through the normal sense apparatus."

[75] On the Buddha's ability to sit motionless for seven days and nights see MN 14 at MN I 94,33 and one of its parallels, EĀ 41.1 at T II 744b17.

In other words, during profound concentrative attainments body and mind appear to have become so much unified in subjective experience that they become complementary facets of a single mode of experience. Such a unified condition can still have a physical dimension, a refined sense of the presence of the body, even though this would be so different from ordinary sensory bodily experience that one in absorption would no longer feel itches and minor bodily pains.

On this assumption, it would depend on the individual meditator to what degree this sense of bodily presence is consciously experienced during absorption. Depending on the subjective stance that informs experience, opposing views regarding the actual condition of absorption attainment and its relation to bodily experience could be based on the same mental condition, viewed differently.

The *Madhyama-āgama* to the *Kāyagatāsati-sutta* describes the bodily dimension of the first absorption as follows:[76]

> A monastic completely drenches and pervades the body with joy and happiness born of seclusion [experienced in the first absorption], so that there is no part within the body that is not pervaded by joy and happiness born of seclusion.
>
> It is just like a bath attendant who, having filled a vessel with bathing powder, mixes it with water and kneads it, so that there is no part [of the powder] that is not completely drenched and pervaded with water.

The simile in the otherwise closely similar Pāli parallel additionally indicates that the ball of bath powder does not ooze.[77]

---

[76] The translated passage is MĀ 81 at T I 555b19 to 555b22; for a translation of the entire discourse see Kuan 2007.

[77] MN 119 at MN III 92,32. Another difference is that MN 119 speaks of a bath attendant or of his apprentice. This is a recurrent pericope

The description in this simile would be related to one of the standard ways of bathing in ancient India by going to a river to take a bath out in the open.[78] When one is out in the open, any soap powder to be used for bathing can easily be scattered by the wind.[79] In such a situation it would obviously be useful if the bathing powder is first moistened and made into a firm ball (ideally one that does not ooze) so that it can be handled easily and without loss when one is bathing in the river. The motif of the powder mixed thoroughly with water conveys the sense of unification of body and mind in the experience of joy and happiness during the first absorption.

In the case of the second absorption, the bodily experience finds its expression as follows:[80]

> A monastic completely drenches and pervades the body with joy and happiness born of concentration [experienced in the second absorption], so that there is no part within the body that is not pervaded by joy and happiness born of concentration.
>
> It is just like a mountain spring that is full and overflowing with clear and clean water, so that water coming from any of the four directions cannot enter it, with the spring water welling up from the bottom on its own, flowing out and flooding the surroundings, completely drenching every part of the mountain so that there is no part that is not pervaded by it.

---

in the early discourses, where a craftsman is usually mentioned together with his apprentice.

[78] E.g., MN 93 at MN II 151,19 and one of its parallels, MĀ 150 at T I 662c26, describe going to a river with bath powder to wash oneself.

[79] This is suggested in a discussion of this simile in the *Vimuttimagga*, T 1648 at T XXXII 417b8.

[80] The translated passage is MĀ 81 at T I 555b27 to 555c2.

The simile in the Pāli parallel instead describes a lake which has water welling up from within.[81] Be it a mountain spring or a lake fed from within, both similes provide an illustration of the welling up of joy and happiness from within, which completely fill the whole body-and-mind complex and pervade it thoroughly.[82] Compared to the first absorption, the joy and happiness are of a different kind, as instead of being merely born of seclusion they are now born of concentration proper and thereby of a superior type, just as there is more water in a spring or lake than in a ball of soap. The practitioner has become so deeply concentrated that joy and happiness just keep welling up from within, similar to water in a spring or lake that wells up from within.

The bodily dimension of the third absorption is described in this way:[83]

> A monastic completely drenches and pervades the body with happiness born of the absence of joy [experienced in the third absorption], so that there is no part within the body that is not pervaded by happiness born of the absence of joy.
>
> It is just like a blue, red, or white lotus which, being born in the water and having come to growth in the water, remains submerged in water, with every part of its roots, stem, flower, and leaves completely drenched and pervaded [by water], with no part that is not pervaded by it.

The Pāli parallel makes the additional point that the water that pervades the lotus is cool,[84] something that in a hot climate like India would have been perceived as attractive. The lotus itself

---

[81] MN 119 at MN III 93,10.

[82] See T 1648 at T XXXII 418c29.

[83] The translated passage is MĀ 81 at T I 555c8 to 555c12.

[84] MN 119 at MN III 94,1.

is a recurrent symbol of transcendence in early Buddhist texts,[85] which in the present context might point to the circumstance that the type of happiness experienced at this juncture comes about by progressive transcendence. Based on earlier having gone beyond sensual pleasures, now even the experience of non-sensual joy is transcended, which in comparison to the non-sensual happiness that remains is comparably gross.

Besides this nuance of a refinement of happiness, the circumstance that the lotus is fully submerged in water conveys a further progression when compared to the water welling up in a spring or lake and the water used to form a soap ball. Here the image depicts a total immersion in water. This at the same time is then a condition of total immersion in happiness; the whole mind is engulfed by the uninterrupted and all-pervading experience of happiness.

The case of the fourth absorption reads like this:[86]

> A monastic mentally resolves to dwell having accomplished a complete pervasion of the body with mental purity [experienced in the fourth absorption], so that there is no part within the body that is not pervaded by mental purity.
>
> It is just like a person covered from head to foot with a cloth measuring seven or eight units, so that no part of the body is not covered.

The version of the simile found in the Pāli discourse does not give the size of the cloth, but indicates that it is white.[87] The description in both versions of being completely covered by

[85] An example is Dhp 58f; which has parallels in the Gāndhārī *Dharmapada* 303f, Brough 1962/2001: 166, the Patna *Dharmapada* 135f, Cone 1989: 138, and the *Udānavarga* 18.12f, Bernhard 1965: 243.

[86] The translated passage is MĀ 81 at T I 555c17 to 555c23.

[87] MN 119 at MN III 94,16; see also below p. 79 note 34.

this cloth seems to exemplify the imperturbable nature of the mind reached at this juncture of meditative absorption. This condition is similar to a body that is well protected from the impact of cold or heat through this cloth,[88] at the same time presumably also being protected from being bitten by mosquitoes, gad flies, etc.

It hardly needs pointing out that these four illustrations of the experience of the embodied mind during absorption are a far cry from regarding the body as the origin of disgust, pain, and evil. Instead, during these meditative experiences the body becomes the rallying point of experiences of incredible joy and happiness.

Although such experiences require the leaving behind of sensual desire, they do not give the impression of being an expression of a deprecation of the body. Instead, they provide an alternative to sensual pleasure which, when viewed from the perspective of the pleasure experienced during absorption, is vastly inferior and exceedingly more coarse.

For one who practices in this way it would probably not be humiliating to have a body, nor are these experiences part of an attempt to escape from corporeal existence. Quite to the contrary, attaining absorption requires that the contemplating practitioner be very much present to his or her bodily existence and free from any negativity toward it, as negativity could easily become a case of succumbing to the mental hindrance of aversion. Be it the hindrance of sensual desire or the hindrance of aversion, the presence of any of these two would make it impossible to attain absorption in the first place.

In this way, the passages surveyed above make it clear that within the realm of early Buddhist meditation practice there is

---

[88] Ps II 323,5 and T 1648 at T XXXII 420c2.

indeed more than one kind of body discourse. The question remains whether these different kinds of body discourse stand in a meaningful relationship to each other.

A central purpose of contemplating the anatomical parts is the development of freedom from infatuation with sensual pleasures. Seen from the perspective of the absorptions, the point here is not a denial of pleasure as such, but rather an attempt to leave behind coarse pleasure in order to be able to access a more refined form of pleasure, which nevertheless is still experienced on a bodily dimension. The leaving behind of sensual pleasure is required because the pleasure born of unification of the mind can only arise once the diversification of searching for gratification through the sense-doors has been at least temporarily left behind. In other words, it is precisely getting out of sensuality that leads to superior happiness.[89]

In this way the two seemingly opposed perspectives on the body, the negative perspective underlying contemplation of the anatomical parts and the positive perspective evident in the bodily experience of the absorptions, stand in a logical continuum.

The same holds from a practical perspective. If the contemplation of the anatomical parts were to be undertaken in such a way as to sense or feel at least some of the parts of the body,[90] then with such practice the internal sensitivity for the body as a whole would increase. Such sensitivity in turn would facilitate being aware of the body in any posture or during any activity, fulfilling precisely the function of awareness of bodily postures and thereby achieving a centering of the mind in the body. Needless to say, being able to remain centered on the

[89] DN 18 at DN II 214,16 and one of its parallels, DĀ 4 at T I 36a27, explicitly describe the gaining of happiness on going beyond sensuality.

[90] For such an approach to contemplation of the anatomical parts see Anālayo 2014d: 76f.

body in spite of sensual distractions depends on the degree to which sensual desire has been diminished. In other words, the more contemplating the anatomical constitution of the body has been successful in removing sensual desire, the easier it will be to carry out contemplation of the bodily postures without succumbing to distraction.

The purpose of mindfulness of the postures of the body is to provide a firm grounding in the body. Such a way of centering oneself, aloof from sensual distraction, is in turn an important precondition for being able to reach deeper levels of concentration with the attainment of absorption. In this way, awareness established firmly on the body in the present moment, supported by having become aware of its anatomical parts and removed sensual desire, and then further strengthened through embodied mindfulness of one's bodily postures and by letting go of any sensory distraction, provides a foundation for being able to experience absorption. Needless to say, absorption attainment requires going beyond sensuality and in turn contributes to a loss of interest in sensuality.[91]

With the attainment of absorption, the happiness generated by a mind that is totally aloof from sensual distractions then pervades the entire body just like mixing soap powder and water, just like water welling up from within a lake or spring, or just like a lotus that is completely immersed in water, eventually resulting in a state of superb imperturbability comparable to being wrapped up from head to toe in a clean cloth.

In this way, the three meditative perspectives on the body surveyed in this part of the present chapter, ranging from a negative attitude via a neutral mode of practice to bodily expe-

---

[91] On the contrast between sensuality and absorption see below p. 128ff.

riences that are clearly positive, can be seen to build on each other and to stand in a logical and practical continuum.

The continuity underlying the three types of bodily discourses finds confirmation in the circumstance that all of the three types of exercises discussed here can be found in the selfsame discourse, the *Kāyagatāsati-sutta* and its parallel. Although the Chinese and Pāli versions of this discourse exhibit some differences regarding what practices should be included under this heading,[92] they agree as far as the above discussed exercises are concerned. That is, from their perspective the negative attitude toward the body when contemplating its anatomical constitution, the neutral mode of practice when being aware of the body in different postures, and the positive experience of the embodied mind during absorption are complementary forms of practicing mindfulness of the body.[93] In the end, from the viewpoint of actual meditation practice these different kinds of body discourse become just one kind of discourse.

Conclusion

Practice or research related to mindfulness needs to be based on a clear understanding regarding what type of mindfulness is

---

[92] *Pace* Kuan 2008: 96, contemplations found only in the *Madhyama-āgama* version do not seem to have a clear relationship to the body and thus can safely be assumed to be later additions; see in more detail Anālayo 2013b: 41–45 (where the discussion is concerned with the same exercises as part of the *Madhyama-āgama* parallel to the *Satipaṭṭhāna-sutta*).

[93] Harris 2012: 116f notes that the *Kāyagatāsati-sutta* "changes mood completely after the cemetery meditations are described. From meditation on corpses, it suddenly turns to joy and rapture" and "the joy and rapture described are not of the mind alone. They are of the body. Every part of the body is said to be flooded with them."

being employed. The early Buddhist conception of mindfulness can involve the use of concepts and evaluations. It can also coexist with unwholesome mental conditions.

Mindfulness has a close relationship to memory, although the two are not identical. Instead, mindfulness appears to be a quality that facilitates and strengthens recall. Such an interpretation enables an appreciation of the clear link to memory and at the same time preserves the important quality of *satipaṭṭhāna* as concerned with what happens in the present moment.

The sixteen steps of mindfulness of breathing appear to have been predominantly associated with formal meditation in a secluded setting. For the challenge posed by everyday situations, mindfulness of the body in the sense of a proprioceptive type of awareness seems to offer a practicable solution for ensuing continuity of mindfulness.

Such embodied awareness reflects one of the different facets of the early Buddhist attitude toward the body, which combines awareness of its lack of inherent sexual attraction with embodied awareness and the experience of intense bodily happiness during absorption under the overarching aim of progress to awakening.

Before turning in more detail to the path to awakening in the next chapter, I would like to conclude the present chapter with a Pāli verse on the potential of mindfulness:

> Those who always proceed with mindfulness …
> proceed evenly among what is uneven.[94]

---

[94] SN 1.18 at SN I 7,20: *ye caranti sadā satā … caranti visame saman ti*; this verse is not found in the parallels SĀ 578 at T II 154a6 and SĀ² 163 at T II 435b8.

The Path

Introduction

In the preceding chapter I argued for a continuity between mindful insight into the body's anatomical constitution, a grounding of awareness in an embodied form of mindfulness during any activity, and the bodily dimension of the experience of deep concentration during absorption attainment. The continuity and complementary nature of these meditation practices related to the body exemplify what I consider to be the general relationship between tranquillity and insight in early Buddhist discourse. In order to explore this topic further and from a broader perspective, in what follows I translated and study the standard description of the gradual path of practice.

A unifying feature of nearly all of the thirteen discourses in the first chapter of the *Dīgha-nikāya*, the Chapter on the Aggregate of Morality, is the giving of an exposition of the gradual path of training that leads from going forth to full awakening.[1] This has a counterpart in the *Dīrgha-āgama* extant in Chinese translation, which has a similar chapter comprising ten discourses.[2] According to current consensus of opinion among scholars, this discourse collection would have been transmitted by reciters of the Dharmaguptaka tradition.[3] The

---

[1] The first discourse, the *Brahmajāla-sutta*, DN 1 at DN I 4,1 to 12,17, has instead an extended exposition on morality in three graded sections.

[2] DĀ 20 to DĀ 29, which forms the third chapter of the collection; see T I 82a6: 第三分.

[3] On the school affiliation of the *Dīrgha-āgama* see, e.g., Demiéville 1951: 252f, Brough 1962/2001: 50, Lü 1963: 242, Bareau 1966,

Dharmaguptaka *Vinaya* is the monastic code still observed nowadays in countries like China, Taiwan, and Korea.

Another version of the gradual-path account can be found in the Sarvāstivāda and/or Mūlasarvāstivāda *Dīrgha-āgama* preserved in Sanskrit fragments. The Mūlasarvāstivāda monastic code is followed today in the Tibetan tradition (reciters of the closely related Sarvāstivāda tradition appear to have been responsible for transmitting the *Madhyama-āgama* extant in Chinese translation,[4] from which I translated passages with descriptions of the bodily dimension of absorption experience in the previous chapter).

Comparable to the Chapter on the Aggregate of Morality in the *Dīgha-nikāya*, the Sarvāstivāda/Mūlasarvāstivāda *Dīrgha-āgama* has a similar chapter, which in its case comprises twenty-three discourses.[5]

The assembling of discourses that in one way or another describe the gradual path of training has obvious advantages for transmission. Such a grouping of discourses is easily memorized for oral recitation, because the substantial amount of text common to the discourses need be learned only once. When transmission shifts to the written medium, the full text need be written out only at its first occurrence and can be abbreviated for subsequent discourses. This saves both time and

---

Waldschmidt 1980: 136, Mayeda 1985: 97, Enomoto 1986: 25, Hirakawa 1987: 513, Schmithausen 1987: 318, Oberlies 2003: 44, Salomon 2007: 354 note 14, and Willemen 2008: 60.

[4] The general consensus among scholars on the school affiliation of the *Madhyama-āgama* has been called into question by Chung and Fukita 2011: 13–34, as well as Chung 2014 and 2017; for critical replies see Anālayo 2012c: 516–521 and 2017d.

[5] For a survey of this collection see Hartmann and Wille 2014 (for a minor correction of their presentation see Anālayo 2014h: 8f note 13).

writing material, the latter probably being an important concern in a manuscript culture.

Besides serving as a factor for conveniently grouping discourses to facilitate their transmission, the gradual-path account also has a much more important practical significance. It offers in schematic fashion answers to such questions as: What are the practices required for progressing from unawakened worldling to fully liberated one? In what way do these practices relate to one another?

By providing information on such matters, the gradual-path account in the early discourses stands at the beginning of a concern with conceptions of the path to liberation that have been of lasting relevance in the development of Buddhist thought and practice.[6]

In what follows, I study the section of the gradual path of training that describes the practices to be undertaken after a foundation in moral conduct has been established and up to gaining the mental imperturbability required for developing supernormal abilities (or else the immaterial attainments, a topic to which I return in the next chapter).[7] In this way, the section of the gradual path I will be examining here extends from sense-restraint to the attainment of the fourth absorption. My study is based on first translating this section from the Dharmaguptaka *Dīrgha-āgama*, in comparison with its parallels. The discourse trans-

---

[6] Buswell and Gimello 1992/1994: 3f point out that "the intrinsic efficacy of mārga generally dominates the whole of Buddhism and leads it to privilege mārga in ways that other traditions do not. Thus many of the most characteristic features of Buddhism appear to derive from its emphasis on mārga."

[7] See below p. 150ff; on the supernormal ability of levitation in particular see Anālayo 2016e and for a discussion of aspects of the section on morality in the *Brahmajāla* and its parallels Anālayo 2014a.

lated is a parallel to the *Ambaṭṭha-sutta* of the *Dīgha-nikāya* and forms the first discourse in the chapter with expositions of the gradual path of training in the Chinese *Dīrgha-āgama*.[8]

After the translation,[9] I survey somewhat differing gradual-path schemes found in the early discourses in general, in order to evaluate their function as a kind of prototype path manual and the impact of such descriptions on conceptions of the relationship between tranquillity and insight in later exegetical works. Based on this, I then critically examine the assumption

---

[8] In the case of the *Dīgha-nikāya*, the full account of the gradual path is instead found in the second discourse, the *Sāmaññaphala-sutta*; hence in my comparative notes I will refer to this discourse. For the Mūlasarvāstivāda version of the gradual path I rely on the account given in a version of the *Śrāmaṇyaphala-sūtra* preserved in the *Saṅghabhedavastu*. As my main concern is to compare versions of the gradual path transmitted by the Dharmaguptaka, Mūlasarvāstivāda/Sarvāstivāda, and Theravāda reciter lineages, I will not take up the gradual-path account in T 22, a discourse parallel to DN 2 that has been preserved as an individual translation.

[9] The translated section is DĀ 20 at T I 84c13 to 85c13; in what follows I note only selected differences between the parallel versions, as an exhaustive study of variations would go beyond the scope of this chapter. I have added numbering to some paragraphs to facilitate the discussion in the study part of this chapter; these numbers are not found in the original. Regarding the account of the gradual path in the *Ambaṭṭha-sutta* and its parallels, Meisig 1993: 234f considers this to be a later addition, since in his opinion it interrupts an otherwise heated debate. According to MacQueen 1988: 180, however, the gradual path fits its context in the *Ambaṭṭha-sutta* and its parallels quite well. Meisig 1987: 35ff (see also Ramers 1996: 6f) makes a similar suggestion for the *Sāmaññaphala-sutta* (DN 2), where one parallel version, EĀ 43.7 at T II 762a7, lacks the account of the gradual path. For a critical reply to the suggestion that in the case of DN 2 the gradual-path account would be a later addition see Freiberger 2000: 73f note 165.

by several modern scholars that the early Buddhist discourses reflect an underlying tension between two competing accounts of the path to liberation.

A Translation of the Gradual Path

1) By cultivating noble virtue [monastics practicing the gradual path of training] are not defiled by attachment in the mind and they harbor joy and happiness within.[10] Although seeing a form with the eye, they do not grasp at its characteristics and their eyes are not bound by forms. Being without any greedy attachment, they are firm and calm, without being distressed and without any evil influxes. They firmly uphold the set of precepts and guard the eye faculty well. The ear, nose, tongue, body, and mind *are also like this*. They tame the six types of contact well, guarding and disciplining them, in order to obtain being at ease.

It is just like a capable trainer [of horses] who drives a chariot with four horses on level ground, holding the whip and the reins, so that they do not stray from the route.[11] In

[10] The Mūlasarvāstivāda and Theravāda parallels speak of an inner experience of the happiness of blamelessness; see Gnoli 1978: 240,18: *adhyātmam anavadyasukhaṃ pratívedayate* and DN 2 at DN I 70,5: *ajjhattaṃ anavajjasukhaṃ paṭisaṃvedeti*. Here and in the remainder of the translation, I employ plural forms to avoid gendered terminology like "he". In view of the Indic parallels, it is highly probable that the original underlying the Chinese translation would have had a single monk as its subject. However, terms like *bhikkhu* and *bhikkhave* do function as general terms of address and do not imply that instructions are meant for male monastics only; see Collett and Anālayo 2014. I hope this justifies my decision to translate as if the passage were speaking of a plurality of monastics.

[11] The simile is not found in the Mūlasarvāstivāda and Theravāda parallels.

the same way monastics tame the 'horses' of the six [sense] faculties [so that] they are at ease and without loss.

2) Possessing noble virtue in this way and achieving noble [restraint] of the [sense] faculties,[12] they know [how to be] moderate in eating and are without greed for flavors.[13] They proceed by nourishing the body so that it does not become afflicted, but not out of pride. They regulate the body so that former painful feelings cease and new painful feelings do not arise,[14] so that the body is at ease and they have strength and are without concerns.

It is just like a person who applies medicine to an ulcer in order to heal the ulcer, not seeking to adorn himself nicely, nor out of personal pride. Young brahmin,[15] in the same way monastics take sufficient food to support the body, without harboring pride.

---

[12] Adopting the variant 諸 instead of 眼.

[13] The Mūlasarvāstivāda and Theravāda parallels proceed from sense-restraint directly to clear comprehension when undertaking various bodily activities (found only at a later point in DĀ 20); see Gnoli 1978: 241,3 and DN 2 at DN I 70,25. They do not cover topics 2 to 4 found in DĀ 20: moderation in eating, wakefulness, and *satipaṭṭhāna*.

[14] The *Visuddhimagga* and the *Yogacārabhūmi* agree that the new feelings to be avoided are those caused by overeating; see Vism 33,2 and Śrāvakabhūmi Study Group 1998: 140,9 or T 1579 at T XXX 410b27 (for a study, edition, and translation of the entire section on contentment with food see also Wayman 1961: 139–162).

[15] The young brahmin, to whom the exposition of the gradual path is addressed, is 阿摩晝, corresponding to Ambaṭṭha in DN 3 at DN I 100,5. For a study of Ambaṭṭha in comparison with Śvetaketu in the *Upaniṣad*s see Black 2011. Bronkhorst 2007: 354f suggests that a possible Sanskrit form of the name as Ambaṣṭha would have signalled to a perceptive audience that he is not of pure brahmin descent (something which, in the course of their discussion, the Buddha reveals so as to humble the overly arrogant young brahmin).

Again it is like lubricating [the axle of] a chariot, wishing to make it movable and usable, so as to use it to transport a load to some place.[16] In the same way monastics take sufficient food to support the body, wishing to practice the path.

3) Young brahmin, being accomplished in noble virtue in this way, achieving noble [restraint] of the [sense] faculties, and knowing [how to be] moderate in eating, in the first and last [watches] of the night monastics are diligently wakeful. Again, during the day they are constantly mindful and with a unified mind, whether walking or sitting, removing the many hindrances.

In the first watch of the night they are constantly mindful and with a unified mind, whether walking or sitting, [85a] removing the many hindrances. On reaching the middle watch of the night, they then lie down on the right side to sleep, constantly mindful of the time for rising again. They fix their perceptions in [mental] clarity and their mind is not confused. On reaching the last watch of the night they rise with attention, being constantly mindful and with a unified mind, whether walking or sitting, removing the many hindrances.

In this way being accomplished in noble virtue, achieving noble [restraint] of the [sense] faculties, knowing [how to be] moderate in eating, in the first and last [watches] of the night monastics are diligently awake, constantly mindful, and with a unified mind that is not confused.[17]

---

[16] DN 2 at DN I 71,6 instead uses the image of a bird that takes its wings along wherever it flies to illustrate a monastic's contentment. The similes of using medicine for a wound and of applying grease to an axle can be found also in SN 35.198 at SN IV 177,1; see as well Vism 33,5 and 32,17.

[17] The practice of wakefulness and the next section on *satipaṭṭhāna* practice are without a counterpart in the two parallel versions.

4) How are monastics with mindfulness that is not confused? In this way, monastics contemplate the internal body as a body, diligently without laxity, with undistracted mindfulness, removing desire and discontent for the world. They contemplate the external body as a body … they contemplate the internal and external body as a body, diligently without laxity, with undistracted mindfulness, removing desire and discontent for the world. They contemplate feeling … mental states … dharmas *also in this way*. This is how monastics are with mindfulness that is not confused.

5) How are they with a unified mind? In this way, when taking a step while walking, when going in or out, when looking to the left or the right, when bending or extending [a limb], when raising or lowering the head, when carrying the robes and bowl, when receiving beverages and food, when defecating or urinating, when falling asleep or waking up, when sitting or standing, when speaking or being silent, at all such times monastics are constantly mindful and with a unified mind, without losing their deportment.[18] This is being with a unified mind.

It is just like a person who walks with a great assembly; whether he walks in front, in the middle or at the back, he constantly comes to be at ease and is without fear.[19]

---

[18] On clear comprehension see Anālayo 2003: 141–145 and 2013b: 51f. At a workshop organized by Gil Fronsdal at Stanford University, April 2014, Jens-Uwe Hartmann pointed out that, whereas DN 2 at DN I 71,14 qualifies such clear comprehension as "noble", *ariya*, in line with the qualification used for morality and sense-restraint, the gradual path account in the *Saṅghabhedavastu* employs instead the qualification "supreme", *parama*; see Gnoli 1978: 241,10.

[19] The two parallels do not employ a simile to illustrate the practice of clear comprehension with various bodily activities.

Young brahmin, in this way when taking a step while walking, when going in or out ... *up to* ... when speaking or remaining silent, monastics are constantly mindful and with a unified mind, without any worries or fears.

6) In this way possessing noble virtue, achieving noble [restraint] of the [sense] faculties, knowing [how to be] moderate in eating, being diligently awake in the first and last [watches] of the night, constantly mindful and with a unified mind that is not confused, monastics delight in being in quiet places, at the foot of a tree, in a cemetery, in a mountain cave, in an open field, or among heaps of garbage.

When the time has come, they beg for food. Upon returning, they wash the hands and feet, put away robes and bowl, and sit down cross-legged with body erect and straight mind, collecting mindfulness in front.[20]

7) They discard avarice and greed, completely dissociating the mind from them. They extinguish anger in the mind and are without the bondage of resentment. They dwell with the mind in purity, constantly harboring *mettā* and empathy.

They discard sloth-and-torpor, fixing their perceptions in [mental] clarity, with mindfulness that is not confused. They remove restlessness-and-worry, completely dissociating the mind from them. Dwelling inwardly at peace, they eliminate restlessness-and-worry from the mind. They remove uncertainty and doubt, going beyond the net of doubt. Their mind is collected and unified in wholesome states.

---

[20] The two parallels do not describe how the monastic begs for food, but just list secluded places and describe sitting down cross-legged with mindfulness in front, *pratimukha/parimukha*; see Gnoli 1978: 241,14 and DN 2 at DN I 71,19; for a discussion of the implications of mindfulness being established "in front" see Anālayo 2003: 128f.

It is just as if a slave has been granted by his master [the right to have his own] family name and is at ease, having been set free and exempted from being a slave. His mind is delighted and he has no more worries and fears.

Again it is like a person who, having been granted wealth [as a loan] to make a living, has gained a great profit in return. He repays the original owner of the goods and the surplus wealth is enough for his needs. He thinks to himself: 'Formerly I was granted wealth [as a loan] and I was afraid that it would not turn out as I wished. Now I have gained profit in return and, having repaid the original owner of the goods, the surplus wealth is enough for my needs.' Having no more worries and fears, [85b] he gives rise to great delight.

[Again] it is like a person who, having been sick for a long time, recovers from his sickness;[21] being [able] to digest beverages and food, and his appearance and strength are satisfactory. He thinks: 'Formerly I was sick but now I am recovered. I am [able] to digest beverages and food, and my appearance and strength are satisfactory.' Having no more worries and fears, he gives rise to great delight.

Again it is like a person who, having been imprisoned for a long time, is released and at ease. He thinks to himself: 'Formerly I was arrested and detained; now I have been liberated.' Having no more worries and fears, he gives rise to great delight.

Again it is like a person who carries much wealth and treasure while passing through a great wilderness. He gets to cross it at ease, without encountering robbers. He thinks to himself: 'Carrying wealth and treasure I have passed

[21] Adopting the variant 瘥 instead of 差.

through this hardship.' Having no more worries and fears, he gives rise to great delight and his mind is at ease.[22]

Young brahmin, when monastics are overcome by the five hindrances themselves, they are constantly worried and fearful. They are again like a slave, like a person in debt, [like] one who for a long time has been sick, [like] one who is imprisoned, [like] one who journeys through a great wilderness. They see themselves not yet free from the hindrances, their mind being covered and darkened, their eye of wisdom not being clear.

8) Then they diligently discard sensual desire, evil and unwholesome states. Being endowed with [directed] awareness and [sustained] contemplation,[23] with joy and happiness arisen from seclusion, they gain entry into the first absorption. Their body is completely pervaded, filled, and drenched by joy and happiness,[24] with no [part] that is not permeated.

It is just like a capable bath attendant who fills a container with much [soap] powder. By drenching it with water, he completely moistens it with water,[25] so that no [part] is not pervaded [by water].[26]

In the same way monastics gain entry into the first absorption, with joy and happiness throughout their body,

---

[22] The sequence of the similes in the Mūlasarvāstivāda version, Gnoli 1978: 241,19, is as follows: loan, sickness, slavery, imprisonment, and dangerous journey. The sequence of the similes in the Theravāda version, DN 2 at DN I 71,31, proceeds in this way: loan, sickness, imprisonment, slavery, and dangerous journey.

[23] For a more detailed discussion of the significance of *vitakka/vitarka* as a factor of the first absorption see below p. 123ff.

[24] Adopting the variant 以 instead of 已.

[25] Adopting the variant 水 instead of 外.

[26] See the discussion above p. 56f.

with no [part] that is not permeated. Young brahmin, in this way this is the first gaining of happiness with the present body. Why is that? Because this is to be gained by being diligent, with mindfulness that is not confused, and by delighting in quietude and seclusion.

Discarding [directed] awareness and [sustained] contemplation,[27] they give rise to confidence,[28] and their mindfulness is collected in mental unification. Being without [directed] awareness and without [sustained] contemplation, with joy and happiness arisen from concentration, they enter the second absorption. Their body is completely pervaded, filled, and drenched by the joy and happiness of mental unification, with no [part] that is not permeated.

It is just like [a pool] on a mountain top with cool spring water that wells up by itself from within, none coming in from outside.[29] The pool itself is in turn soaked by the clear water that wells up from within, with no [part] that is not pervaded.

---

[27] Adopting the variant 捨 instead of 於.

[28] The two parallels qualify such confidence as "internal", *ajjhattaṃ/adhyātmam*; see DN 2 at DN I 74,14 and Gnoli 1978: 243,12. This qualification gives the impression that the inner stability reached with the absence of the first absorption factors *vitakka/vitarka* and *vicāra* is a central factor in the arising of such inner confidence.

[29] The Mūlasarvāstivāda parallel, Gnoli 1978: 243,18, also specifies that this pond is located on top of a mountain. This location explains why it would not receive water flowing in from outside. In the context of the simile, the location on top of a mountain illustrates the mental aloofness experienced with the second absorption. According to the *Vimuttimagga*, T 1648 at T XXXII 418c27, the absence of water flowing in from the outside illustrates the absence of *vitakka/vitarka* and *vicāra*, and the welling up of water from within stands for the welling up of joy and happiness born of concentration.

Young brahmin, in the same way monastics enter the second absorption, with no [part of their body] that is not permeated by the joy and happiness born of concentration. This is their second gaining of happiness with the present body.

Discarding joy, they dwell in equipoise and with mindfulness that is not confused. With their whole being experiencing acute happiness they enter the third absorption,[30] which is spoken of by noble ones as a [condition of] equipoise, mindfulness, and happiness.[31] Their body is completely pervaded, filled, and drenched by happiness that is without joy, with no [part] that is not permeated.

It is just like *uppala* lotuses, *paduma* lotuses, *kumuda* lotuses, [or] *puṇḍarīka* lotuses, which have emerged from the mud, but have not emerged above the water. Their roots, stems, stalks, and flowers are soaked in the water, with no [part] that is not pervaded [by the water].[32]

---

[30] My translation is based on the assumption that a reference to 身 here renders an instrumental *kāyena* in the Indic original, which in such contexts functions as an idiomatic expression to convey personal and direct experience; see Schmithausen 1981: 214 and 249 ad. note 50, Radich 2007: 263, Harvey 2009: 180 note 10, and Anālayo 2011: 379f note 203.

[31] Adopting a variant without 起.

[32] As mentioned above p. 59, the total immersion in water reflects a progressive deepening of concentration reached at this juncture: from active kneading with water to form a soap ball (illustrative of the joy and happiness of the first absorption), via the welling up of spring water (illustrative of the experience of joy and happiness of the second absorption), to total immersion in water (representing the stable happiness of the third absorption, which is without the mental motion of joy). The water imagery continues in relation to full awakening, which DĀ 20 at T I 86c8 illustrates with the exam-

Young brahmin, in the same way monastics enter the third absorption and dwell with their body soaked with happiness that is secluded from joy, with no [part] that is not pervaded. [85c] This is their third gaining of happiness with the present body.

Discarding ⟨pain⟩ and happiness,[33] sadness and joy having previously ceased, being without pain and without happiness, with purity of equipoise and mindfulness, they enter the fourth absorption. Their body is completely filled and drenched with mental purity, with no [part] that is not pervaded.

---

ple of seeing in clear water plants and pebbles, as well as fish moving in various directions. The Mūlasarvāstivāda version, Gnoli 1978: 251,1, only lists the items seen, without referring to the possibility of motion. Motion is mentioned in DN 2 at DN I 84,16, which describes seeing fish that are moving or stationary. During the Stanford workshop (mentioned above p. 72 note 18), Paul Harrison pointed out that the water has to be very clear in order for an observer to be able to see fishes not only when they are moving, but also when they are motionless. A point conveyed by this detail would thus be the supreme clarity of vision gained with full awakening.

[33] My translation is based on an emendation, indicated by the use of angle brackets ⟨ ⟩. The original at T I 85c2 reads: 彼捨喜樂, 憂喜先滅 (the character 喜 is the problematic one). This clearly is an error, since the standard formulation in the early discourses in general and also elsewhere in the same *Dīrgha-āgama* speaks of discarding *pain* and happiness, instead of *joy* and happiness (which makes no sense, since the same description indicates that joy had been discarded earlier); see, e.g., DĀ 2 at T I 23c23: 捨滅苦樂, 先除憂喜, DĀ 6 at T I 42b9: 捨滅苦樂, 先除憂喜, DĀ 9 at T I 50c22: 離苦樂行, 先滅憂喜, DĀ 17 at T I 75a24: 樂盡苦盡, 憂喜先滅, DĀ 21 at T I 93c5: 樂滅苦滅, 先除憂喜, DĀ 28 at T I 110b3: 捨苦捨樂, 先滅憂喜. Hence I emend the present passage to read: 彼捨苦樂, 憂喜先滅, assuming that due to a scribal error 苦 has been confused with 喜.

It is just like a person who has taken a bath and is clean. He covers his body with a new white cloth, demonstrating the cleanness of his body.[34]

Young brahmin, in the same way monastics enter the fourth absorption and permeate their body with mental purity, with no [part] of it that is not pervaded.

9) Again, having entered the fourth absorption their mind is imperturbable, without increase or decrease. They dwell without craving or aversion in the stage of imperturbability.

It is just like a private room that has been plastered inside and outside, and whose door has been firmly shut and locked,[35] with no wind or dust [entering]. Inside a lamp has been lit, which nobody touches or agitates. The flame of that lamp rises quietly and without perturbation.[36]

Young brahmin, in the same way monastics have entered the fourth absorption and their mind is imperturbable, without increase or decrease. They dwell without craving or aversion in the stage of imperturbability. This is their fourth gaining of happiness with the present body. Why is that? Because this is to be gained by being diligent without

---

[34] The specification that the person in this way demonstrates the cleanness of the body is not found in the two parallels, nor do they mention that the person has taken a bath (the corresponding part has not been preserved among the Sanskrit fragments of the *Saṅghabhedavastu*, but the same is found in the Tibetan translation of the *Bhaiṣajyavastu*, D 1 *kha* 76b7 or Q 1030 *ge* 71b2, which additionally specifies the size of the cloth). The specifications given in DĀ 20 help to bring out an aspect of the simile emphasized in the *Yogācārabhūmi*, T 1579 at T XXX 339c8, according to which the whiteness of the cloth represents the purity of the mind reached with the fourth absorption.

[35] Adopting the variant 扃 instead of 嚮.

[36] The simile is not found in DN 2.

laxity, being with mindfulness that is not confused, and delighting in quietude and seclusion.

A Study of the Gradual Path

The table below surveys the differences in the descriptions of the gradual path in the three parallel versions.[37]

Theravāda DN 2	Dharmaguptaka DĀ 20	Mūlasarvāstivāda Sanskrit fragment
1) sense-restraint	1) sense-restraint & simile	1) sense-restraint
	2) food moderation & simile	
	3) wakefulness	
	4) *satipaṭṭhāna*	
5) comprehension	5) comprehension & simile	5) comprehension
6) seclusion	6) seclusion	6) seclusion
7) hindrances & similes	7) hindrances & similes	7) hindrances & similes
8) absorption & similes	8) absorption & similes	8) absorption & similes
9) imperturbability	9) imperturbability & simile	9) imperturbability & simile

Common to the three versions is the starting point in sense-restraint (1) and the final section, which proceeds from clear comprehension (5) to seclusion (6), the removal of the hindrances (7), the attainment of the four absorptions (8), and the gaining of mental imperturbability (9). Here the parallel versions differ only in the degree to which they illustrate aspects of the gradual path of training with similes. The Dharmaguptaka version translated above offers a simile for sense-restraint

[37] Here and below, the tables proceed from the Theravāda Pāli version, probably more familiar to most readers, to the parallels.

(1), which depicts a charioteer keeping his horses in check so that the chariot does not stray from the road. Another of its similes describes a person who walks fearlessly with a great assembly as an illustration of the practice of clear comprehension (5). In the case of imperturbability, the Dharmaguptaka and Mūlasarvāstivāda versions have a simile that involves a sheltered room or house.

Another and more pronounced difference is that moderation with food (2), wakefulness (3), and *satipaṭṭhāna* (4) are taken up only in the Dharmaguptaka version. This raises the following question: What to make of the absence of moderation with food, wakefulness, and *satipaṭṭhāna* in the Theravāda and Mūlasarvāstivāda versions?

Now in the case of another gradual-path account in the *Cūlahatthipadopama-sutta* of the *Majjhima-nikāya* (MN 27) and its parallel in the *Madhyama-āgama* (MĀ 146),[38] a collection that appears to have been transmitted by Sarvāstivāda reciters, these practices are also not mentioned.

Theravāda MN 27	Sarvāstivāda MĀ 146
1) sense-restraint 5) comprehension 6) seclusion 7) hindrances 8) absorption 9) imperturbability	1) sense-restraint 5) comprehension 6) seclusion 7) hindrances 8) absorption 9) imperturbability

However, in the case of yet another gradual-path account found in these same two discourse collections, namely in the *Mahā-assapura-sutta* (MN 39) and its *Madhyama-āgama*

[38] MN 27 at MN I 180,19 and MĀ 146 at T I 657b27; on the school affiliation of the *Madhyama-āgama* see above p. 66 note 4.

parallel (MĀ 182),[39] moderation with food (2) and wakefulness (3) are mentioned in the Theravāda version, but absent from the Sarvāstivāda version.

Theravāda MN 39	Sarvāstivāda MĀ 182
1) sense-restraint	1) sense-restraint
2) food moderation	
3) wakefulness	
5) comprehension	5) comprehension
6) seclusion	6) seclusion
7) hindrances & similes	7) hindrances
8) absorption & similes	8) absorptions
9) imperturbability	9) imperturbability

In this case the Theravāda version (MN 39) covers moderation with food (2) and wakefulness (3), two practices that are not included in another discourse in the same *Majjhima-nikāya* collection, the *Cūlahatthipadopama-sutta* (MN 27).

The *Mahā-assapura-sutta* (MN 39) shows that taking into account these two practices is not specific to the Dharmaguptaka tradition alone, as in the present case the Theravāda account also covers them. The *Mahā-assapura-sutta* (MN 39) is not unique in this respect, as another version of the gradual path account in the *Gaṇakamoggallāna-sutta* (MN 107) also covers moderation in eating (2) and wakefulness (3).

[39] MN 39 at MN I 273,3 and MĀ 182 at T I 725a25 (the absorptions are abbreviated, making it uncertain if this version also had the similes). Another parallel, EĀ 49.8 at T II 802a3, has only sense-restraint, moderation with food & simile, and wakefulness. Since the school affiliation of the *Ekottarika-āgama* is uncertain (see in more detail Anālayo 2016c: 172–178 and 211–214), for the present comparison I leave this version aside.

Theravāda MN 107	Sarvāstivāda MĀ 144
	4) *satipaṭṭhāna*
1) sense-restraint	1) sense-restraint
2) food moderation	
3) wakefulness	
5) comprehension	5) comprehension
6) seclusion	6) seclusion
7) hindrances	7) hindrances
8) absorption	8) absorption

The case of the *Gaṇakamoggallāna-sutta* (MN 107) is of further significance in regard to the reference to *satipaṭṭhāna* (4) already found in the Dharmaguptaka *Dīrgha-āgama*. Such a reference occurs also in the *Madhyama-āgama* parallel (MĀ 144) to the *Gaṇakamoggallāna-sutta*.[40] Here the *Madhyama-āgama* account of the gradual path of training not only mentions *satipaṭṭhāna*, it even distinguishes between *satipaṭṭhāna* practice as such and the same done in the absence of thought. This distinction is also found in the *Dantabhūmi-sutta* of the *Majjhima-nikāya*, as well as in its *Madhyama-āgama* parallel.[41]

So the circumstance that the above translated Dharmaguptaka *Dīrgha-āgama* discourse stands alone among the long discourse versions of the gradual path of training in mentioning moderation with food (2), wakefulness (3), and *satipaṭṭhāna* (4) does not mean that these practices were not seen as being required for progress on the path to awakening among Theravāda and Mūlasarvāstivāda reciters. But for whatever reason these practices have not always been included in versions of the gradual path found in discourses transmitted by these reciter traditions.

[40] MN 107 at MN III 2,14 and MĀ 144 at T I 652b4.

[41] MN 125 at MN III 136,20 and MĀ 198 at T I 758b15.

The variations that have emerged so far are bewildering if one conceives of differences between parallel versions as invariably the products of intentional editorial decisions taken under the influence of school affiliation. The differences found here, and also in the course of other comparative studies, point to the need to take into account the impact of oral transmission on the texts instead of just focusing on sectarian agendas.

Another example illustrating the same point is the topic of contentment. In the case of the *Dīrgha-āgama* discourse translated above, contentment with one's robes and almsfood, exemplified with the help of a simile of a bird, occurs in the midst of the section on morality.[42] The same is the case in the Mūlasarvāstivāda parallel, which also combines its description of contentment with the simile of a bird that takes its wings along wherever it goes.[43] In the Theravāda version, however, contentment together with the simile occurs at a later juncture, after sense-restraint and clear comprehension.[44]

Notably, an exposition of the gradual path in the Theravāda *Cūlahatthipadopama-sutta* of the *Majjhima-nikāya* agrees in this respect with the Dharmaguptaka and Mūlasarvāstivāda sions just mentioned, since it also places contentment before sense-restraint and clear comprehension.[45]

This shows that the positioning of contentment vis-à-vis sense-restraint and clear comprehension is also not school specific, as within the same Theravāda tradition we get different sequences. In the *Dīgha-nikāya* the sequence is:

sense-restraint – clear comprehension – contentment.

---

[42] DĀ 20 at T I 84a5; see also the discussion in Meisig 1987: 60f.

[43] Gnoli 1978: 233,18.

[44] DN 2 at DN I 71,4.

[45] MN 27 at MN I 180,19.

But in the *Majjhima-nikāya* the sequence is:

contentment – sense-restraint – clear comprehension.

In a detailed study of the gradual path of training in the Pāli discourses,[46] Bucknell (1984: 10) points out that the practice of the various aspects of the path is "both sequential and cumulative". The sequential character can be seen in the final part of the gradual-path account, which proceeds from seclusion (6) to imperturbability (9). What comes before that, however, is cumulative.

The final part is sequential insofar as seclusion (6) and the removal of the hindrances (7) are required for the attainment of absorption (8), which in all versions also requires having taken the sitting posture.[47] Only when the four absorptions have been attained one after the other will imperturbability (9) be reached. This part is clearly sequential; each practice forms the foundation for the next one and it would not be possible to cultivate one mentioned later in the list before having practiced one mentioned earlier.

This sequential part from sitting in seclusion (6) via the removal of the hindrances (7) to the attainment of the four absorptions (8) and therewith the gaining of mental imperturbability (9) is found throughout the versions surveyed so far. The only exception is the *Gaṇakamoggallāna-sutta* and its *Madhyama-āgama* parallel where, due to the circumstances of the presentation, the gradual-path account is taken only up to the fourth absorption. Therefore the stage of imperturbability

---

[46] On the gradual path see also Franke 1917: 50–80, Eimer 1976: 26–34, Meisig 1987: 35–80, Crangle 1994: 149–152, Ramers 1996, Freiberger 2000: 71–86, Sujato 2005: 157–159, and Melzer 2006: 12–24.

[47] After emerging from absorption, however, walking meditation can be done in such a way as to maintain the collectedness of the mind that has been gained during the sitting; see also below p. 123 note 28.

(9) is not explicitly mentioned. The same can safely be assumed to be implied, however, since both versions do mention the fourth absorption, which in the early discourses corresponds to reaching meditative imperturbability.[48]

Thus the essentially sequential character of sitting in seclusion (6), removing the hindrances (7), attaining the absorptions (8), and gaining mental imperturbability (9) as practices that invariably follow one another would have served as a fixed model during teaching and transmission, hence this part remained stable throughout different presentations.

The same is not the case for the cumulative practices that come before this sequential part. Practices like sense-restraint (1), moderation with food (2), wakefulness (3), clear comprehension (5), etc., are essentially cumulative, in that they are practiced together and do not build on each other in the way the sequential aspects of the path do. It would not be reasonable to assume that only after one has practiced sense-restraint (1) is one ready to be cultivating moderation with food (2); only after having accomplished such moderation has the time come to practice wakefulness (3); and only after one has practiced wakefulness is one finally set for engaging in the practice of clear comprehension (5). From a practical perspective this clearly does not make much sense.

Although one might imagine that a neophyte to the training is introduced to these step by step, once that has happened, all of these practices are to be undertaken in conjunction. In fact wakefulness by way of meditating in the early and late parts of the night would be something to be undertaken as soon as possible, just like moderation with food, which in fact supports wake-

[48] For a more detailed discussion of imperturbability see Anālayo 2012c: 195–200.

fulness, as overeating will lead to sleepiness. Again sense-restraint needs to be cultivated right away, and clear comprehension should be practiced throughout. Both are also to some degree interrelated, since restraint of the senses is an aspect of acting with clear comprehension and such clear comprehension in turn is empowered if one has established sense-restraint.

Given the essentially cumulative character of these practices, it becomes a matter of choice how many of them are listed in a particular exposition. A need to select naturally arises once one moves from actual practice to theoretical description, since what is practiced simultaneously cannot be described simultaneously. Some features of the practice need to be selected and listed sequentially to represent the whole.

This in turn suggests that there need not be a deeper significance in the variations observed above. Such differences, in the words of Bucknell (1984: 32), simply make "use of different, though essentially equivalent, summarizing lists of stages".

This perhaps explains the curious fact that *satipaṭṭhāna* (4) is mentioned only rarely, in spite of its indubitable importance for cultivating the path to liberation. The reason is simply that those responsible for early versions of the gradual path did not feel a need to mention *satipaṭṭhāna* explicitly.

Mindfulness in some form or another would in fact be required for all aspects of the gradual path. In particular sense-restraint (1) and clear comprehension (5) necessarily imply mindfulness practice, so that it would be misleading to assume that training in mindfulness was not part of the gradual path in actual practice. Given that the early path descriptions were not meant to be all-comprehensive and invariably fixed, the absence of an explicit reference to *satipaṭṭhāna* would not have been perceived as problematic. Perhaps such absence could even be understood to reflect an awareness of the all-pervasive need for mindfulness for each of the different aspects of the gradual path, from establishing sense-restraint all the way through to absorption attainment and beyond.

In later times, path manuals tend to adopt a more fixed form and strive for greater comprehensiveness. Although this results in neat theoretical presentations, without the type of variations observed above, it is not without problems. The kind of problems that can arise from adopting a fixed model can be seen in relation to the basic division of the path into the threefold training in morality, concentration, and wisdom.

As part of a presentation of the threefold training in morality, concentration, and wisdom, the *Mahāparinibbāna-sutta* indicates that concentration that is conjoined with and supported by morality is very fruitful, just as wisdom that is conjoined with and supported by concentration is very fruitful, and such wisdom will lead to the destruction of the influxes.[49] Some of these interrelations are also reflected in its Mūlasarvāstivāda parallel,[50] whereas the Dharmaguptaka version mentions only the threefold training as such, without detailing the interrelations among the three.[51]

---

[49] DN 16 at DN II 91,7: *iti sīlaṃ iti samādhi iti paññā. sīlaparibhāvito samādhi mahapphalo hoti mahānisaṃso. samādhiparibhāvitā paññā mahapphalā hoti mahānisaṃsā. paññāparibhāvitaṃ cittaṃ sammadeva āsavehi vimuccati.*

[50] The Mūlasarvāstivāda parallel has a similar formulation, although without the link from concentration to wisdom; see Waldschmidt 1951: 160 (§8.6): *itīmāni bhikṣavaḥ śīlāny ayaṃ s(amādhir iyaṃ prajñā), śīlaparibhāvitaḥ samādhiś cirasthitiko bhavati, prajñāparibhāvitaṃ cittaṃ samyag eva vim(u)cyate.*

[51] DĀ 2 at T I 13a3 just introduces noble morality, noble concentration, noble wisdom, and noble liberation as four profound teachings or states, 有四深法: 一曰聖戒, 二曰聖定, 三曰聖慧, 四曰聖解脫; see also T 6 at T I 178b5.

Although these three trainings clearly build on one another, this does not imply a rigid separation. According to a simile in the *Soṇadaṇḍa-sutta* and its *Dīrgha-āgama* parallel, the relationship between morality and wisdom, for instance, can be illustrated with two hands that wash each other.[52] Similarly, morality and wisdom support each other.

With later tradition the interrelations among the three trainings have not always remained as prominent a characteristic as in this simile. Shankman (2008: 86) points out that since the "standard gradual path of practice proceeds progressively through the threefold division of … morality, concentration and wisdom", this then "is used to support the notion of two distinct types of meditative developments as presented in the Visuddhimagga". In other words, the fixing of path descriptions, in the case of the Theravāda tradition by the time of the *Visuddhimagga*, contributes to a separation of what in the early discourses are two complementary aspects of meditative cultivation, namely tranquillity and insight.[53]

Such are the possible pitfalls of fixed path accounts taken literally. Keeping in mind such possible repercussions offers a perspective on the variations in the path accounts surveyed above. Given that variations are found within a single reciter tradition and even within a single discourse collection, it seems clear that path descriptions were not considered as having to conform to one single model and that they served a didactic rather than strictly normative purpose. With complementary perspectives standing side by side, the tendency to latch on to one particular list as the only right way is deprived of a founda-

---

[52] DN 4 at DN I 124,5 and DĀ 22 at T I 96b18 (where the simile is spoken by the Buddha himself); on this simile see Gombrich 1984: 99.

[53] In Anālayo 2003: 88–91 and 2012a: 229–235 I already stressed the interrelation of these two in early Buddhist thought.

tion. After all, any description of the gradual path of training is simply a map, whose purpose is to provide guidelines to be put into practice in the particular teaching context within which it evolved. In this way, variations in the gradual-path accounts are like various fingers pointing to the moon. Attention should not be paid to a particular finger, but to the direction in which it points, in order to see the moon for oneself.

In sum, a comparison of accounts of the gradual path of training from sense-restraint to imperturbability shows several variations, even between discourses pertaining to the same reciter tradition. Closer inspection suggests that such variations need not be seen as reflecting contending accounts of the path of practice. Instead, they can more fruitfully be viewed as complementary. From the viewpoint of the tendency of later path accounts to become more fixed, such a tendency to variation has the advantage of being less prone to misinterpretation, in the sense of mistaking what for the purpose of communication is presented separately as reflecting actually disconnected types of practices.

The Theory of Two Paths to Awakening

The idea that the early discourses reflect actually separate types of practice, to the extent that two competing accounts of the path to awakening can be discerned, has been a recurrent theme in academic scholarship. In what follows I briefly take up the main arguments that have been proposed in support of the notion that there is evidence for an irreconcilable conflict between the advocates of two distinct paths to liberation in early Buddhist discourse. After examining the main arguments proposed for this theory, I discuss problems with one of its main planks, the belief that the scheme of the four noble truths stands for an intellectual form of understanding only. Another main plank is the consequent assumption that absorption attainment equals the gaining of liberating insight. This is a topic to which I return in the next chapter, in which I argue that the idea that absorption attainment is in and of itself liberating cannot be sustained in light of certain basic understandings of absorption in the early discourses.

The theory of two contrasting paths to liberation harkens back to an article published by de La Vallée Poussin in 1929, in which he argued that a discourse in the *Aṅguttara-nikāya* (AN 6.46) opposes meditators to those who reach liberation by mere reflection.[54] By way of background to his taking up this position, it could be pertinent that 1929 falls within the period in which de La Vallée Poussin must have been working on his remarkable annotated translation of Vasubandhu's *Abhidharmakośa*, published in six volumes from 1923 to 1931.[55] This makes it fairly probable that his approach and thinking were influenced by Buddhist exegesis as expressed by scholars such as Vasubandhu.

As the above study of gradual-path accounts would have shown, a clear-cut division between tranquillity and insight of the type found regularly in Buddhist exegetical works (best known in this respect is probably the *Visuddhimagga* by Buddhaghosa) does not necessarily correspond to the situation in the early discourses, where *samatha* and *vipassanā* are rather interrelated qualities, instead of representing two separate meditation practices.[56] Needless to say, this does not mean that there could not be discernible differences and even tensions

[54] AN 6.46 at AN III 355,1; see de La Vallée Poussin 1929.

[55] De La Vallée Poussin 1923/1971, 1924/1971, 1926/1971, 1925/1980a, 1925/1980b, and 1931/1980.

[56] See, e.g., Bergonzi 1980, Cousins 1984, Sujato 2001: 23–30, Gangajot 2016, and above p. 89 note 53.

between an emphasis on tranquillity or on insight in actual practice. The point I intend to make is only that the assumption of two conflicting approaches to liberation, the one requiring a mode of intellectual reflection and the other being based solely on ecstatic absorption, does not accurately reflect what the early discourses convey. Nor does such a position accord particularly well with the bulk of later exegesis, but this is not what I am at present concerned with, which is only to contrast the notion of two paths to liberation with the position taken in the early discourses.

Further details on the basic assumption underlying the theory of two paths to awakening emerge with another article by de La Vallée Poussin, which appears to have had a formative influence on subsequent scholars. According to his presentation, early (as well as later) Buddhist sources testify to the existence of two mutually opposed theories. One of these theories sees liberation as the result of intellectual means, whereas the other considers it to be the result of ascetic and ecstatic disciplines.[57] The first theory of intellectual means finds exemplification in insight into the four truths and knowledge of things as they really are. Following the approach of ecstatic discipline one instead proceeds through the four absorptions and the four immaterial spheres up to the attainment of cessation.

The two-paths theory relies on four main passages, which I now briefly introduce and then take up one after the other for critical evaluation. I number these four passages consecutively in order to facilitate the discussion.

---

[57] De La Vallée Poussin 1936/1937: 189f: "on peut … discerner dans les sources bouddhiques, anciennes ou scolastiques, deux théories opposées … la théorie qui fait du salut une œuvre purement ou surtout intellectuelle; la théorie qui met le salut au bout des disciplines ascétiques et extatiques."

1) Among the early discourses, de La Vallée Poussin sees the discourse on Susīma as proving that there were arahants who had reached liberation by a purely intellectual approach.[58]

2) Another discourse shows in his view that a monk by the name of Nārada, even though he has the same insight as an arahant monk by the name of Musīla, does not consider himself an arahant because he lacks the direct experience of Nirvāṇa that is possible with the attainment of cessation.[59]

3) In the paper already mentioned earlier, de La Vallée Poussin had taken up a discourse in the *Aṅguttara-nikāya*, which according to his assessment opposes meditators to those who reach the final goal by reflection.[60]

4) In addition to this, another passage from the *Aṅguttara-nikāya* has at times been taken to have similar implications,

---

[58] De La Vallée Poussin 1936/1937: 202: "il y a des Arhats délivrés par la *prajñā*, par la connaissance purement intellectuelle"; see also Pande 1957: 537f.

[59] De La Vallée Poussin 1936/1937: 218: "Nārada, qui possède les mêmes savoirs que Musīla, ne se considère pas comme Arhat parce que le contact avec le Nirvāṇa (qu'on obtient dans la *nirodhasamāpatti*) lui manque."

[60] De La Vallée Poussin 1929. Griffith 1981: 616 then sees the same discourse as evidencing "an acrimonious debate" between "those who practice concentrative meditation" and "those zealous for *dhamma* [which] are 'those who, penetrating by means of wisdom, see the profound goal'" (see also below p. 96 note 66). Griffith 1981: 617 sums up that "the *nibbāna* realized by insight meditation is simply not the same as the *nibbāna*-in-life (*diṭṭhadhammanibbāna*) which is the result of concentrative meditation." Clough 2012: 23 similarly concludes that this discourse proves two separate paths leading to two distinct goals, where "the noble person who is liberated of mind is freed from craving as a result of the cultivation of samatha. The noble person who is liberated by insight is freed from ignorance through the cultivation of vipassanā."

since it indicates that tranquillity overcomes passion and insight overcomes ignorance.[61]

In what follows I take up each of these four cases in turn.

1) Regarding the first of these four passages, the assessment by de La Vallée Poussin that the discourse involving Susīma features arahants who reached liberation by a purely intellectual approach seems to be based on a misunderstanding. The Pāli version of the discourse and its parallels show variations inasmuch as the need for attaining all four absorptions to reach liberation is concerned.[62] But even those versions that do not stipulate absorption attainment do clearly refer to meditation practice.[63] None of them supports the idea that a purely intellectual approach could lead to full awakening, without having cultivated a level of tranquillity that at the very least borders on absorption attainment.

---

[61] According to Gombrich 1996: 114, this passage seems "to suggest two paths to nirvana".

[62] For a detailed study see Bodhi 2007 and 2009.

[63] In SN 12.70 at SN II 123,26 and in a discourse quotation in the Mahāsāṅghika *Vinaya*, T 1425 at T XXII 363a14, the arahants deny that they attained supernormal powers or the immaterial attainments and then explain that they are liberated by wisdom. This leaves open that they could have attained absorption. In SĀ 347 at T II 97a9 and in discourse quotations in the *Vibhāṣā*s translated by Xuánzàng (玄奘) and Buddhavarman, T 1545 at T XXVII 572c16 and T 1546 at T XXVIII 408a28, the arahants even deny having attained any of the four absorptions. Nevertheless, SĀ 347 at T II 97c2 clearly indicates that they meditated, as they reached liberation after having dwelled alone and in seclusion, with single-minded attention and being established in diligence, 彼諸善男子獨一靜處, 專精思惟, 不放逸住, 離於我見, 不起諸漏心善解脫. According to the *Vibhāṣā*s, they attained liberation based on what appears to be access concentration, T 1545 at T XXVII 572c25: 然彼五百應真苾芻依未至定得漏盡 and T 1546 at T XXVIII 408b9: 彼諸比丘先依未至禪盡漏.

2) Turning to the second passage, featuring the two monks Nārada and Musīla, closer inspection shows that this discourse is not about a juxtaposition of two monks, one of whom has not reached cessation attainment, contrary to the assumption by de La Vallée Poussin. In fact the attainment of cessation does not feature at all in any of the different extant versions of the discourse.

In all versions the monk Nārada employs the simile of seeing water that one is unable to reach physically to illustrate that, even though one has already seen the goal, one therefore need not have fully reached it.[64] In other words, the simile conveys that he has reached a stage of awakening that falls short of being arahantship. This conclusion finds confirmation in the commentary, which reports that Nārada was a non-returner.[65] Thus this discourse is about the difference between one who has already experienced Nirvāṇa when attaining a lower level of awakening, a trainee (*sekha*), and an arahant who has reached full awakening. In sum, the difference between the monks Nārada and Musīla is not one of different paths, but only concerns different levels of the path.

3) In the case of the discourse in the *Aṅguttara-nikāya* that de La Vallée Poussin sees as contrasting meditators to those who reach the final goal by mere reflection, his reading seems also to be based on a misunderstanding. The discourse does indeed set meditators (*jhāyin*) in opposition to those who devote themselves to Dharma (*dhammayoga*), but of these only

---

[64] SN 12.68 at SN II 118,4, SHT II 680a 95R9–10, Waldschmidt et al. 1968: 39, and SĀ 351 at T II 98c27; for critical assessments of the assumptions by de La Vallée Poussin and others in relation to this discourse see also Swearer 1972: 369, Gómez 1999: 700–703, and Bodhi 2003.

[65] Spk II 123,11.

the first are reckoned to have actually reached a level of awakening. Whereas the meditators dwell having personally experienced the deathless element, which would imply they must at the very least be stream-enterers, those who devote themselves to Dharma have only reached a wise understanding.[66] This does not imply any level of awakening, let alone turning them all into arahants.

4) The last of the four passages to be examined is the indication in another discourse in the *Aṅguttara-nikāya* that tranquillity overcomes passion and insight overcomes ignorance.[67] This presentation does not imply that these are two different goals, because passion and ignorance are interrelated problems. Passion exists because of ignorance and one way in which ignorance expresses itself is precisely through passion.

A discourse in the *Saṃyutta-nikāya* and its *Saṃyukta-āgama* parallel define penetrative understanding (*pariññā*), the opposite of ignorance, as the destruction of passion.[68] Another discourse in the *Saṃyutta-nikāya* and its *Saṃyukta-āgama* parallel indicate that insight into impermanence eradicates passion, whereby

---

[66] AN 6.46 at AN III 356,14 (of which no parallel is known to me) indicates that the *jhāyin*s "dwell having directly experienced the deathless element", *amataṃ dhātuṃ kāyena phusitvā viharanti*, whereas the *dhammayoga* monks "see having penetrated with wisdom a profound meaningful saying", *gambhīraṃ atthapadaṃ paññāya ativijjha passanti* (the rendering by Griffiths 1981: 616 of *gambhīraṃ atthapadaṃ* as "profound goal" seems to me to be misleading; for other translations of this expression see, e.g., Bodhi 2012: 919: "a deep and pithy matter", or Nyanatiloka 1907/1984: 208: "einen tiefgründigen Lehrgegenstand"). The passage does not juxtapose two types of arahants and therefore does not support the two-paths theory; see also Gómez 1999: 695–699 and Cousins 2009.

[67] AN 2.3.10 at AN I 61,4.

[68] SN 22.106 at SN III 160,1 and its parallel SĀ 72 at T II 19a8.

liberation is reached.[69] Needless to say, such insight into impermanence is precisely what counters ignorance. The difference between sensual passion and ignorance relates to their total removal, as a non-returner has completely emerged from sensual passion, but not yet totally removed all ignorance.

Elsewhere ignorance is reckoned the nutriment for craving.[70] This implies that one who removes ignorance will thereby automatically go beyond passion and craving. The same is also evident from the standard description of dependent arising (*paṭicca samuppāda*) in the cessation mode, where the removal of the first link of ignorance leads to the cessation of the ensuing links, including the links of craving and clinging.

Descriptions of the attainment of arahantship similarly point to this interrelation between the problem posed by passion, sensual desires, and craving on the one hand and the problem of ignorance on the other hand. These descriptions specify that with full awakening the influxes of sensuality (*kāmāsava*) and [desire for] existence (*bhavāsava*) are overcome just as well as the influx of ignorance (*avijjāsava*).[71] It is the combined removal of

---

[69] SN 22.51 at SN III 51,12 and SĀ[3] 12 at T II 496b24.

[70] AN 10.62 at AN V 116,19 and its parallels MĀ 52 at T I 487c29, MĀ 53 at T I 489b1, T 36 at T I 819c26, and T 37 at T I 820b25; the exposition is in particular concerned with craving for becoming. Carrithers 1983: 66 explains that "the relationship between craving, ignorance and suffering is rather like the relationship between heat, oxygen and fire. Heat is the motive force, but without oxygen fire could not arise." Regarding such 'oxygen' supply, Matilal 1980: 163 notes that the problem of ignorance is not just a matter of lacking some theoretical knowledge, given that "*avidyā* is said to be the guiding force of our action. But certainly mere lack of knowledge does not motivate us to act."

[71] One out of numerous examples would be the account of the gradual path in DN 2 at DN I 84,8 and its parallels DĀ 27 at T I 109b8 (to be

craving and of ignorance which makes one an arahant, not only the one or the other. In the words of Gethin (1997: 221),

> what Buddhist thought seems to be suggesting ... is that what is logically distinct – the cognitive and affective, fact and value – is empirically inextricably bound up together: a mind that does not see in accordance with the truth is a mind that tends to grasp.

In this way the last of the four passages, the *Aṅguttara-nikāya* discourse on tranquillity and insight, is not about two different paths, but about two complementary aspects of the path to liberation. This conclusion finds confirmation in the *Ekottarika-āgama* parallel, which clarifies that what leads to full awakening is insight.[72] Eliade (1958: 176, originally published in French in 1954) concludes that, according to the *Aṅguttara-nikāya* discourse on tranquillity and insight,

> the two methods ... are equally indispensable for obtaining arahantship ... the 'experimental knowledge' given by the four *jhāna*s and the *samāpatti*s does not lead to *nirvāṇa* unless it is illuminated by 'wisdom'.

---

supplemented from DĀ 20 at T I 86c6), T 22 at T I 275c25, and the *Saṅghabhedavastu*, Gnoli 1978: 250,28.

[72] EĀ 20.7 at T II 600b6; for a translation and more detailed discussion see Anālayo 2015c: 63–65. This is in line with a general pattern described by Gimello 1978: 185 as follows: "in all versions of the story of the Buddha's life and in all systematic curricula of meditation, it is discernment, or its perfection as insight (*prajñā*), which is the proximate cause of enlightenment, not *śamatha* or *samādhi*." Bergonzi 1980: 327 concludes that the need for both tranquillity and insight to reach full awakening has been evident since the most ancient Buddhist texts, "fin dai più antichi testi buddhisti si insiste spesso sulla necessità – ai fini della liberazione – di combinare in un'unica struttura fondamentale le due diverse tecniche meditative di *samatha* e *vipassanā*."

Keown (1992/2001: 79 and 82) points out that

> there exist two techniques of meditation precisely because the obstacles to enlightenment are themselves twofold ... the two techniques exist precisely because final perfection can only be achieved when both dimensions ... the emotional and the intellectual, are purified.

Not only full awakening, but also the attainment of cessation requires that the two supposedly different paths are combined. A discourse in the *Saṃyutta-nikāya* and its *Saṃyukta-āgama* parallel explicitly state that to reach the attainment of cessation requires both tranquillity and insight.[73] As summed up by Stuart (2013: 44) in a discussion of the attainment of cessation that, even though there may seem to be

> a 'fundamental difference' between a mindless state of cessation and a mindful realization of the Four Noble Truths, the practice said to lead to these states may very well have originally been singular.

In sum, it seems clear that the four main passages recurrently quoted in support of the theory of two competing paths to liberation fail to support it. Nevertheless, this theory has had a continuous impact on the way the discourses are read and interpreted in discussions among scholars and practitioners.

Recent examples are the suggestion that the sequence of *Majjhima-nikāya* discourses related to the Buddha's awakening reflects an emphasis on the path of insight alone,[74] or else

---

[73] SN 41.6 at SN IV 295,29 and its parallel SĀ 568 at T II 150c5.

[74] Sferra 2011: 97 sees the sequence of discourses in the *Majjhima-nikāya*, where MN 4 (account of the Buddha's awakening) is followed by MN 19 (description of the Buddha's pre-awakening overcoming of unwholesome thoughts), as indicating that the

the supposition that the account of the Buddha's awakening by attaining the four absorptions and the three higher knowledges shows the possibility of attaining full awakening by tranquillity alone.[75] Both suggestions are, as far as I can see, cases of reading the two-paths theory into material that simply does not warrant such an interpretation.[76]

Theravāda tradition emphasizes insight over yogic practices, in contrast to the Mūlasarvāstivāda tradition as reflected in the *Saṅghabhedavastu*, which reports his attainment of supernormal abilities as part of the account of the Buddha's awakening, "l'implicito è abbastanza evidente: la sequenza dei *sutta* suggerisce che per ottenere il risveglio i Theravādin ritengono necessario coltivare la consapevolezza (*sati*) e l'*insight* (*vipassanā*) … i Mūlasarvāstivādin, lo yoga e le *siddhi*."

[75] According to Clough 2012: 129, part of the Buddhist tradition "saw attainment of the jhāna states alone, without subsequent vipassanā practice, as sufficient for liberation", since "the only description of the Buddha's meditative practice prior to his directing his mind to these three higher knowledges is that of a cultivated progression through each of the four jhānas … there is no reference whatsoever in these importantly paradigmatic passages (they are describing *the* ultimate event in the religion, after all) to the soon-to-be Buddha diverting himself to any identifiable or distinguishable vipassanā technique."

[76] Regarding the first theory by Sferra 2011 (see above note 74), the sequence of discourses in the *Majjhima-nikāya* does not follow a chronological order, in contrast to accounts of the Buddha's progress to awakening in *Vinaya* narratives. Moreover, the Buddha's attainment of supernormal abilities, described in the *Saṅghabhedavastu*, Gnoli 1977: 116,20, is also reported in MN 12 at MN I 69,10, which in fact stands between MN 4 and MN 19. Thus the sequence of discourses in the *Majjhima-nikāya* does not have the implication attributed to it by Sferra. Regarding the second theory by Clough 2012 (see above note 75), the three higher knowledges are precisely about the cultivation of insight. The first and the second higher knowledge

The same influence continues, although at times without the individual protagonist being consciously aware of this influence, in modern-day attempts to present absorption attainment itself as productive of liberating insight, a topic to which I return in more detail in the next chapter.

As far as I can see, the two-paths theory might best be set aside as an erroneous projection of the Western contrast between the thinker and the mystic onto material that does not warrant such an interpretation. Of course, others will not necessarily agree with my assessment. Yet, those who wish to uphold this theory or one of its two main assumptions need to engage seriously with the criticism that has been voiced, rather than ignoring it. At the very least, the notion of two conflicting paths can no longer be taken as representing scholarly consensus, but needs first to be argued by addressing in detail the different objections that have been raised.

In the remainder of this chapter I take up the first of the two major assumptions that appear to be underlying the theory of two separate paths to liberation. The two assumptions are:

1) the idea that in the early discourses the comprehension of the four noble truths is just a matter of intellectual reflection,[77]

2) the notion that the attainment of absorption was considered as liberating in and of itself, to be discussed in the next chapter.

---

have the potential to disclose dependent arising, and the third higher knowledge corresponds to the highest level of insight possible (for a survey of different aspects of the Buddha's pre-awakening cultivation of insight which then came to their culmination on the night of his awakening see Anālayo 2010: 18f). In sum, the suggestions by Sferra and Clough are not supported by the textual evidence and appear to be the result of being influenced by the two-paths theory.

[77] On the attribute "noble" in relation to the four truths see in more detail Anālayo 2016c: 239–248.

Insight into the Four Noble Truths

In a recent attempt to argue the two assumptions just mentioned, Polak (2016: 89f) correctly notes that the four noble truths correspond to right view, which forms a precondition for the cultivation of the noble eightfold path. He then sees this precursory role as standing in contrast to passages that present the four noble truths as an expression of the attainment of the final goal.

Here it needs to be kept in mind that a preliminary understanding of the four noble truths as a guiding principle for setting out on the practice of the noble eightfold path need not correspond to the level of insight into the four noble truths gained with awakening. The *Dhammacakkappavattana-sutta* and its Chinese parallels in fact present insight into the four noble truths as requiring sustained practice, expressed in terms of three turnings applied to each truth. In what follows I translate excerpts from this exposition in the *Saṃyukta-āgama* parallel to the *Dhammacakkappavattana-sutta*, which sets in after the first "turning" of a basic understanding of the four noble truths has already been described:[78]

> The noble truth of *dukkha* should be further understood with knowledge ... having understood the noble truth of the arising of *dukkha*, it should be eradicated ... having understood this noble truth of the cessation of *dukkha*, it should be realized ... having understood this noble truth of the path to the cessation of *dukkha*, it should be cultivated ...
>
> Having understood this noble truth of *dukkha*, it has to be understood completely ... having understood this noble

[78] SĀ 379 at T II 103c17 to 104a1; for a survey of the parallels to this discourse, as well as a detailed critical discussion of the assumption by some scholars that the teaching given in this discourse is late, see Anālayo 2015e: 347–388 and 2016c: 267–299.

> truth of the arising of *dukkha*, it has to be eradicated completely ... having understood the noble truth of the cessation of *dukkha*, it has to be realized completely ... having understood the noble truth of the path to the cessation of *dukkha*, it has to be cultivated completely ...

In the above extract, for the sake of readability I have employed ellipses to dispense with a repeated occurrence of the expression "when I gave proper attention to it, vision, knowledge, understanding, and realization arose." This expression is found after each of the individual statements. The formulation reinforces what already emerges from the passage itself, namely the need to deepen one's understanding of the four noble truths. This implies that there are different levels of profundity in realizing the four noble truths, which can extend from the initial appreciation of one who has just embarked on the path all the way to the profound insight of one who has gained full awakening. The *Saṃyukta-āgama* version concludes this part of its exposition with the Buddha's statement:[79]

> [So long as] in regard to these four noble truths in three turnings and twelve modes I had not given rise to vision, knowledge, understanding, and realization, I had not yet attained ... deliverance, release, and liberation.

From a comparative perspective, a difference in the *Dhammacakkappavattana-sutta* is that, instead of applying one turning to all four truths and then moving on to the next turning, it rather applies all three turnings to one truth and then moves on to the next truth.[80] This is a recurrent difference among the parallel versions of the discourse with which, according to

---

[79] SĀ 379 at T II 104a2 to 104a4.
[80] SN 56.11 at SN V 422,3.

tradition, the Buddha set in motion the wheel of Dharma.[81] In fact one version found in the *Ekottarika-āgama* just mentions the three turnings and the resulting twelve modes, without working through them in detail.[82]

Alongside such variations, however, the basic notion of three turnings that need to be applied to each of the four truths is clearly common ground among the *Dhammacakkappavattana-sutta* and its parallels. This implies that, from the time of what tradition regards as the first sermon given by the recently awakened Buddha, engagement with the four noble truths was quite definitely *not* presented as an intellectual exercise in reasoned understanding only. Rather, it was considered to involve a prolonged cultivation, expressed with the metaphor of "three turnings". It is only with the completion of this prolonged cultivation that according to the *Dhammacakkappavattana-sutta* and its parallels the Buddha felt qualified to claim he had reached full liberation.

Besides, judging from the above passage and its parallels the four noble truths are not the actual content of the experience of awakening. That is, to describe the realization of awakening with the help of the scheme of the four noble truths does not imply that such realization takes place in a way that directly involves the formulations employed for describing these four truths. In other words, the presentation in the *Dhammacakkappavattana-sutta* and its parallels does not require us to imagine the Buddha at the moment of awakening mentally saying to himself: "This is *dukkha*, this is the arising of *dukkha*…" etc.

Instead of describing intellectual reasoning at the moment of awakening, the formulation of the four noble truths rather ap-

---

[81] For a survey of these different patterns see Anālayo 2016c: 298.
[82] EĀ 24.5 at T II 619b3.

pears to be a description that draws out the implications of what happened, based on a scheme apparently taken over from ancient Indian medical diagnosis.[83] The realization itself at the moment of awakening is the experience of Nirvāṇa. This finds expression in the circumstance that the three turnings mentioned in the *Dhammacakkappavattana-sutta* use the terminology of realization only in relation to the third truth.[84] It is with the realization of Nirvāṇa that the cessation of *dukkha* is realized.

The terminology in the passage above clarifies also the relationship between the third noble truth and the other three. With the "realization" of the cessation of *dukkha* = 3rd truth, *dukkha* is fully "understood" (when one has once experienced its complete absence) = 1st truth; the arising of *dukkha* has been "eradicated" = 2nd truth; and the path leading to the cessation of *dukkha* has been "cultivated" to its fulfillment = 4th truth.

In this way, what the entire set of four truths points to is a realization experience, which is described by analogy with a medical scheme of diagnosis. This fourfold scheme serves to explain the implications of the realization and at the same time to enable others to follow up and reach the same realization.

Understood in this way, the four noble truths can fulfill their diagnostic function at the outset of the path, when an initial appreciation of the fact of *dukkha*, its cause, the possibility of its cessation, and the vision of a practical path to this end motivates

---

83 See Anālayo 2015e: 27–40. As noted by Shulman 2014: 40, verbal accounts of experiences like cessation could simply be part of a "post-meditation process of reflection". Other aspects of his discussion of the four noble truths, however, are less convincing.

84 The suggestion by Batchelor 2015: 79f that the third truth does not refer to a distinct realization as the outcome of meditative practice, but just to 'beholding' the momentarily absence of reactivity, does not do justice to the original.

someone to set out to cultivate the path. They can continue to encapsulate the motivation and deepening insight of the one who walks the path, and they can eventually function as an expression of the arrival at the goal.

In sum, this plank of the theory of two paths to awakening, the idea that insight into the four noble truths is a matter of intellectual reasoning, is unconvincing. In the next chapter I will argue that the same holds also for the other plank, the belief that absorption is in itself the path to liberation.

By way of summing up, I can do no better than quote the assessment of the two-paths theory by two eminent scholars. Cox (1992/1994: 65f) notes that

> prior studies of early Buddhist religious praxis … presume that the tension between knowledge and meditative concentration evident in certain textual descriptions of the path reflects an actual divergence in techniques and historical traditions of religious praxis … [yet, there is instead] an alternative explanation, neglected in previous studies, to this tension between the cognitive and the meditative – namely, a final goal that subsumes knowledge and concentration as equally cooperative means rather than mutually exclusive ends … extensive textual evidence … argues that this – not concentration or knowledge alone – represents the final goal.

Gethin (1992/2001: xiv) clarifies that,

> contrary to what is sometimes suggested, there are not two radically different conceptions of the Buddhist path vying with each other: there is no great struggle going on between the advocates of the way of 'calm' (*samatha*) and 'meditation' (*jhāna*) on the one hand, and the advocates of the way of 'insight' (*vipassanā*) and understanding (*paññā*) on the other. In fact it turns out that the characteristically early

Buddhist conception of the path leading to the cessation of suffering is that it consists precisely in the combining of calm and insight.

Conclusion

Descriptions of the gradual path in the early discourses show several variations, in particular in relation to those practices that are of a cumulative character rather than being sequential. In later exegesis, depictions of the path tend to become more fixed and reflect a drive toward comprehensiveness.[85] As an almost inevitable result, the intrinsic interrelation between complementary aspects of the path, such as concentration and wisdom or tranquillity and insight, can be lost out of sight.

The same tendency has been taken considerably further in modern scholarship, leading to the assumption that the early Buddhist discourses reflect an irreconcilable conflict between advocates of two different paths to liberation. One of these two paths presumably involves an intellectual insight into the four noble truths, whereas the other path cultivates absorption attainment as in and of itself productive of liberating insight.

Closer inspection of the main passages quoted in support of this theory makes it safe to conclude that such suggestions do not reflect the early Buddhist position in this respect and appear to be the result of projecting the Western contrast between the thinker and the mystic onto material that does not warrant such an interpretation.

Insight into the four noble truths can take place at various depths, ranging from an initial appreciation that inspires one to

[85] On the tendency toward comprehensive coverage as an influential element in the arising of Abhidharma thought see Anālayo 2014c.

embark on the path all the way to the profound insight of one who has reached the final consummation of this path.

In relation to the moment of awakening, the scheme of four truths functions as a description of the Buddha's realization of Nirvāṇa. Apparently inspired by an ancient Indian scheme of medical diagnosis, such a pragmatic form of description serves to flesh out the implications of the experience of awakening in relation to the overarching task of finding a way out of the predicament of *dukkha* and at the same time serves to convey in a succinct manner the main elements of the path to be adopted by those who are in quest of the supreme health of Nirvāṇa.

Contrary to the assumption underpinning one of the chief planks of the theory of two separate paths to awakening, full realization of the four noble truths appears to be very much a matter of meditative cultivation, rather than being the result of intellectual reflection only. It is to the other main plank of this theory, the notion that absorption attainment is in itself liberating, that I turn in the next chapter.

By way of a poetic conclusion to this chapter, here is a verse from the *Dhammapada* on the four noble truths:

> The eightfold one is foremost of paths,
> The four [noble truths] of statements of truths,
> Dispassion is foremost of qualities,
> One with vision of two-footed ones.[86]

---

[86] Dhp 273; which has similarly worded parallels in the Gāndhārī *Dharmapada* 109, Brough 1962/2001: 134 (which in the last line speaks of "living beings" in general, instead of "two-footed ones"), the Patna *Dharmapada* 358, Cone 1989: 198, and the *Udānavarga* 12.4, Bernhard 1965: 192. Counterparts preserved in Chinese, which show some variations, can be found in T 210 at T IV 569a18, T 212 at T IV 682a25, and T 213 at T IV 783a22.

Absorption

Introduction

Whereas the notion that comprehension of the four noble truths is merely a matter of intellectual reflection has been of appeal mainly in scholarly circles, the idea that absorption attainment has an inherently liberating role in the early Buddhist path to awakening has won a wider following, presumably due to its attractiveness among practitioners of meditation.

Positions taken in this respect range from considering absorption (Pāli: *jhāna*, Sanskrit: *dhyāna*) as being in itself a form of insight to suggestions that insight into impermanence, etc., can be practiced while one is immersed in absorption. A proper appreciation of what relevant early discourse passages offer in this respect also requires ascertaining what according to these texts it means to be in absorption, wherefore in what follows I will alternate between studying arguments made in favor of the insight potential of absorption and features that in the early discourses characterize its attainment.

I begin by examining the assumption that absorption is in itself productive of liberating insight and then take up the question of what type of insight could be cultivated while one is immersed in an absorption. This then leads me on to exploring the nature of absorption attainment, in particular the role of *vitakka* and the significance of seclusion from sensuality in contrast to the happiness and joy experienced during deep concentration.

I also discuss the question of whether according to the early texts sound can be heard during absorption attainment, then argue that the immaterial spheres stand in a coherent meditative continuity with absorption attainment, and finally survey a few early discourse passages that appear to consider absorption to have been a pre-Buddhist type of practice.

Absorption as a Form of Insight

Regarding the idea that in the early discourses absorption is considered to be in itself liberating,[1] an argument in support of this notion has been made by Arbel (2015: 203), who suggests that in the *Cūḷavedalla-sutta* "the nun Dhammadinnā explains to Visākha that entering the *jhāna*s is the way to abandon the underlying tendencies (*anusaya*; M I 303–304)."[2] If that should be the case, the passage would indeed point to insight being an intrinsic quality of absorption attainment.

From a comparative perspective, it needs be noted that the corresponding passage in the Tibetan parallel to the *Cūḷavedalla-sutta* does not use the term "underlying tendency" at all. The relevant passage simply states, in relation to feelings experienced during the first, second, and third absorptions, that "such pleasant feelings do not increase (literally: "spread out") desire, but abandon it."[3]

In the case of the *Cūḷavedalla-sutta* itself, the passage in question describes that by attaining the first absorption "one

---

[1] E.g. Polak 2016: 85, whose suggestions regarding the four noble truths I examined in the previous chapter, considers "liberating insight as an intrinsic quality of the *jhāna* meditative state".

[2] For critical replies to Arbel 2015 and Polak 2016 respectively see Anālayo 2016a and 2016h.

[3] D 4094 *ju* 10a5 or Q 5595 *tu* 11a8: *'di ni bde ba'i tshor ba la 'dod chags rgyas par mi 'gyur zhing spong bar 'gyur ba zhes bya'o* (the key term here is *rgyas pa*, whereas for *anusaya* one would expect a term like *bag la nyal* or *phra rgyas*); for a translation of the Tibetan version see Anālayo 2012c: 40–55.

abandons lust and the underlying tendency to lust does not underlie that."[4] According to a parallel in the *Madhyama-āgama*, the feeling experienced in the first absorption "is reckoned a pleasant feeling that does not have the underlying tendency to sensual desire". It adds that this is so "because it abandons sensual desire".[5] The *Cūḷavedalla-sutta* and its *Madhyama-āgama* parallel do not explicitly take up the second or the third absorption, unlike the Tibetan version. Nevertheless, the position they take for the first absorption would hold implicitly for the pleasant feelings experienced during those higher absorptions in which such feelings are present.

Now the descriptions given in these two discourses in relation to the first absorption convey the sense not of a final abandoning of the underlying tendency to sensuality, but only of a temporary abandoning of sensuality. That is, the difference compared to the Tibetan version, according to which "such pleasant feelings do not increase desire, but abandon it" is a matter of formulation only, not a difference of meaning. In this respect the *Cūḷavedalla-sutta* and its parallels appear to be stating the same as a discourse in the *Dīgha-nikāya* and its parallels, according to which with the first absorption all previous perceptions of sensuality are abandoned.[6]

Arbel (2015: 203) argues that Dhammadinnā, after having discussed the first absorption, "further states that in the next two *jhāna*s one will abandon aversion". Now the *Cūḷavedalla-sutta* and its *Madhyama-āgama* parallel do not even mention the "next two *jhāna*s", which are only taken up in the Tibetan

4 MN 44 at MN I 303,32: *rāgan tena pajahati, na tattha rāgānusayo anuseti*.

5 MĀ 210 at T I 789c12: 是謂樂覺非欲使也. 所以者何? 此斷欲故.

6 DN 9 at DN I 182,18, with parallels in a Sanskrit fragment, Melzer 2006: 254 (417v1), and in DĀ 28 at T I 110a25.

version, where they receive the same treatment as the first. This is in fact to be expected, since it is hard to see how the pleasant feeling of the first absorption could have a substantially different function from the pleasant feeling of the second absorption, or the happiness felt with the third absorption.

The topic of aversion, be it as an "underlying tendency" or just as something that "increases", comes up in the *Cūḷavedalla-sutta* and its parallels in relation to a form of reflection, namely the aspiration to reach awakening. None of the three versions relates this aspiration in any way to absorption attainment. In this way, the suggestion that "in the next two *jhāna*s one will abandon aversion" seems to be a case of reading into a passage something that is not found there at all.

Now a proper appreciation of absorption in early Buddhist discourse would require a systematic reading of all relevant texts, even if one only takes into account the Pāli versions.[7] Besides the *Dīgha-nikāya* passage already mentioned, a systematic reading will sooner or later lead to several discourses that highlight the potential drawbacks of absorption attainment. Such discourses imply that the early Buddhist texts did not consider absorption attainment to be in itself productive of liberating insight.

One such passage is found in a discourse in the *Aṅguttara-nikāya* which, in agreement with its *Madhyama-āgama* parallel, describes a monastic who is an attainer of absorption and subsequently gets so overwhelmed by sensual desire as to disrobe. Here is the relevant part from the *Aṅguttara-nikāya* discourse:[8]

> A certain person ... attains the first absorption. [Thinking]: 'I am an attainer of the first absorption', [this person] dwells

---

[7] On the notion of a "systematic" reading see below p. 186f.

[8] AN 6.60 at AN III 394,11 to 394,14 (the original is abbreviated).

> associating closely with monks, nuns, male lay disciples, female lay disciples, kings, royal ministers, other teachers, and the disciples of other teachers. Associating closely and becoming intimate with them, dwelling uncontrolled and intent on talking, lust invades the mind. The mind being invaded by lust, [this person] gives up the [monastic] training and returns to the lower [lay] life.

The *Madhyama-āgama* parallel proceeds in this way:[9]

> Suppose there is a person who attains the first absorption. Having attained the first absorption, [this person] in turn remains at ease himself and does not strive further with a wish to attain what has not yet been attained, with a wish to obtain what has not [yet] been obtained, with a wish to realize what has not [yet] been realized. Later [this person] in turn associates frequently with laypeople, makes fun, becomes conceited, and engages in various types of impetuous conversations.
>
> As [this person] associates frequently with laypeople, makes fun, becomes conceited, and engages in various types of impetuous conversations, sensual desire in turn arises in the mind. Sensual desire having arisen in the mind, the body and the mind in turn become heated up [with passion]. The body and mind having become heated up, [this person] in turn gives up the [monastic] precepts and quits the path.

Both discourses continue with the same type of description for the higher absorptions. The two versions also illustrate the case of each absorption with a simile, where they exhibit some differences in the relationship they establish between a simile and the level of absorption this simile is meant to illustrate.

---

[9] MĀ 82 at T I 558b2 to 558b8.

In the case of the first absorption, the *Aṅguttara-nikāya* discourse describes dust on a road that disappears after rain (an image used in the *Madhyama-āgama* for the second absorption),[10] whereas the *Madhyama-āgama* discourse describes no longer seeing pebbles (etc.) in a pond that has become full of water after rain (a simile used in the *Aṅguttara-nikāya* for the second absorption).[11] It seems that at some point during oral transmission the similes related to the first and second absorptions changed places in one of these two versions.

Alongside such variations, however, the two discourses agree in their basic assessment that a monastic who has attained absorption can subsequently become so overwhelmed with sensual desire as to give up the training. This is hardly compatible with the idea that absorption is in itself productive of insight, that its attainment constitutes "the way to abandon the underlying tendencies" of sensuality, etc. Instead, it shows that absorption attainment needs to be combined with the cultivation of insight, and that the temporary aloofness from sensuality gained during such absorbed experience does not suffice to ensure that sensual passion will no longer overwhelm the mind on a later occasion.

Another discourse in the *Aṅguttara-nikāya* and its *Saṃyukta-āgama* parallel illustrate the limitations of deep concentration attainments with the example of taking hold of gum with one's hand, as a result of which the gum sticks to the hand.[12] This illustrates the predicament of someone who has become so attached to the concentration experienced that inspiration to pro-

---

[10] AN 6.60 at AN III 394,15 and MĀ 82 at T I 558c2.

[11] AN 6.60 at AN III 395,5 and MĀ 82 at T I 558b8 (which has a slightly longer list of things to be seen in the pond, compared to those mentioned in AN 6.60).

[12] AN 4.178 at AN II 165,23 and its parallel SĀ 492 at T II 128b5.

gress to liberation has been lost. Rather than being itself the means to liberation, here deep concentration has actually become the source for attachment that obstructs progress to total freedom of the mind.

Needless to say, this does not imply that absorption does not have much to offer for progress on the path to awakening. The point I am making is only that, to offer this contribution, absorption needs to be combined with insight and in particular to be practiced without giving rise to attachment.

The danger of attachment comes up for comment also in the *Uddesavibhaṅga-sutta* and its *Madhyama-āgama* parallel, just to provide another example. This danger manifests when a practitioner develops attachment to the sublime pleasure experienced when in absorption.[13] The warning sounded in this way reflects a recurrent cautionary attitude expressed in the early discourses in regard to absorption experience. Although the absorptions are regularly presented as crucial for progress on the path to full awakening, at the same time the possibility of getting stuck in them is also a repeated theme.

The same warning recurs in another discourse in the *Majjhima-nikāya* and its *Ekottarika-āgama* parallel, which describe different accomplishments that fall short of being the final goal, such as material gains, fame, moral conduct, or becoming accomplished in concentration. To mistake deep concentration for the final goal is, according to an illustration provided in these discourses, comparable to someone in search of heartwood who, mistakenly believing to have found heart-

---

[13] MN 138 at MN III 226,15 points out that due to attachment to the pleasure experienced the mind gets stuck internally; MĀ 164 at T I 695a25 indicates that the mind will not become internally settled due to such attachment; see in more detail Anālayo 2011: 788 note 152.

wood, only takes along the inner bark or else the roots of a tree.[14]

Insight Meditation During Absorption

Although the above passages make it in my view safe to conclude that the early Buddhist discourses did not consider absorption attainment as being in itself a form of liberating insight, the question remains how far insight can and should be cultivated while one is immersed in absorption attainment.

An example for insight contemplation related to absorption attainment can be seen in the *Mahāmāluṅkya-sutta* and its *Madhyama-āgama* parallel, which apply their respective instructions to the four absorptions and the three immaterial attainments.[15] The *Mahāmāluṅkya-sutta* follows a description of the attainment of the first absorption with the following instruction:[16]

> Whatever there is therein – [be it] pertaining to form, pertaining to feeling, pertaining to perception, pertaining to formations, pertaining to consciousness – one contemplates those states as impermanent, *dukkha*, a disease, a tumor, a dart, a calamity, an affliction, alien, disintegrating, empty, and not self; one turns the mind away from those states.
>
> Having turned the mind away from those states, one inclines the mind toward the deathless element: 'This is peaceful, this is sublime, namely the calming of all constructions (*saṅkhāra*), the letting go of all supports (*upadhi*), the extinction of craving, dispassion, cessation, Nirvāṇa.' Being established on that, one attains the destruction of the influxes.

---

[14] MN 29 at MN I 194,25 and its parallel EĀ 43.4 at T II 759b26.

[15] See in more detail Anālayo 2011: 357f.

[16] MN 64 at MN I 435,31 to 436,4.

The *Madhyama-āgama* version presents a different insight contemplation of the first absorption, which proceeds as follows:[17]

> In dependence on this attainment, one contemplates the rise and fall of feelings. Having contemplated the rise and fall of feelings in dependence on this attainment and become established in it, one will certainly attain the destruction of the influxes.

In this way, the *Madhyama-āgama* version turns in particular to the impermanent nature of feelings, whereas the *Mahāmāluṅkya-sutta* takes up all of the five aggregates and moreover encourages cultivating a variety of insight perspectives. In addition to impermanence, these perspectives also bring in the other two characteristics of *dukkha* and not self in several ways. Another noteworthy difference is that the *Mahāmāluṅkya-sutta* directly encourages inclining the mind toward Nirvāṇa. The main point that is common to the two versions is the need to contemplate the impermanent nature of absorption attainment.

This raises the question of the way in which the impermanent nature of an absorption experience should be cultivated so as to safeguard against the potential drawbacks of attachment to deep concentration attainments. The above descriptions could be read in two ways. Either one undertakes such insight contemplation while still being in the attainment, or else one does so retrospectively, after having emerged from the absorption itself but while still being in a mental condition close to it in concentrative depth.

The relationship between absorption attainment and insight can be further explored with the help of the *Anupada-sutta*, which describes Sāriputta cultivating insight in relation to a

---

[17] MĀ 205 at T I 779c19 to 779c21.

range of concentration attainments, from the first absorption through the immaterial spheres all the way up to the attainment of cessation.[18]

This discourse has regularly been quoted in support of the ability to contemplate the impermanent nature of the mental constituents of an absorption while being in the actual attainment.[19] In other words, whereas passages like the *Mahāmāluṅ-*

---

[18] MN 111 at MN III 25,9 introduces the whole exposition with the Buddha's indication that during the period of a fortnight Sāriputta practiced *vipassanā* in this way.

[19] E.g. Crangle 1994: 238 supports his assessment that "wisdom is applied from within *jhâna*" by referring in his note 150 to the insight passage in the *Anupada-sutta* as discussed by Schmithausen 1981: 231 note 117 (whose position to my mind reads considerably more cautiously in this respect than Crangle seems to think). In an article on whether one needs to emerge from absorption in order to cultivate insight, Gunaratana 2007: 47 and 60 explains that according to the *Anupada-sutta* "Sāriputta knew the arising, presence and passing away of all mental states from the first *Jhāna* up through the base of nothingness", thus "Sāriputta knew them when they were present, when they arose and when they disappeared. He was fully mindful of it when any mental state was present. He was completely aware while he was going through these *Jhānic* states." Gunaratana 2007: 67f concludes that "Ven. Sāriputta not only saw the mental factors of each *Jhāna* in turn, he did it without leaving the *Jhānic* state." Similarly, Shankman 2008: 85 argues that according to this discourse it seems that "Sāriputta was able to recognize, investigate, and develop insight into each of the jhānas and the first three āruppas while still in the particular meditative state." Shankman 2008: 101f concludes that from the early discourses to the commentarial tradition "the understanding of jhāna evolved from being a state of undistracted awareness and profound insight into the nature of changing phenomena to states of extreme tranquillity in which the mind is utterly engrossed in the mental qualities of the jhāna itself." Thus "jhāna in the suttas is a state of heightened mindfulness and aware-

kya-sutta and its *Madhyama-āgama* parallel, etc., in principle allow the two different readings mentioned above, in the case of the *Anupada-sutta* the situation is seen as being clear-cut in favor of insight practiced while one is in an absorption. If this were to be the case, then the *Anupada-sutta* would provide a model for interpreting other passages, such as the *Mahāmāluṅkya-sutta*.

The reason why the *Anupada-sutta* takes such a prominent role in relation to discussions of insight during absorption attainment appears to be the formulation the discourse uses when describing Sāriputta's cultivation of insight in relation to the attainments of neither-perception-nor-non-perception and of cessation. Here the discourse speaks of having emerged from the respective attainment and of contemplating those states that are past, have ceased, and have changed.[20] Since such specifications are not used in relation to the four absorptions and the three lower immaterial spheres, this naturally gives the impression that these are not concerned with states that are past and have ceased, but rather with states that are present.

The presentation in the *Anupada-sutta*, a discourse without a parallel in the discourse collections of other traditions and therefore of somewhat limited validity for reconstructing early Buddhist thought, is not without problems. The description of the mental-factor analysis in the *Anupada-sutta* shows signs of having undergone some later expansion in line with evolving Abhidharma thought, evident in an apparent expansion of the listing of some mental factors.[21]

---

ness of an ever-changing stream of experiences." Van Oosterwijk 2012: 98 similarly affirms that "in *jhāna* a monk may see the elements of existence as impermanent."

[20] MN 111 at MN III 28,17+28: *dhammā atītā niruddhā vipariṇatā.*

[21] The added portion appears to be the following part of the list of mental factors: "contact, feeling, perception, volition, mind, desire,

Nevertheless, in what follows I will take a closer look at the *Anupada-sutta* to see if the discourse, even if it should only reflect later ideas of its Theravāda reciters, does imply that insight into impermanence is to be practiced while one is immersed in an absorption. Here is the description of the insight contemplation undertaken by Sāriputta in relation to the first absorption (leaving the factor *vitakka* without translation for the time being, as I will discuss its significance later on):

> The states in the first absorption were determined by him one by one: *vitakka*, [sustained] application, joy, happiness, mental unification, contact, feeling, perception, volition, mind,[22] desire, determination, energy, mindfulness, equipoise, and attention. Known these states arise, known they remain, known they disappear.
>
> He understood thus: 'Indeed, in this way these states, which have not been, come into being; having been, they disappear.'
>
> Not being in favor of or against these states, he dwelled being independent, without being bound to them, being freed from them, being released from them, with a mind that is without confines. He understood: 'There is an escape beyond this.'[23]

According to the above description in the *Anupada-sutta*, "known these states arise, known they remain, known they disappear", *viditā uppajjanti, viditā upaṭṭhahanti, viditā abbhatthaṃ gacchanti*. This provides an important indication for a proper appreciation of the discourse, which clearly depicts a

---

determination, energy, mindfulness, equipoise, attention"; for a more detailed discussion see Anālayo 2014c: 100–110.

[22] The Siamese edition (S^e) has "consciousness" instead of the "mind".

[23] MN 111 at MN III 25,14 to 25,24.

mode of contemplation where Sāriputta is aware of these states arising and, after they have remained for a while, he is also aware when they disappear.

To cultivate such awareness of these mental qualities arising and disappearing while being in an absorption is impossible, because the very presence of these qualities is required for there to be an absorption in the first place and for it to continue being a state of absorption.[24]

The formulation used in the discourse makes it clear that the passage does not intend to refer to the momentary change of mental qualities. The *Anupada-sutta* clearly specifies that Sāriputta observes the arising of mental qualities which "have not been, come into being", *ahutvā sambhonti*, and he contemplates their disappearance when "having been, they disappear", *hutvā paṭiventi.*[25] The notion of momentariness, according to which phenomena pass away on the spot at every moment, is in fact a relatively late development in Buddhist thought.[26] It can safely be set aside as not forming the backdrop of the early discourses.

So when these states have not yet come into being or disappear, a practitioner inevitably is not yet or no longer in the absorption, simply because the absorption lasts only as long as all of the mental qualities that characterize it are fully present. Therefore to observe the arising of these mental qualities and

---

[24] This has in fact already been pointed out by Vetter 1988: 69: "it is certainly not possible to observe, as is stated in the text, the disappearance of these qualities in any of these states [i.e., the absorptions], because they are constituted by these qualities."

[25] The PTS edition (E^e) uses *paṭivedenti* instead of *paṭiventi.*

[26] According to von Rospatt 1995: 15–28, the doctrine of momentariness manifests fully only at a time after the closure of the canonical Abhidharma collections.

their disappearance could only happen before an absorption is attained or after the attainment has come to an end.

The circumstance that in relation to the attainments of neither-perception-nor-non-perception and of cessation the *Anupada-sutta* speaks of emerging from the respective attainments and of contemplating mental qualities that are past, have ceased, and changed must then be related to the particular nature of these two attainments.

In the case of these two attainments, either perception has been subdued to the extent that it is no longer possible to cognize or else the mind has come to cease.[27] Therefore there is no continuity of perceptual awareness from before the time one entered these attainments to emergence from them, comparable to the way this would be possible with the absorptions and the other immaterial attainments. In the case of attaining neither-perception-nor-non-perception or cessation, practitioners could only know that at some time in the past they entered and that by now they have emerged.

The same is not the case for the four absorptions and the lower three immaterial attainments, where practitioners can and in fact should be aware of the condition of the mind during actual attainment. But such awareness is concerned with a stable condition of the mind, a stability of continuously knowing the meditation object. The coming into being of that mental condition and its disappearance, in contrast, can only happen when one is not yet or no longer in the actual attainment.

This in turn shows that the *Anupada-sutta*'s description does not depict insight into impermanence practiced while a practi-

---

[27] In these two cases, MN 111 at MN III 28,16+27 in fact no longer lists any mental qualities, unlike the cases of the four absorptions and the lower three immaterial attainments, where the discourse each time lists the mental qualities of which Sāriputta was aware.

tioner is immersed in an absorption. Instead, the presentation in this discourse supports a reading according to which contemplation of the impermanent nature of the mental constituents of an absorption takes place before or on emerging from the attainment. In both cases a considerable degree of concentration has already been established or still remains present.[28] In such a condition of a concentrated mind, close to actual absorption, insight contemplation has its place by way of comparison with the mental condition experienced during the actual attainment.[29]

The Role of *vitakka*

The topic of insight reflection during absorption leads me on to the related question of whether any reflection takes place when one is immersed in absorption. This relates in particular to the significance of *vitakka* as a factor of the first absorption. The term *vitakka* is etymologically related to *takka*, which stands for logical reasoning and thought. This at first sight suggests that conceptual thought continues during the first level of absorption.[30]

---

[28] Such continuity seems to be implied in the standard description of wakefulness, according to which one keeps the mind in a condition free from the hindrances during sitting and walking meditation; cf., e.g., AN 3.16 at AN I 114,10 and its parallel EĀ 21.6 at T II 604a15. An example illustrating such continuity is AN 3.63 at AN I 182,27, a discourse without parallel, according to which the Buddha, with his exceptional meditative expertise, was able to maintain the collectedness of mind, gained earlier through attainment of the four absorptions, when doing walking meditation; see also above p. 85 note 47.

[29] Ajahn Brahm 2006: 178 concludes that "one cannot gain deep insight while experiencing jhāna. This is because the jhāna states are too still for the mental activity of contemplation to occur … after emerging from a jhāna … it is then that deep insight is possible."

[30] This is a position taken by Griffiths 1983: 60, Stuart-Fox 1989: 82, and Bucknell 1993: 397.

In fact a discourse in the *Madhyama-āgama* describes a progression of practice where merely leaving behind thought leads on to the attainment of the second absorption.[31] This seems to lend support to the impression that the first absorption corresponds to a condition of the mind in which thought is still present. Comparative study, however, brings to light that the corresponding passage in the Pāli parallel does mention the first absorption, before coming to the second absorption.[32] The converse occurs in another instance, where a Pāli discourse proceeds directly from leaving behind thought to the second absorption, whereas in this case the *Madhyama-āgama* parallel mentions the first absorption.[33]

Now in these two cases the reference to the first absorption could in principle be an addition due to the leveling tendency of oral transmission. Conversely, the absence of this reference could equally well be the result of an error during oral transmission, since in both cases a leaving behind of *vitakka* has just been mentioned. This could have misled the reciters into continuing with the standard formulation of the second absorption, which mentions leaving behind *vitakka*, thereby unintentionally omitting to recite the description of the first absorption.[34]

---

[31] MĀ 102 at T I 589c9.

[32] MN 19 at MN I 117,6.

[33] MN 125 at MN III 136,27 and MĀ 198 at T I 758b26.

[34] MN 125 at MN III 136,25 reads: *mā ca … vitakkaṃ vitakkesī ti. so vitakkavicārānaṃ vūpasamā*. From the viewpoint of recitation, the negative injunction not to think "thoughts" could easily have led on to the idea of stilling of "thoughts". What makes such a shift even more probable is the circumstance that in this way, after two instances of the word *vitakka* (*vitakkaṃ vitakkesī*), a third repetition of the same term is made (*vitakkavicārānaṃ*). Given the repetitive nature of the early Buddhist oral tradition, this flows more naturally than continuing after *mā ca … vitakkaṃ vitakkesīti* with

In sum, to take these two discourses as canonical support for assuming that the first absorption is comparable to ordinary thinking activity is doubtful, as the apparent progression from such an ordinary state of mind directly to the second absorption, without ever having experienced the first absorption, could just be the result of a transmission error.

Another indication relevant to the present theme is that the second absorption constitutes a noble type of silence.[35] Since speech has ceased before the attainment of the first absorption,[36] the reference to "silence" here cannot mean that only with the second absorption one stops speaking (I return below to the question of hearing sound while being in the second absorption). The point behind the idea of a "noble silence" would rather reflect that with the attainment of the second absorption, the mental factors *vitakka* and *vicāra* (application) have been left behind. These two are elsewhere qualified as verbal formations,[37] since they are required for being able to speak. However, the same two mental factors of *vitakka* and *vicāra* can also be employed in a way that does not involve breaking into

---

so vivicc' eva kāmehi, etc. On repetition as a central characteristic of the early Buddhist texts, see e.g. von Simson 1965: 5ff, Allon 1997: 273ff, Weeratunge 2004, Anālayo 2007: 8ff, and Gethin 2007.

[35] SN 21.1 at SN II 273,14: *dutiyaṃ jhānam upasampajja viharati, ayaṃ vuccati ariyo tuṇhībhāvoti*, and its parallel SĀ 501 at T II 132a19: 第二禪具足住, 是名聖默然.

[36] SN 36.11 at SN IV 217,5: *pathamaṃ jhānaṃ* (B^e^ and C^e^: *paṭhamaṃ jhānaṃ*, S^e^: *paṭhamajjhānaṃ*) *samāpannassa vācā niruddhā hoti* and its parallel SĀ 474 at T II 121b2: 初禪正受時, 言語寂滅.

[37] SN 41.6 at SN IV 293,15: *vitakkavicārā vacīsaṅkhāro* and its parallel SĀ 568 at T II 150a24: 有覺, 有觀, 名為口行. Another occurrence of this definition in MN 44 at MN I 301,21 has a similarly worded Tibetan counterpart in D 4094 *ju* 8a5 or Q 5595 *tu* 9a5: *rtog pa dang dpyod pa ni ngag gi 'du byed ces bya'o.*

speech, merely standing for a directing of the mind toward a theme or object and sustaining it there.[38]

For evaluating the meaning of *vitakka* appropriate to the first absorption, the *Upakkilesa-sutta* and its parallels can be consulted, which report the Buddha's own struggle through various mental obstructions before he was able to attain even just the first absorption. The same discourse indicates that Anuruddha experienced similar difficulties; in fact the Buddha relates his own struggle precisely to help Anuruddha and his friends to deepen their concentration.[39] This is noteworthy in view of the fact that, according to the canonical listings of eminent disciples, Anuruddha excelled all other monk disciples of the Buddha in the exercise of the divine eye and thereby in an ability that requires considerable concentrative mastery.[40] For him to have needed the Buddha's personal intervention to attain just the first absorption, and for the Buddha on that occasion to relate his own difficulties in this respect, implies that already the first absorption involves a level of concentration that requires a considerable amount of meditation practice and expertise, even in the case of gifted practitioners.

The impression that in the context of absorption attainment *vitakka* does not refer to conceptual thought appears to have

---

[38] Cousins 1992: 139 speaks of *vitakka* as "the activity of bringing different objects into firm focus before the mind's eye – be these objects thoughts or mental pictures." Shankman 2008: 40 notes that, although in the context of the first absorption *vitakka* and *vicāra* must refer to some degree of mental activity, they "should never be understood as thinking or musing in the ordinary sense".

[39] MN 128 at MN III 157,27, MĀ 72 at T I 536c18, and D 4094 *ju* 276a2 or Q 5595 *thu* 20a3; for a comparative study see Anālayo 2011: 734–741.

[40] AN 1.14 at AN I 23,20 and EĀ 4.2 at T II 557b9; see also T 126 at T II 831a22.

been also the understanding of the translators of the Chinese *Āgamas*, who in descriptions of absorption attainment regularly employ the term "awareness" (覺) to render this particular absorption factor.[41] By using this Chinese character, instead of any of the characters that could render "thought", the translators seem to express their understanding of the practical implications of *vitakka* in the context of the first absorption.[42] The understanding evident in their rendering supports an interpretation of the absorption factor *vitakka* as conveying the idea of an application of the mind, in the sense of a directing of the quality of awareness that can take place in rather subtle ways, beyond the employment of conceptual thought.

In sum, it seems that *vitakka* as a factor of the first absorption need not be taken to imply that thinking and reflection continue while one is in the actual attainment. This suggestion finds further support in other indications regarding the nature

---

[41] 有覺 as the counterpart to *savitakka* in the descriptions of the first absorption is found in DĀ 9 at T I 50c19 (parallel to DN 33 at DN III 222,5), MĀ 2 at T I 422b12 (parallel to AN 7.65 at AN IV 118,21), SĀ 483 at T II 123b1 (parallel to SN 36.29 at SN IV 236,3), and EĀ 31.1 at T II 666b13 (parallel to MN 4 at MN I 21,35). Hirakawa 1997: 1062 lists √*budh*, √*jñā*, and √*vid* for 覺, which Soothill and Hodous 1937/2000: 480 translate as "to awake, apprehend, perceive, realize" and also as to be "aware".

[42] An example would be the description of the first absorption in MĀ 102 at T I 589c9, which uses 覺, but in the same line of the text MĀ 102 employs a different character to refer to "thoughts". The parallel MN 19 at MN I 116,35 and 117,7 uses *vitakka* for both types of occurrence. The use of different characters for what in the Pāli parallel (and presumably also in the Indic original underlying MĀ 102) is the same term conveys the impression that the translator(s) was/were aware of the difference between these two types of *vitakka* and endeavored to render them in such a way that they would not be confused with each other.

of absorption attainment in the early discourses, which in what follows I examine in turn.

Seclusion

Another qualification of the first absorption is "seclusion", explicitly mentioned in the introductory phrase to the first absorption, which specifies that such attainment that takes place *vivicc' eva kāmehi vivicca akusalehi dhammehi*, "secluded from sensual pleasure, secluded from unwholesome states".[43] This phrase has been taken by Arbel (2015: 190) as a pointer to a liberating function inherent in absorption attainment, as "according to the Sanskrit dictionary, the first meaning of *viveka* is 'discrimination'."

A problem with this argument, based on consulting Monier-Williams' Sanskrit dictionary, is that *vivicca* in the above phrase is the gerund of the verb *viviccati*, so that it would be more natural to look for a related Sanskrit term in the dictionary by consulting the entry *vi-√vic* instead of *viveka*. The dictionary by Monier-Williams (1899/1999: 987) begins the entry on *vi-√vic* by listing the following meanings: "to sift (esp. grain by tossing or blowing), divide asunder, separate from (instr. or abl.)". Only later does it also give "to discern" as another alternative, and this alternative is not related to the use of the instrumental.

Since in the Pāli phrase in question the terms *kāmehi* and *akusalehi dhammehi* are in the instrumental, the proper conclusion to be drawn from consulting this dictionary is that the relevant sense of the Sanskrit term concerns being "separate from" the object or condition that comes in the instrumental case. Similarly to the case of the underlying tendencies, the present argument also appears to be a misreading, this time of a dictionary.

[43] On the term "wholesome", *kusala/kuśala*, see, e.g., Cousins 1996 and Schmithausen 2013.

According to the Pāli commentarial tradition, whose understanding would be at least as pertinent as a Sanskrit dictionary, the expression *vivicc' eva kāmehi* conveys a sense of separation.[44] This also corresponds to the understanding that underlies translations of this phrase in the Chinese *Āgama*s.[45]

The obstruction caused by sensual pleasures to the gaining of the inner peace of deeper concentration is in fact a recurrent topic in the early discourses. An example would be a passage in the *Māgandiya-sutta* and its parallels, in which the Buddha addresses a wanderer of apparently hedonist views. The Pāli version offers the following assessment:[46]

---

[44] The commentary Ps I 124,22 on an occurrence of the phrase in MN 4 at MN I 21,34 refers to the *Visuddhimagga* for a full explanation; Vism 139,13 then explains *vivicc' eva kāmehī ti kāmehi viviccitvā, vinā hutvā, apakkamitvā*, translated by Ñāṇamoli 1975/1991: 137 as "*quite secluded from sense desires* means having secluded himself from, having become without, having gone away from, sense desires."

[45] An example from the *Dīrgha-āgama* would be DĀ 21 at T I 93b20 (parallel to DN 1 at DN I 37,1): 去欲, 惡不善法, which conveys the sense of "being apart from sensual pleasures, from evil and unwholesome qualities". In discourses in the *Madhyama-āgama* and *Saṃyukta-āgama* one can find the expression 離欲, 離惡不善法, "separated from sensual pleasures, separated from evil and unwholesome qualities"; see, e.g., MĀ 2 at T I 422b11 (parallel to AN 7.65 at AN IV 118,22) or SĀ 483 at T II 123a29 (parallel to SN 36.29 at SN IV 236,2). An example from the *Ekottarika-āgama* would be EĀ 31.1 at T II 666b12 (parallel to MN 4 at MN I 21,34): 無貪欲想, "free from perceptions of sensual desire". D 4094 *ju* 10a2 or Q 5595 *tu* 11a4 (parallel to MN 44 at MN I 303,30), reads: *'dod pa las dben pa, sdig pa mi dge ba'i chos las dben pa*, "being free from sensual desire and free from evil and unwholesome states".

[46] MN 75 at MN I 508,21 to 508,26. That the wanderer in question would have been holding hedonist views suggests itself from the

> Whatever recluses or brahmins dwelled [in the past], dwell [now] or will dwell [in future] with a mind internally at peace and free from thirst [for sensual pleasures], they all … [do so] by abandoning craving for sensual pleasures and removing the fever of sensual pleasures …

The *Madhyama-āgama* parallel proceeds as follows:[47]

> Without having abandoned sensual desires, without being separated from craving for sensual pleasures, that [one] should have dwelled, shall dwell [in future] or should be dwelling now with a mind internally at peace, that is impossible.

The two versions describe the predicament of indulging in sensual pleasures with the example of a leper who scratches his wounds. Although the leper experiences satisfaction in this way, his wounds will only get worse by being scratched. Indulging in sensual pleasures is similar, the two discourses point out, as it will likewise provide momentary satisfaction at the cost of increasing one's tendency to crave for more of the same.

A series of stark images illustrating the disadvantage of sensual pleasures can be found in the *Potaliya-sutta* and its

---

outset of the discourse, where he criticizes the Buddha as a "destroyer of being", MN 75 at MN I 502,15: *bhūnahuno* (on this term see also Barua 1921/1981: 355, Saksena 1936: 713, Bhagwat 1946: 64, Horner 1946: 287, Alsdorf 1965: 46–47, Vetter 2000: 132 note 45, and Norman 2004: 81), with its counterpart in MĀ 153 at T I 670b17: 壞敗地. The Pāli commentary, Ps III 211,5, explains that this wanderer was particularly opposed to the Buddha's teachings on sense-restraint; see also the comment by Bodhi in Ñāṇamoli 1995/2005: 1281 note 740: "his view thus seems close to the contemporary attitude that intensity and variety of experience is the ultimate good and should be pursued without inhibitions or restrictions."

[47] MĀ 153 at T I 671c12 to 671c13.

Madhyama-āgama parallel. One of these images compares indulging in sensual pleasures to a hungry dog that gnaws a meatless bone.[48] This simile conveys a sense of brief pleasure without lasting satisfaction; although the dog enjoys gnawing the bone, its hunger will not be appeased.

Another simile compares sensual pleasures to holding a burning torch against the wind; one will get burned unless one quickly lets go of the torch. Such unskillful handling of a burning torch illustrates that, from an early Buddhist perspective, searching for happiness among sensual objects is similarly unskillful. Yet another simile illustrates the evanescent nature of sensual pleasures with the example of experiences during a dream; all vanish as soon as one wakes up.

These passages flesh out why the initial stipulation in the standard account of the first absorption points to the need to leave behind concern with sensual pleasures in order to be able to access the inner peace of absorption attainment. This is so simply because sensual desire is a major obstacle to entry into absorption.

The same perspective would also be relevant to the import of a description of the faculty of concentration in a discourse in the *Saṃyutta-nikāya*. This description employs the phrase "having made release the object", *vossaggārammaṇam karitvā*, and then continues with the standard description of the four absorptions.[49]

Arbel (2015: 186f) argues that the phrase found in this discourse implies the cultivation of the awakening factors and thereby points to the intrinsically insight-related nature of ab-

---

[48] MN 54 at MN I 364,12 and MĀ 203 at T I 774a20; for a translation of the similes in MĀ 203 see Anālayo 2013b: 74–76.

[49] SN 48.10 at SN V 198,24; translation by Bodhi 2000: 1672.

sorption attainment. In evaluating this suggestion, in addition to noting that the description given in this Pāli discourse is not found in its *Saṃyukta-āgama* parallels, it also needs to be kept in mind that in other Pāli discourses the term *vossagga* can convey various meanings.

One example is when a householder hands over responsibilities to his wife, whereby he engages in "relinquishment of authority", *issariya-vossagga*. Another example is when the same householder at the right time grants his workers "leave", *vossagga*.[50] Such forms of relinquishment do not require the cultivation of the awakening factors. It follows that occurrences of the term *vossagga* need not invariably refer to the awakening factors.

In the standard descriptions of the cultivation of the awakening factors, *vossagga* does not stand on its own, but rather comes combined with the term *pariṇāmin*, "ripening in" or "maturing in". Moreover, such ripening or maturing is introduced as something that takes place dependent on seclusion, dependent on dispassion, and dependent on cessation, *vivekanissita*, *virāganissita*, and *nirodhanissita*. The whole phrase appears to describe a progressive series, where in dependence on seclusion, dispassion, and cessation the cultivation of the awakening factors ripens or matures in relinquishment, *vossagga*.[51]

The description of the faculty of concentration in the discourse mentioned above does not use the set of terms *vivekanissita*, *virāganissita*, and *nirodhanissita*, leaving hardly a basis for assuming that this description must refer to the type of *vossagga* that comes about through cultivating the awakening

---

[50] DN 31 at DN III 190,6 and 191,4; for a survey of meanings of the term *vossagga* see Anālayo 2012a: 266–268.

[51] See Gethin 1992/2001: 166 and Anālayo 2013b: 219–226.

factors. Now the awakening factors would not be required when a householder grants authority to his wife and leave to his workers, even though these are forms of *vossagga*. This in turn shows that to take the occurrence of the term *vossagga* on its own in the description of the faculty of concentration as necessarily implying that absorption attainment is to be "achieved by the cultivation of the seven factors of awakening", to use the wording employed by Arbel (2015: 187), is not convincing.

Instead, the term *vossagga* in the description of the faculty of concentration can more fruitfully be understood as making basically the same point as the phrase "secluded from sensual pleasure" (etc.), in that one needs to relinquish concern with sensuality, as well as any other unwholesome condition, in order to be able to attain absorption. From a practical perspective, such *vossagga* can serve as an entrypoint into absorption.

The standard description of the first absorption refers back to this same need with the qualification of the joy experienced during actual attainment as *vivekajaṃ*, "born of seclusion". This conforms to a standard encouragement in the discourse that one should develop the pleasure of deep concentration, whereas the pleasure of sensuality should be shunned. The contrast between these two types of happiness can be seen in two passages in the *Araṇavibhaṅga-sutta* and its parallel. The first passage in the Pāli discourse reads as follows:[52]

> In dependence on the five sensual pleasures there arises happiness and pleasure, which is reckoned sensual happiness, a dung-like happiness, the happiness of a worldling, an ignoble happiness, it should not be engaged in, it should not be cultivated, should not be made much of; I say that this happiness should be feared.

---

[52] MN 139 at MN III 233,20 to 233,24 and MĀ 169 at T I 702c6 to 702c9.

The *Madhyama-āgama* parallel similarly explains:

> In dependence on the five sensual pleasures there arises joy, there arises happiness. This happiness is an ignoble happiness, the happiness of an ordinary worldling … it should not be cultivated, should not be practiced, should not be made much of; I say that it should certainly not be cultivated.

In contrast to this stands the happiness of absorption attainment, which the *Araṇavibhaṅga-sutta* describes as follows:[53]

> This is reckoned the happiness of renunciation, the happiness of seclusion, the happiness of peace, the happiness [leading to] complete awakening, it should be engaged in, it should be cultivated, it should be made much of; I say that this happiness should not be feared.

The *Madhyama-āgama* parallel similarly proclaims that:

> This happiness is a noble happiness, the happiness of dispassion, the happiness of seclusion, the happiness of peace, the happiness that leads to complete awakening … which should be cultivated, should be practiced, should be made much of; I say that it certainly should be cultivated.

For a full appreciation of the practical significance of seclusion from sensuality as a quality of absorption attainment, it is helpful to take into account that the experience of joy and happiness is not merely a signpost marking the attainment of the first absorption. Rather, the cultivation of such joy and happiness appears to be instrumental for achieving the attainment. In other words, it seems to be precisely the experience of non-sensual happiness that leads the mind into absorption attainment. Owing to the attraction joy and happiness exert on the

---

53 MN 139 at MN III 233,31 to 234,1 and MĀ 169 at T I 702c13 to 702c15.

mind, relinquishing and remaining secluded from sensuality and any other unwholesome condition takes place naturally and results in absorption attainment.

The cultivation and gradual refinement of happiness that in this way comes about through absorption attainment have their roots in those practices that lay the foundation for concentration, delineated in the canonical accounts of the gradual path, which I discussed in the second chapter of this book. Of crucial importance in this respect is the maintenance of ethical conduct, which according to the *Kandaraka-sutta*, a discourse without parallels, causes the happiness of blamelessness (*anavajjasukha*).[54]

Another significant aspect of the gradual path is the practice of sense-restraint. Countering the natural tendency for sensual distraction and extroversion lays the foundation for the seclusion from sensual pleasures mentioned in the description of the first absorption. By dint of being properly undertaken, according to the *Kandaraka-sutta* sense-restraint leads to an unimpaired type of happiness (*abyāsekhasukha*).[55]

An important source of happiness can also be found in contentment,[56] whose potential for leading to a deepening of concentration can hardly be overestimated. In fact, contentment

---

[54] MN 51 at MN I 346,10; see also above p. 69 note 10.

[55] MN 51 at MN I 346,23.

[56] The happiness of contentment has found a poetic expression in SN 4.18 at SN I 114,22 and its parallel SĀ 1095 at T II 288a23, which indicate that those who own nothing live happily; see also Dhp 200, with Indic language parallels in the Gāndhārī *Dharmapada* 168, Brough 1962/2001: 145, in the Patna *Dharmapada* 257, Cone 1989: 170, and in the *Udānavarga* 30.49, Bernhard 1965: 405; on *santuṭṭhi* in general see also Anālayo 2006b. This verse appears to express a pan-Indic attitude, as it has a counterpart in the *Mahābhārata* 12.268.4, Bevalkar 1954: 1466, and in the *Uttarājjhayaṇa* 9.14, Charpentier 1922: 96.

directly feeds into concentration, which is but the outcome of a mind that is contentedly resting within instead of being on a quest for sensual distraction and entertainment.

The cultivation of happiness continues to lead to a progressive deepening of concentration. Subsequent to the happiness of seclusion experienced during attainment of the first absorption, with the second absorption one experiences joy and happiness that are "born of concentration", as explicitly indicated in the standard descriptions of this absorption. With the third absorption, joy is left behind and pure happiness remains.

The presence of this happiness disappears with the fourth absorption, which nevertheless is an experience that is still reckoned to be "a dwelling in happiness here and now".[57] This other form of happiness of the fourth absorption is superior to the type of happiness experienced in the lower three absorptions.[58]

In sum, the absorptions as the consummation of such progressive refinement of happiness indubitably have a transformative role and rightly deserve to be considered an integral aspect of the path to awakening. This does not mean, however, that they are productive of insight in and of themselves. Moreover, the actual experience of being in an absorption does not even seem to be compatible with insightful reflection or contemplation of impermanence, simply because the mind at such

[57] MN 8 at MN 41,18: *diṭṭhadhammasukhavihāra*, which has a counterpart in MĀ 91 at T I 573b29: 現法樂居.

[58] That the happiness of the fourth absorption is superior to the happiness of the lower absorptions emerges from SN 36.19 at SN IV 226,28 and its parallels in SĀ 485 at T II 124b6 and Sanskrit fragment SHT II 51 folio 41 V7–8, Waldschmidt et al. 1968: 10 (in both cases the section on the fourth absorption is given only in abbreviation).

a time is too "absorbed" to engage in such activities. Instead, it appears to be on emerging from absorption that the proper time for insight into its impermanent nature has come.

Absorption and Hearing Sound

Given that from the viewpoint of the early discourses a practitioner who has fully entered absorption attainment appears to be in a condition where thoughts and the conceptual activity corresponding to fully formulated thoughts have become stilled, this brings up the related question of whether one who has entered the second absorption and thus a noble type of silence, as mentioned above, will still be able to hear sound.[59] This question that raised discussions among practitioners and scholars already during the period of Buddhist exegetical activity.[60]

The possibility of being clearly aware while in a deep state of absorption, yet be unaware of any sound, finds exemplification in an episode reported in the *Mahāparinibbāna-sutta* and its parallels. In the episode in question the Buddha describes an occasion when he had been in deep meditation while a terrible storm was raging. The parallels agree that the Buddha explained that he had been fully awake, yet he did not hear anything.[61]

---

[59] In what follows my discussion of the possibility of "hearing sound" concerns the mental processing of sound waves created externally in such a way that these are understood for what they are. The question at stake is thus whether a mind immersed in the second absorption can at the same time, while remaining in the absorption attainment, be conscious of a particular sound.

[60] See in more detail Dessein 2016.

[61] DN 16 at DN II 132,12, Waldschmidt 1951: 276,8 (§28.36), DĀ 2 at T I 19b2, T 5 at T I 168b18, T 6 at T I 184a1, and T 7 at T I 198a29. Bronkhorst 1993/2000: x sees a contradiction between the approving attitude shown in the present passage toward deeper states of con-

A story recorded in a range of *Vinaya*s appears to provide a different perspective, as here Mahāmoggallāna reports having heard the sound of elephants while he was immersed in a deep level of concentration corresponding to the fourth absorption or to being in one of the immaterial attainments. Other monks think that he has committed a breach of the *pārājika* rule by making a false claim to having been in such high attainment.[62] When the matter is brought before the Buddha, however, he exonerates Mahāmoggallāna and makes it clear that the statement made did not involve a breach of the *pārājika* rule. This at first sight gives the impression that one can hear sound even while being in the fourth absorption.[63]

---

centration during which sights or sounds are no longer experienced and the criticism of the "development of the faculties" by avoiding sights and sounds, raised in MN 152 (for a comparative study see Anālayo 2011: 849–853). Yet, the point made in MN 152 is how to relate to everyday experience, in fact the expression "development of the faculties", *indriyabhāvanā*, is an obvious counterpart to "restraint of the faculties", *indriyasaṃvara*. The exposition in MN 152 is not a criticism of deeper stages of concentration during which sensory experience is absent, but rather a criticism of attempting to deal with sensory impact during daily life by simply trying to avoid it, instead of developing equanimity toward whatever is experienced; for a criticism of Bronkhorst's arguments see also Pāsādika 2009: 92f.

[62] The actual term used is *uttarimanussadhamma*, on which see in more detail Anālayo 2008. My study of this episode has benefitted from Syinchen 2010.

[63] According to Ṭhānissaro 2012: 227: "as for the assertion that a person in jhāna cannot hear sounds, this point is clearly disproven by an incident in the … discussion of Parājika 4 in the Vinaya. There, Ven. Moggallāna states that he can hear sounds when entering the formless attainments. A group of monks object to his statement, convinced that he is making a false claim … so they report his statement to the Buddha. The Buddha's reply: Moggallāna's ex-

In agreement with the Theravāda version, the Dharmaguptaka *Vinaya* reports the Buddha's explanation that Mahāmoggallāna's attainment had been "impure".[64] According to the Theravāda commentarial tradition, the expression "impure" here means that he had not properly purified his mind from the obstructions to concentration. Being seated in the fourth absorption, he heard sounds when having momentarily lost the absorption and then thought he had heard them while still being in the attainment.[65]

The commentarial explanation receives support from other *Vinaya*s that cover the same event. The Mahāsāṅghika *Vinaya* reports the Buddha's explanation that Mahāmoggallāna did not properly understand the characteristics of emerging and entering (absorption). It was when he had emerged from the concentration that the hearing had occurred; he did not hear while being in the concentration attainment.[66]

According to the Mūlasarvāstivāda *Vinaya*, the Buddha clarified that Mahāmoggallāna had quickly emerged and then quickly re-entered (the absorption). Even though he actually had emerged from the concentration, he thought he had remained in the concentration.[67]

The Sarvāstivāda *Vinaya* has such an indication already as part of its actual report of what happened. According to this

---

perience of those attainments was not pure; however, that impurity was not enough to make the statement false. He actually was experiencing the formless attainments."

[64] Vin III 109,12: *aparisuddho* and T 1428 at T XXII 985a3: 不清淨.

[65] Sp II 514,1: *samādhiparipanthike dhamme na suṭṭhu parisodhetvā … catutthajjhānaṃ appetvā nisinno, jhānaṅgehi uṭṭhāya nāgānaṃ saddaṃ sutvā, antosamāpattiyaṃ assosin ti evaṃ saññī ahosi.*

[66] T 1425 at T XXII 466a6: 不善知出入相, 出定聞, 非入定聞.

[67] T 1442 at T XXIII 680b8: 速出, 速入, 雖是出定, 謂在定中.

report, Mahāmoggallāna took hold well of the characteristic of entering concentration, but not of the characteristic of emerging from it. He actually had emerged from the concentration when he heard the sound of elephants. Having heard it, he had then quickly entered the concentration again.[68]

The circumstance that the other monastics thought Mahāmoggallāna had made a false claim to attainment implies that for them it was self-evident that one cannot hear sound and at the same time be in deep absorption. Thus the Mahāmoggallāna incident in the different *Vinaya*s does not entail that, from the perspective of these texts, one can hear sound when being actually immersed in the fourth absorption or one of the immaterial attainments. It does show, however, that they envisage the possibility of mistaking a condition as being absorption attainment when this condition actually falls short of being the full attainment, properly speaking.

The inability to hear sound appears to apply also to lower levels of absorption, judging from a discourse in the *Aṅguttara-nikāya* and its *Madhyama-āgama* parallel. The narration that precedes the actual exposition in these two discourses revolves around some senior disciples who considered sound to be an obstacle to entering deep concentration, to the extent that they left to avoid some noisy visitors. The Buddha confirms their assessment and then elaborates by presenting a series of obstacles in terms of their being "thorns". The relevant part reads as follows in the *Aṅguttara-nikāya* discourse:[69]

---

[68] T 1435 at T XXIII 440c22: 善取入定相, 不善取出定相. 從三昧起, 聞薩卑尼池岸上大象聲; 聞已, 還疾入三昧; the Buddha repeats this when explaining to the monastics what happened; see T XXIII 441a4.

[69] AN 10.72 at AN V 134,26 to 135,2. The term used is *sadda*, which means "sound" in general; for conveying the sense of "noise", the term *sadda* needs to be additionally qualified as *ucca* or *mahant*.

> Sound (*sadda*) is a thorn to the first absorption; application (*vitakka*) and its sustaining (*vicāra*) is a thorn to the second absorption; joy (*pīti*) is a thorn to the third absorption.

The *Madhyama-āgama* parallel similarly proclaims that:[70]

> Sound is a thorn for one entering the first absorption; [directed] awareness and [sustained] contemplation is a thorn for one entering the second absorption; joy is a thorn for one entering the third absorption.

The thorns mentioned in the two versions before coming to the three lower absorptions differ. The *Aṅguttara-nikāya* discourse lists delight in socializing as a thorn to seclusion, pursuing the appearance of beauty as a thorn to cultivating the [notion] of the absence of beauty, going to see shows as a thorn to guarding the senses, and keeping company with females as a thorn to leading the celibate life (this refers to the situation of a heterosexual male, of course).

The *Madhyama-āgama* parallel lists breaches of morality as a thorn to maintaining morality, bodily adornments as a thorn to guarding the senses, the appearance of beauty as a thorn to cultivating the [notion] of the absence of beauty, anger as a thorn to cultivating *mettā*, the drinking of liquor as a thorn to abstaining from liquor, and looking at the female form as a thorn to leading the celibate life (again, this holds for the case of a heterosexual male).

After the fourth absorption, which in both versions has its thorn in inhalations and exhalations, the *Aṅguttara-nikāya* discourse mentions perceptions and feelings as thorns to cessation and then concludes with the thorns of lust, hatred, and delusion which an arahant has overcome.

---

[70] MĀ 84 at T I 561a7 to 561a9.

The *Madhyama-āgama* discourse additionally refers to the four immaterial attainments, where in each case the lower attainment is a thorn to the higher one, then mentions perception and knowing as thorns to the attainment of cessation, and finally also takes up the three thorns of lust, hatred, and delusion, which an arahant has left behind.

The differences in the two listings give the impression that an original exposition predominantly concerned with thorns to absorption practice, which is the topic broached in the introductory narration, has been subsequently expanded by way of the addition of other thorns.

It is against the variations between the two versions that their similar exposition of thorns to absorption attainment emerges as evidence for the early Buddhist understanding of the nature of absorption attainment, given that this is found in the same way in expositions that otherwise differ. Such common ground can reasonably be expected to be early.

Now to attain the second absorption one needs to overcome *vitakka* and *vicāra*, application and its sustaining, and to attain the third absorption it is necessary to leave behind joy (*pīti*). In fact a recurrence of these factors implies that the respective level of absorption has been lost. It follows that from the perspective of these two discourses proper attainment of the first absorption requires leaving behind the hearing of sound.[71]

A statement confirming the incompatibility of the first absorption with the hearing of sound can be found in a discourse in the *Dīrgha-āgama*, of which no parallel is known. The relevant passage states:[72]

---

[71] In line with this indication, Ajahn Brahm 2006: 273 note 9 concludes that "sound can disturb the first jhāna, but when one actually perceives the sound one is no longer in the jhāna."

[72] DĀ 11 at T I 59a7, a statement made similarly in DĀ 10 at T I 56c29.

When entering the first absorption, the thorn of sounds ceases.

A passage in the *Poṣadhavastu* of the Mūlasarvāstivāda *Vinaya* also speaks of the thorn of sounds. Here this comes as part of a description of meditating monastics who were unable to develop unification of the mind because of the thorn of sounds.[73] This supports the impression that suggests itself from the above early discourses in the way these have been preserved by the Dharmaguptaka, Sarvāstivāda, and Theravāda reciter traditions.

In fact, according to a passage found in the *Mahāvedalla-sutta*, already with the first absorption one reaches a condition of "mental unification", *cittekaggatā*.[74] The same indication is made in the Chinese and Tibetan parallels to the *Cūḷavedalla-sutta*,[75] a difference in placement that reflects a general tendency of the two *vedalla* discourses to have exchanged some doctrinal discussions with each other in various transmission lineages. Once with the removal of *vitakka* the second absorption has been attained, a condition of "internal stillness", *ajjhattaṃ sampasādanaṃ*, obtains and one has reached a still deeper condition of "unification", *ekodibhāva*. For a mind unified within, an act of hearing would constitute an external disturbance.

Elsewhere in the Pāli discourses the qualification *ekodibhāva* refers to a deeply concentrated condition of the mind, capable of developing direct knowledge (*abhiññā*) or super-

---

[73] Hu-von Hinüber 1994: 264,3 (§6.4): *dhyāyināṃ kaṇṭakaśabdena cittaikāgryaṃ na labhante*; with the Tibetan counterpart in ibid. note 2: *bsam gtan dag gi tsher ma ni sgra yin pas, sems rtse gcig pa nyid kyang mi thob pa'i skabs te.*

[74] MN 43 at MN I 294,31.

[75] MĀ 210 at T I 788c20 and D 4094 *ju* 8a2 or Q 5595 *tu* 8b8, which are parallels to MN 44.

normal abilities (*iddhi*).[76] This differs from the usage of the similar term *ekaggatā*, which for want of a better alternative I also render as "unification".

Later texts like the *Abhidhammatthasaṅgaha* consider *ekaggatā* to be one of the seven mental factors present in every mental state (*sabbacittasādhāraṇa*).[77] This differs from the to some extent comparable definition of "name", *nāma*, in the discourses, which does not mention *ekaggatā*.[78] In other words, it is only by the time of Abhidharma analysis that some degree of mental unification was held to be a general characteristic of the mind.[79] This is not what *ekodibhāva* stands for in the early discourses. Here mental unification does not refer just to a momentary focus on an object present in the mind, but rather to a condition of the mind that is unified for a considerable stretch of time.

A discourse in the *Saṃyukta-āgama* states that, even though the senses and their objects are present and one is perceptive during the attainment of the first absorption, the objects of these

---

[76] Most occurrences of the qualification *ekodibhāva* in the four Pāli *Nikāya*s seem to be concerned with the second absorption. Two cases that offer further information are AN 3.100 at AN I 254,33, which relates a mental condition that is *ekodibhāvādhigato* to the ability to realize direct knowledge, and AN 6.70 at AN III 426,8, which describes a *samādhi* that is similarly specified as *ekodibhāvādhigato* as enabling the attainment of *iddhi*s. Thus *ekodibhāva* seems to have a more restricted range of meaning than *cittekaggatā*.

[77] Abhidh-s 2.2; Bodhi 1993: 80 explains that this refers to "the unification of the mind on its object".

[78] SN 12.2 at SN II 3,34 and its parallel EĀ 49.5 at T II 797b28 list feeling, perception, attention, contact, and intention. The *Abhidhammatthasaṅgaha* list of universal factors adds to these five the two factors of the life faculty and *ekaggatā*.

[79] See Dhs 9,8.

senses will not be experienced (in the ordinary way).[80] Although this discourse does not have a Pāli parallel, properly speaking,[81] a related position is taken in a discourse in the *Aṅguttara-nikāya*, which has a parallel preserved as a Sanskrit fragment. According to the relevant passage, dwelling in the first absorption one dwells at the end of the "world", which the same discourse explains to refer to pleasurable objects of the five senses.[82]

In practical terms, the passages surveyed above seem to imply that one who hears sound would not at that very same time be fully immersed in the unified mental condition of an "absorption", *jhāna/dhyāna*, of the type described in the early discourses. This could be either because of having temporarily risen from the attainment of absorption, or else because of mistaking a level of concentration that borders on absorption as being already the full attainment itself.[83] Here the story of

[80] SĀ 559 at T II 146c6; on the bodily dimension of absorption, which indeed differs from ordinary bodily touch sensation, see above p. 54ff.

[81] Akanuma 1929/1990: 61 lists SN 35.192 as a parallel to SĀ 559, yet the two discourses are too different to be reckoned parallels.

[82] AN 9.38 at AN IV 430,22; see SHT VI 1326 folio 212, Bechert and Wille 1989: 82f. Now AN 9.37 at AN IV 427,13 states that the five senses and their objects are not experienced in the immaterial attainments. Yet, the parallel SĀ 559 at T II 146c6 affirms the same for the four absorptions. As SĀ 559 explicitly mentions the change of speaker, unlike AN 9.37, perhaps the latter has lost a portion of text.

[83] Catherine 2008: 156 explains that at times meditators may have an experience wherein "the jhanic factors are strongly established but ... it is not full absorption. To understand the quality of this phase, imagine yourself standing on the threshold of your house. You are looking inside through the open front door, but you have not yet stepped inside ... this phase marks a natural transition; I would not call it jhana until a deeper immersion has occurred. When conditions for absorption do occur, the experience is like entering the house and closing the door behind."

Mahāmoggallāna's hearing of sound provides a good example for appreciating how different understandings of the nature of absorption can arise. In fact the dividing line between absorption and levels of concentration bordering on absorption is not always easily drawn in subjective experience.

Just as with hearing sound, it would similarly be quite possible to contemplate the impermanent nature of different factors of the mind while being deeply concentrated and experiencing the presence of absorption factors, such as non-sensual joy and happiness, although strictly speaking this would have to be reckoned a condition of having temporarily risen from full absorption attainment or else a condition of not yet having fully reached it.

With the above discussion I certainly do not intend in any way to be devaluing experiences where absorption factors are present and one is still able to hear or think, which can indeed be very powerful and subjectively empowering. My intention is only to enable the drawing of a clear distinction between absorption proper of the type described in the early discourses and states bordering on this type of absorption. Such a distinction has considerable practical significance, simply because overestimating the absorbed condition of the mind that one has been able to reach can lead to underestimating the potential of going deeper.[84]

In this context I think it is also relevant to allow some space to reflect on the basic purpose of descriptions of the absorptions from the viewpoint of actual meditation practice. This purpose is reflected in a *Madhyama-āgama* discourse without

---

[84] Catherine 2008: 155 advises that "should you choose to apply the term jhana liberally to states lightly saturated by jhanic factors, please don't presume such states represent the full potential of jhana. The early discourses … describe very deeply secluded states."

a Pāli parallel that describes how someone who has attained the first absorption by dint of further practice reaches the second absorption. Not recognizing this experience for what it is, the practitioner comes to a mistaken conclusion and then loses the attainment:[85]

> [The practitioner thinks]: 'I have lost the first absorption, my concentration has ceased.' That practitioner of absorption does not understand as it really is: 'By cultivating right intention my mind, joyful and calm, has progressed from the first absorption to the second absorption, which is superior in calmness.' Not having understood this as it really is, [the practitioner] turns back the mind [from the second absorption] and then loses the concentration. In this way a practitioner of absorption, [who had actually] progressed, thinks to be regressing.

The converse can also happen, when someone prematurely attempts to progress from the first to the second absorption and thereby even loses the level of concentration earlier attained. Mistakenly believing to have reached the second absorption,[86]

> in this way a practitioner of absorption, [who has] regressed, thinks to be progressing.

Although this *Madhyama-āgama* discourse is without a Pāli parallel, a somwhat similar point is made in a discourse in the *Aṅguttara-nikāya*.[87] The discourse compares an attempt to reach the second absorption without having properly developed the first absorption to a foolish cow which, trying to get to a new

---

[85] MĀ 176 at T I 714a2 to 714a6.
[86] MĀ 176 at T I 714c4.
[87] AN 9.35 at AN IV 418,6.

place on a mountain without firmly planting her feet in the place she had been, is neither able to reach the new place nor able to safely return to where she was before.

In this way, the listing of key aspects of the absorptions in the standard descriptions in the early discourses has the purpose of helping to recognize the experience and avoiding any wrong assessments of one's progress or regress, because this can undermine one's proper practice.[88]

The function of such listings goes further, since the key aspects they enumerate are indications about how to enter absorption, and the successful putting into practice of these indications is what makes for the actual attainment, as already mentioned above. Such providing of directions on how practice should be undertaken comes to the fore in another discourse in the *Madhyama-āgama*, also without a Pāli parallel, which describes a practitioner who has attained the first absorption and is unable to maintain it:[89]

> One does not keep that practice, is not mindful of its characteristic marks, one is only mindful of and has perceptions related to the characteristics of engaging in sensual pleasures; one completely regresses.

Here regression happens because a crucial aspect of the first absorption, "seclusion" from sensuality, has not been properly maintained. Failure to keep up this quality of seclusion when faced by the temptation of sensual pleasures and distractions inevitably leads to regress. Another type of practitioner, how-

---

[88] The same principle is also reflected in AN 6.71 at AN III 427,1, which highlights the importance of properly recognizing what leads to decline and what leads to progress, etc., although the exposition does not explicitly mention the attainment of absorption.

[89] MĀ 177 at T I 716b23 to 716b24.

ever, acts differently and is able to stabilize the attainment of the first absorption:[90]

> One does keep that practice and is mindful of its characteristic marks, one establishes mindfulness in accordance with the Dharma so as to dwell with a unified mind.

This passage highlights how clear awareness of the "characteristic marks", which in the present case is in particular seclusion from sensuality, is of considerable importance in order to be able to stabilize the ability to enter absorption.[91]

Keeping in mind this pragmatic orientation of the descriptions of absorption attainment in the early discourses helps to avoid misinterpretations, influenced by the assumption that such descriptions must be mentioning all the factors that are present in the respective experience. An attempt to provide comprehensive descriptions is not a concern of the early discourses, but much rather a tendency of later exegesis.

An example in case is unification of the mind, already mentioned above. Although unification of the mind is attributed to the first absorption in the *Mahāvedalla-sutta* and the parallels to the *Cūḷavedalla-sutta*, as well as in the extract from the *Anupada-sutta* translated above, the same quality is not mentioned in the standard description of the first absorption. Nevertheless, it would be a misunderstanding to assume that the first absorption is without unification of the mind just

---

[90] MĀ 177 at T I 716b28 to 716b29.

[91] This is also reflected in SN 40.1 at SN IV 263,15, which describes how Mahāmoggallāna's attainment of the first absorption was disturbed by the arising of perceptions related to what is sensual and giving attention to them, *kāmasahagatā saññā manasikārā samudācaranti*, whose removal was required to stabilize his attainment.

because this is not explicitly mentioned in the standard description. In fact, on adopting the same type of reasoning one would have to conclude that the first and the second absorption are also without the presence of mindfulness, just because mindfulness is only mentioned in the standard description of the third and fourth absorptions.

Instead of presenting an exhaustive inventory of all mental factors and qualities of a particular absorption experience, in line with the predominant concern in later exegesis, the standard descriptions in the early discourses pragmatically focus on those qualities considered particularly relevant for enabling successful attainment and proper recognition of an absorption. To expect such descriptions to be comprehensive seems a case of reading later exegetical attitudes into the early discourses.

The Immaterial Attainments

The same pragmatic attitude also underpins the description of the immaterial attainments to be reached based on successful mastery of the four absorptions. Yet, some scholars believe they have identified incoherencies in such descriptions, wherefore in what follows I critically examine the suggestions made in this respect.

An example for such suggestions regarding a supposed lack of coherence is Heiler, who considers the immaterial spheres to be too different in character from the four absorptions to fit a meditative progression that covers both. According to his assessment, whereas the four absorptions are a contemplation of religious truths, the immaterial spheres are merely an intellectual abstraction.[92]

---

[92] Heiler 1922: 29: "Den Ausgangspunkt der vier *jhâna* und *appamaññâ* bildet die ernste Betrachtung der religiösen Wahrheiten …

Another argument by Falk considers the four immaterial attainments to be lacking inner coherence, since the first two occur also among the *kasiṇa*s, whereas the last two are mere negations. According to Falk, this makes it probable that these four were put together based on two unrelated sets of two in order to arrive at the same count of four as in the case of the four absorptions.[93]

The distinctions drawn by Heiler and Falk seem to be based on misunderstandings of the nature of the respective experiences. The main difference between the four absorptions and the four immaterial spheres is related to their respective objects. The four absorptions can be cultivated with a variety of objects, hence no specific object is mentioned when these are described. The immaterial spheres involve a transcending of whatever object has been used for attaining the fourth absorption,[94] consequently the descriptions refer to such transcend-

---

den Ausgangspunkt der *arûpa* hingegen bildet die gedanken- und gefühlose Konzentration der Aufmerksamkeit auf ein bedeutungsloses äußeres Objekt oder die rein intellektuelle Abstraktionstätigkeit, deren Stoff außerreligiöse neutrale Vorstellungen abgeben ... dort echtes und tiefes religiöses Erleben – hier eine äußerliche Psychotechnik."

[93] Falk 1939/2004: 340: "La serie dei quattro arūpadhyāna é a sua volta composita. I primi due elementi ... ricompaiono in un'altra classe di esercizi meditativi, nella classe dei *kasiṇa* ... gli ultimi due ... sono invece definiti per mera negazione ... non hanno però nessun chiaro rapporto con i primi due ... appare probabile che due gruppi di due elementi siano stati saldati insieme per riempire uno schema numericamente preformato, per ottenere quattro dhyāna dell'*ārūpya-dhātu* correspondenti, in posizione superiore, ai quattro dhyāna del *rūpadhātu*."

[94] King 1980/1992: 41 explains that "*'jhāna' is a mode of meditative concentration not a content*, whereas the immaterial states represent a *content*."

ence. This does not mean that the experience itself is a mere intellectual abstraction.

In the case of the four absorptions, the differences between them concern the depth of concentration reached. The early discourses describe this deepening of concentration in two complementary ways.

The more commonly found descriptions are concerned with the type of happiness experienced. This proceeds from the joy and happiness of seclusion in the first absorption, via the joy and happiness of concentration in the second absorption and the happiness devoid of joy in the third absorption, to a culmination point reached with the deep equanimity of the fourth absorption.

Another presentation focuses on the role of *vitakka* and its sustaining (*vicāra*), resulting in a threefold distinction:

1) both are required,

2) only sustaining is required,

3) neither is any longer required.[95]

---

[95] E.g. MN 128 at MN III 162,14: *savitakkam pi savicāraṃ samādhiṃ … avitakkam pi vicāramattaṃ samādhiṃ … avitakkam pi avicāraṃ samādhiṃ*, with a counterpart in MĀ 72 at T I 538c3: 有覺有觀定 … 無覺少觀定 … 無覺無觀定. Stuart-Fox 1989: 93 holds that the descriptions of the second type of concentration in MN 128 and MĀ 72 differ, as according to him in MĀ 72 "the second *samādhi* is described as one in which *vitakka* is absent and *vicāra* is *reduced.* In the Pāli version, *vicāra* is simply stated to be present." Yet, the character 少 used in MĀ 72 to qualify 觀 probably renders an equivalent to the qualification *-matta* in the Pāli version, the translator apparently taking *-matta* in the sense of qualifying *vicāra* to be reduced in strength, so that the two versions rather seem to agree in their descriptions This is confirmed by the fact that the expressions *saddhāmattakena* and *pemamattakena* in MN 65 at MN I 444,28 have their counterpart in MĀ 194 at T I 749a3 in 少信 and 少愛, showing that

Numbers 1 and 2 correspond to the first absorption in the fourfold scheme; number 3 covers the rest of the four.

With the fourth absorption attained, the standard description in the early discourses considers the mind to have reached an acme of concentration that is "imperturbable".[96] With such imperturbability reached, according to early Buddhist meditation theory various options for further practice present themselves.

A practitioner might decide to proceed toward the gaining of the threefold knowledge or the six higher knowledges. Both of these sets include the attainment of awakening, alongside various other supernormal abilities that are in themselves not considered necessary for reaching awakening.

An alternative route to be taken based on the fourth absorption is to cultivate the immaterial spheres. These are at times

---

in the *Madhyama-āgama* 少 can render *matta* or *mattaka*; in fact Hirakawa 1997: 398 under 少 lists *mātra* and *mātraka*; see also Bucknell 2010: 49f. References to a stage of concentration where *vitakka* has been overcome but *vicāra* still persists occurs in several other Pāli discourses, see, e.g., DN 33 at DN III 219,18, SN 43.3 at SN IV 360,11, and AN 8.63 at AN IV 300,5. In the case of DN 33, the fragments of the *Saṅgīti-sūtra* have preserved a reference to these three levels of concentration, K 484 Vc, Stache-Rosen 1968: 23, treated in full in the *Saṅgītiparyāya*, T 1536 at T XXVI 389b4. Whereas SN 43.3 does not appear to have a Chinese parallel, in the case of AN 8.63 a similar presentation can be found in the parallel MĀ 76 at T I 543c20. The same three levels of concentration recur in Abhidh-k 8.23 as an exposition "given in the discourses", Pradhan 1967: 448,18: *trayaḥ samādhayaḥ uktāh sūtre: savitarkaḥ savicāraḥ samādhiḥ, avitarko vicāramātraḥ, avitarko'vicāra.*

[96] See, e.g., DN 2 at DN I 76,15 and its parallels DĀ 20 at T I 85c7, T 22 at T I 275a13, and Gnoli 1978: 245,15. Such imperturbability stands according to MN 66 at MN I 454,28 and its parallel MĀ 192 at T I 743b2 in contrast to the "perturbation" caused by the mental factors still present in the lower absorptions.

individually or collectively reckoned to be forms of imperturbability, reflecting the fact that they are based on the degree of concentrative imperturbability reached with the fourth absorption.[97] Progress toward the immaterial spheres takes place by way of a change of the meditative object or perception that has been the basis for the previous cultivation of the four absorptions.[98] This is first to be replaced by the meditative expe-

---

[97] All four immaterial spheres are presented as ways to reach the imperturbable in AN 4.190 at AN II 184,29. Yet MN 105 at MN II 255,5, as well as MN 106 at MN II 263,13 and its parallels MĀ 75 at T I 542c10 and D 4094 *ju* 228a6 or Q 5595 *tu* 260b5, proceeds from imperturbability to the third immaterial sphere, so that here imperturbability would stand for the lower two immaterial spheres. The third immaterial sphere is then qualified as imperturbable in MN 102 at MN II 230,2 and its Tibetan parallel, Skilling 1994: 318,3. Whereas there evidently is some variation in the application of the term "imperturbable", it nevertheless seems clear that the four immaterial spheres are based on the level of imperturbable concentration reached with the fourth absorption. As Gunaratana 1985/1996: 108f explains, progression "from one formless attainment to another is brought about by changing the object of concentration, not by eliminating or replacing component factors … the fourth fine material *jhāna* and the four immaterial [spheres] … contain the same basic constellation of mental concomitants … and the same two *jhāna* factors, namely one-pointedness and neither-painful-nor-pleasant feeling." Govinda 1961/1991: 96 points out that "from the stand point of consciousness (cetasika), the arūpa-jhānas can be classified" under the fourth absorption, "with which they agree in the elimination of the first four factors (vitakka, vicāra, pīti, sukha)".

[98] Polak 2011: 52–58 argues that the description in AN 11.9 at AN V 324,1 criticizes the taking of a perceived object as a support for absorption attainment. The passage actually does not use the noun *jhāna*, but only the verb *jhāyati*, "to meditate" (glossed at Mp V 79,16 with *cinteti*, "to think"). Moreover, this passage describes a form of meditative reflection, *jhāyati*, during which the five hindrances are still

rience of the mental space that this object had occupied. This space can then be attended to as being experienced by one's own consciousness. This in turn can be seen as insubstantial and thus in a way "nothing". Eventually even this concept can be given up, resulting in a condition where the mind is neither perceptive nor imperceptive.

There is thus indeed a difference between the four absorptions and the four immaterial spheres, but all of these eight experiences are meditative experiences and none of them involves mere intellectual abstraction.

There is also indeed a difference between the first two and the last two of the four immaterial spheres, but there is also a difference between the first and the second, as well as between the third and the fourth immaterial sphere. All four, however, are part of a continuous meditative dynamic whose trajectory is based on the progression that results from these differences, instead of being the outcome of an artificial construction with the aim to arrive at a total count of four.

Heiler, based on the assumption that the four absorptions and the four immaterial spheres are incompatible with each other, comes to the conclusion that the immaterial spheres must be a later addition, resulting in an arbitrary and merely theoretical combination of two completely different forms of meditation practice.[99] He finds confirmation for his assessment in

---

present, whose absence is required for true absorption attainment. A verse, which follows the description of one who meditates without an object, makes it clear that this refers to an awakened one, *purisuttama*, in line with the commentarial explanation, Mp V 80,13, that such meditation takes Nirvāṇa as its 'object'. Thus AN 11.9 does not imply a general criticism of absorption based on a perceived object.

[99] Heiler 1922: 29 comments in relation to "die ganze Konstruktion dieser *jhâna* und *arûpa* umfassenden Versenkungsleiter. Es handelt

the fact that the *Sāmaññaphala-sutta* does not mention the immaterial spheres. Moreover, the *Ariyapariyesanā-sutta* reports the Buddha's rejection of the immaterial spheres taught by his first teachers, which according to Heiler shows that the immaterial spheres were not accepted by the Buddha himself, but only taken over by later dogmatists.[100]

Regarding the *Sāmaññaphala-sutta*, it needs to be kept in mind that the topic of this discourse is a description of "the fruits of recluseship" to a contemporary king. Therefore it is only natural that, out of the alternative routes to be taken after the fourth absorption,[101] the description focuses on supernormal abilities and knowledges, instead of taking up the immaterial spheres. Within the narrative context, descriptions of such supernormal abilities are a better way of impressing on the king that the life of a recluse is indeed fruitful.

---

sich um die willkürliche und künstliche, rein theoretische Kombinierung zweier völlig verschiedener Versenkungsmethoden." Yet, as pointed out by King 1980/1992: 50, "the jhānic series leads naturally, even inevitably, into the formless or immaterial-base meditations."

[100] Heiler 1922: 45 comments that in this way "schweigt die dogmatische Darstellung des Heilspfades, das *Sâmañña-phala-Sutta*, von ihr [d.h. von der Stufenleiter der *arûpa*] vollständig. Ja, das *Ariyapariyesana-Sutta* des *Majjhima-Nikâya* berichtet uns ebenso wie *Lalita Vistara* sogar von einer förmlichen Absage Buddhas an die Methode der abstrakten Versenkung ... aus dieser alten und glaubwürdigen Erzählung geht hervor ... daß die Theorie und Praxis des *arûpa jjhânam* nicht von Buddha selbst, sondern erst von der späteren Ordensdogmatik übernommen und weiter ausgestaltet wurde."

[101] The exposition of the various meditative attainments is not found at all in one of the versions of the discourse, EĀ 43.7 at T II 762a7 (the other parallels are listed above p. 153 note 96). As mentioned above, p. 68 note 9, Meisig 1987: 35f takes this to be an indication that the whole exposition is a later addition.

Given that the immaterial spheres are only one of the routes of mental cultivation possible after successful mastery of the fourth absorption, this also explains why in other passages at times the four absorptions are mentioned, but the immaterial spheres are absent.

In fact, at times neither the immaterial spheres nor supernormal abilities and knowledges are mentioned. Depending on the context, a reference to the four absorptions can suffice to cover the concentrative development of the mind. This does not mean that those responsible for these passages were unaware of the possibility of attaining the immaterial spheres or of the supernormal knowledges. Such a conclusion would be similar to misunderstanding the function of the standard descriptions of the four absorptions as having to provide a comprehensive account of all mental factors present in the attainment, mentioned above. Here and elsewhere, it needs to be kept in mind that the attempt at constructing complete maps and comprehensive descriptions, however much a central concern of later exegetical texts, does not necessarily inform descriptions of meditative attainments in the early discourses.

In the present case, on adopting the methodology of assuming that passages that do not mention the immaterial spheres or the supernormal knowledges reflect an unawareness of their existence, one would also have to conclude, for example, that when the *Sallekha-sutta* and its *Madhyama-āgama* parallel list the four absorptions and the immaterial sphere without following this with a reference to awakening,[102] this implies that the possibility of reaching awakening was unknown among the reciters responsible for transmitting this discourse. This is hardly convincing. It seems considerably more reasonable to grant the possibility

---

[102] MN 8 at MN I 40,27 and its parallel MĀ 91 at T I 573b26.

that shorter references, which do not exhaustively cover all aspects of the early Buddhist meditative path, could simply be due to the context in which the respective exposition occurs.[103]

In the case of the *Ariyapariyesanā-sutta*, the point at stake does not seem to be a wholesale rejection of the immaterial spheres.[104] Instead, the Pāli discourse and its *Madhyama-āgama* parallel only report that the Buddha-to-be considered the third and fourth immaterial spheres he had learned from his teachers Āḷāra Kālāma and Uddaka Rāmaputta to fall short of leading him to the final goal of his aspiration.

In fact once the Buddha had reached awakening, according to the same discourse's narration he thought that his former teachers would easily understand what he had found and wished to share his discovery with them.[105] This description,

---

[103] This would explain the observation by Bronkhorst 1993/2000: xiii that some summary listings of meditational states cover the four absorptions, but not the immaterial spheres. This certainly does not imply that "the most plausible explanation is again that the Formless States were not accepted during the earliest period of Buddhism." It would also explain why the definition of *uttarimanussadhamma* in relation to the fourth *pārājika* at Vin III 91,30 just mentions *jhāna*, etc., but does not refer to the immaterial spheres. This does not mean, as assumed by Zafiropulo 1993: 59, that at the time of the formulation of this explanation the immaterial spheres were not part of the known practices. It would be impossible to claim having attained an immaterial sphere without at the same time implicitly claiming to have attained *jhāna*. Therefore the context does not require an additional listing of the immaterial spheres, since the way it reads already suffices to cover false claims to having attained an immaterial sphere.

[104] *Pace* Senart 1900: 347, who even speaks of "une attitude d'hostilité intransigeante".

[105] MN 26 at MN I 170,6+19 and its parallel MĀ 204 at T I 777a25 and 777b3.

where Āḷāra Kālāma and Uddaka Rāmaputta are the first whom the Buddha wants to teach, reflects a rather high value accorded to the immaterial spheres, however much they are considered to fall short of being the final goal.[106]

Whereas Heiler takes the description in the *Ariyapariyesanā-sutta* to be plausible, a similar argument regarding the supposed lateness of the immaterial spheres has been made by Bronkhorst on the assumption that the bodhisattva's period of apprenticeship under Āḷāra Kālāma and Uddaka Rāmaputta is a later invention.[107]

Such a suggestion had already been made earlier by Bareau, based mainly on the fact that the Mahīśāsaka *Vinaya* does not report the apprenticeship of the future Buddha under Āḷāra Kālāma and Uddaka Rāmaputta, but only his post-awakening wish to share his discovery with them.[108]

---

[106] This has already been pointed out by Wynne 2007: 21f, who notes that "the teachers' meditative practices are not denigrated, and it is implied that they must be of some soteriological benefit, for the Buddha is in no doubt as to the teachers' spiritual qualities", thus the discourse is "not a total condemnation of the teachers' meditative methods".

[107] Bronkhorst 1985: 308 suggests that "the meditational states covered by the term *ārūpya* do not appear to have been originally part of Buddhist meditation … the Bodhisattva learned from them [his two teachers] the *ākiñcanyāyatana* and the *naivasaṃjñānāsaṃjñāyatana* respectively, but rejected these states since they did not lead him to the desired end. This story does not appear to be historical and was intended as a denouncement of these two states, and consequently of the 4 *ārūpya*."

[108] Bareau 1963: 16 notes that this episode, found in MN 26 at MN I 163,31, MĀ 204 at T I 776b8, and the Dharmaguptaka *Vinaya*, T 1428 at T XXII 780b8, is absent from the Mahīśāsaka *Vinaya*, which nevertheless does report the intention to teach them, T 1421 at T XXII 104a11. Bareau 1963: 20 then concludes that therefore

This supposed discrepancy is simply due to the fact that the Mahīśāsaka *Vinaya* proceeds from the bodhisattva's meeting with King Bimbisāra directly to his attainment of awakening.[109] The narrative emphasis adopted in this *Vinaya* makes it only natural that neither the apprenticeship under Āḷāra Kālāma and Uddaka Rāmaputta nor the practice of austerities is mentioned.

The same Mahīśāsaka *Vinaya* reports, however, that after the Buddha first wanted to disclose his discovery to Āḷāra Kālāma and Uddaka Rāmaputta, he then decided to approach his five former companions from the time of his ascetic practices.[110] It is thus obvious that the reciters of the Mahīśāsaka *Vinaya* were aware of what tradition generally associates with the period that precedes the Buddha's awakening, and it is only due to its narrative emphasis that this *Vinaya* does not provide a full account of these as part of its report of the pre-awakening sequence of events.

Ārāḍa Kālāma and Udraka Rāmaputra "sont probablement fictifs", a conclusion accepted by Vetter 1988: xxii. Several arguments raised in support of this hypothesis have already been successfully refuted by Zafiropulo 1993: 22–29 and Wynne 2007: 9–26; so in what follows I only intend to supplement their discussions by taking a look at the Mahīśāsaka *Vinaya* passage in question.

[109] T 1421 at T XXII 102c14 describes that the bodhisattva, after King Bimbisāra had left, approached the *bodhi* tree and asked a person nearby for some grass to sit on. Applying Bareau's mode of interpretation consistently, one would have to conclude that the Mahīśāsaka *Vinaya* presents an alternative account in which the bodhisattva attained awakening right away, without any need to search for a way to attain it and without any practice of asceticism. This would not match the remainder of the narration in this same *Vinaya*.

[110] T 1421 at T XXII 104a19 reports that the Buddha reflected that he could teach his five former companions and at T XXII 104b20 records that they refer to his former asceticism when expressing their disbelief in his awakening.

In fact the Theravāda *Vinaya*, in the way it has come down to us, does not mention any of the pre-awakening events.[111] To be sure, this does not imply that the Theravāda *Vinaya* reciters were not aware of the tradition concerning events believed to have preceded the Buddha's awakening.

Thus the absence of a full account in some *Vinaya*s need not be taken as having any deeper significance beyond reflecting the narrative choice of the reciters responsible for the respective texts.

The future Buddha's apprenticeship under Āḷāra Kālāma and Uddaka Rāmaputta is in fact also mentioned in texts that Bareau did not take into account in his study, namely the *Mahāvastu*,[112] a *Vinaya* text of the Mahāsāṅghika Lokottaravāda tradition,[113] and the *Saṅghabhedavastu* of the Mūlasarvāstivāda *Vinaya*.[114]

In sum, the various arguments proposed to support the assumption that the immaterial spheres are a later addition to descriptions of meditative practice in the early discourses are unconvincing.

Another passage even establishes a relationship between the Buddha's mastery of the immaterial attainments and his awakening. This passage is found in a discourse in the *Aṅguttaranikāya*, of which no parallel is known. According to its presentation, the Buddha reported of himself that he attained the four absorptions, the four immaterial spheres, and cessation, where-

---

[111] Vin I 1,1 begins only with the awakening already attained; see the discussion in Zafiropulo 1993: 24.

[112] Senart 1890: 118,6; the wish to teach them is then found in Senart 1897: 322,11.

[113] On the *Vinaya* nature of this text see Tournier 2012.

[114] Gnoli 1977: 97,4; the wish to teach them is found in Gnoli 1977: 130,16.

upon his influxes were destroyed.[115] The eight concentrative attainments that precede cessation are specified to have each taken place at a different time, *aparena samayena*.[116] In other words, the discourse covers an extended time period, not a single meditation session. This form of presentation would indeed be appropriate for the Buddha's pre-awakening meditation cultivation.

The last in this series could imply that the Buddha's actual realization of Nirvāṇa on the night of his awakening should be understood to have taken place by attaining the cessation of perception and feeling.[117] For one who has mastery of the four absorptions and the immaterial spheres, it would presumably be possible to attain full awakening through entry into cessation.

The next discourse in the *Aṅguttara-nikāya* begins with a verse, according to which the Buddha awakened to absorption,

---

[115] AN 9.41 at AN IV 448,7: *āsavā parikkhayaṃ agamaṃsu*, which thus uses an aorist form that differs from the standard formulation *parikkhīṇā honti*. Somaratne 2003: 216 explains that the reading *āsavā parikkhayaṃ agamaṃsu* in AN 9.41 implies that here "the Buddha is talking about a past experience where he achieved the cessation for the first time."

[116] The qualification *aparena samayena* is found in all editions I have been able to consult; the remark in Bodhi 2012: 1832 note 1947 refers only to a doubling of this expression in E[e].

[117] Commenting on AN 9.41, Bronkhorst 2009: 54 reasons that "since no mental processes take place in the cessation of ideation and feeling, the highest enlightenment cannot take place" in this attainment. Yet, as pointed out by Wynne 2002: 31, the description in AN 9.41 indeed "means that the Buddha attained liberation whilst in the state of cessation", and thus by way of the most complete and thorough mode of experiencing Nirvāṇa. As Somaratne 2006: 750 explains, the ability to attain cessation means that "one is able to experience *nibbāna* physically here and now in its completeness."

and then depicts the same series of nine successive stages culminating in cessation.[118] Although of this discourse, too, no parallel seems to be known, the verse recurs in the *Saṃyutta-nikāya* and in the two *Saṃyukta-āgama*s which present the Buddha in conversation with a *deva*. In the complete *Saṃyukta-āgama* (T 99), the *deva* refers in verse to the Buddha's realization of what is to be realized in relation to absorption. In the other *Saṃyukta-āgama* (T 100), the verse by the *deva* speaks of his realization on emerging from absorption.[119]

Alongside differences in formulation, the point common to the parallel versions of this verse appears to be that an integral aspect of the Buddha's awakening was his penetrative insight into the nature of absorption, which was based, of course, on having earlier mastered it.

The main point made in the second *Aṅguttara-nikāya* discourse that also has this verse appears to be the same as in the preceding *Aṅguttara-nikāya* discourse, in that the Buddha's awakening took place after he had mastered the four absorptions and the four immaterial spheres and, in a way, after he had seen through them. It is by such seeing through that he was able to proceed further and attain cessation.

Pre-Buddhist Absorption

The need to see through the absorptions brings me back to the topic of their role in the early Buddhist path to awakening. The passages surveyed so far in this chapter would have made clear that cultivation of absorption, as well as of the immaterial at-

---

118 AN 9.42 at AN IV 451,20.

119 SN 2.7 at SN I 48,29: *jhānam abuddhi*, B^{e}: *jhānam abujjhi*, C^{e}: *jhānam budhā*, new E^{e} ed. by Somaratne 1998: 110: *jhānam abudhā*, and its parallels SĀ 1305 at T II 358c3: 禪思覺所覺 and SĀ^{2} 304 at T II 477a25: 從禪出覺了.

tainments, is not in itself considered as productive of insight. This suggestion receives further support from the fact that some early discourses give the impression that absorption was considered to be a pre-Buddhist practice.

The *Aggañña-sutta* and its parallels, for instance, present the practice of absorption as something undertaken by ancient brahmins during an early stage in the evolution of human society. According to the report in the *Aggañña-sutta*, some brahmins in the distant past were engaged in absorption practice. Other brahmins, who were unable to attain absorption, abandoned the secluded lifestyle required for such practice and instead went to live in villages and taught recitation.[120]

It is noteworthy that the parallel versions use the unspecified expression *jhāna* (禪), without bringing in the analysis into different types, discussed above. This leaves open the possibility that such analysis of absorption into different levels, based on identifying its most significant mental factors, might have been considered to be the more specifically Buddhist contribution to the topic of absorption attainment, in line with a general tendency toward analysis evident in the early discourses.

---

[120] According to DN 27 at DN III 94,17, these brahmins were unable to attain such absorption, *taṃ jhānaṃ anabhisambhuṇamānā*. The parallel DĀ 5 at T I 38c9 refers to brahmins "who did not delight in seclusion and giving attention to sitting in meditation/absorption", 不樂閑靜坐禪思惟者. An individual translation, T 10 at T I 221a6, reports that these brahmins decided to return to the village after (presumably unsuccessfully) "having first cultivated meditation/absorption", 初修禪已. Another parallel, MĀ 154 at T I 676b1, reports that these brahmins "trained in meditation/absorption, but did not attain meditation/absorption", 學禪不得禪. Gethin 2014: 69 comments that "the *Aggañña-sutta* suggests that study of the Vedas is in fact the occupation of those brahmins who failed in precisely the way of life that Buddhist monks now successfully pursue."

Another relevant passage is the *Cūlasakkuludāyi-sutta* and its *Madhyama-āgama* parallel, which feature contemporaries of the Buddha apparently familiar with an ancient practice related to the attainment of the third absorption.[121] Notably, these practitioners are depicted as being ignorant of the way of practice that leads to what they considered as the highest goal. In other words, this discourse seems to reflect the existence of an ancient form of practice that led up to the attainment of the third absorption.[122] However, by the time of their meeting with the Buddha, the actual practice to be undertaken to reach that goal had apparently fallen into oblivion.

Also to be kept mind here is that, during the time of his quest for awakening, the Buddha-to-be trained under the guidance of the two teachers Āḷāra Kālāma and Uddaka Rāmaputta, as already mentioned above. For Āḷāra Kālāma and Uddaka's father Rāma to have reached the third and fourth immaterial attainment respectively would imply that they must have been acquainted with absorption practice at a time long before the Buddha reached awakening.[123]

---

[121] MN 79 at MN II 37,16 and MĀ 208 at T I 786a24.

[122] This is explicitly stated in the commentary, Ps III 275,2; Bodhi in Ñāṇamoli 1995/2005: 1287f note 784 explains that according to the commentary these practitioners "knew that in the past meditators would ... attain the third jhāna".

[123] MN 26 at MN I 165,12 and 166,31 indicates that the attainments the bodhisattva reached under the two teachers would lead to the corresponding rebirth, making it clear that the description refers to the full attainment of the respective immaterial sphere. The same is also evident in the parallel MĀ 204 at T I 776b12+24, where Āḷāra and Uddaka describe the attainments taught by them as a going beyond the respective lower immaterial sphere. Thus the assumption by Ireland 1998: 195 that the "experiences the Buddha had with these two former teachers had no relation to the *jhāna*s as later taught by

In fact according to the *Mahāsaccaka-sutta* and its Sanskrit fragment parallel, the bodhisattva himself had an experience of the first absorption long before going forth.[124] The *Mahāsaccaka-sutta* and its parallel report that, once the bodhisattva had recognized that his ascetic striving was not fruitful, he reflected on alternative approaches and realized that the first absorption, experienced before he had gone forth, was the path to awakening.

Needless to say, the first absorption is not in itself the whole path to awakening, otherwise the Buddha-to-be would have already been well acquainted with the path to awakening since his early youth, without any need later on to search for the way that could lead him to liberation.

The whole path to awakening in early Buddhist thought is rather the noble eightfold path, where in the standard definition all of the four absorptions are but one of the eight factors leading to progress to liberation. However, in the context of

---

him" is unconvincing. It would in fact be difficult to find corroboration for the idea that the immaterial spheres can be reached without previous training in absorption, since the discourses present the four absorptions as what leads up to the immaterial spheres and from there to the attainment of cessation; see, e.g., MN 25 at MN I 160,8 and its parallel MĀ 178 at T I 720a22 (just to mention one occurrence). Such an assumption would also not square too well with the indication that Uddaka himself had not reached what he taught, which had only been accomplished by his father Rāma; see the discussion in Skilling 1981 and Wynne 2007: 14–16. This indication only makes sense if the immaterial attainment he taught did indeed require a high degree of meditative expertise.

[124] MN 36 at MN I 246,31 and fragment 336v6, Liú 2010: 222; cf. also, e.g., the Dharmaguptaka *Vinaya*, T 1428 at T XXII 781a5, the *Mahāvastu*, Senart 1890: 130,15, and the *Saṅghabhedavastu*, Gnoli 1977: 107,27, and for further references Anālayo 2011: 240f.

the situation depicted in the *Mahāsaccaka-sutta*, the recollection of the former experience of the first absorption was the first step on the path to awakening, since it seems to have triggered the decisive insight that the pleasure of such absorption is not something to be feared. This point is made explicitly in the Pāli version, according to which the bodhisattva reflected on why he was afraid of a form of pleasure that is apart from sensuality and unwholesome states.[125]

In this way, the recollection of his absorption experience appears to have corroborated the bodhisattva's dawning insight that the path to freedom does not require just engaging in pain and avoiding all forms of pleasure and happiness, which the fruitlessness of his asceticism had already made plain to him.[126]

Another discourse suggestive of the existence of absorption meditation practices in the ancient Indian setting before the advent of the Buddha is the *Brahmajāla-sutta*, which together with its parallels examines a range of various views. The *Brahmajāla-sutta*'s exposition on views is one of the few instances where a discourse is quoted by name in another Pāli discourse, a clear token of the *Brahmajāla-sutta*'s antiquity.[127] Many of

---

[125] MN 36 at MN I 246,37; on the significance of the Buddha's pre-awakening recollection of an absorption experienced in his youth see the discussion in Anālayo 2011: 240–243 and 2017c.

[126] In MN 85 at MN II 93,15 the Buddha states that, before his awakening, he had believed that progress to happiness required going through pain (not in the parallel fragment 342r, Silverlock 2009: 77). After having reached awakening he of course knew better.

[127] SN 41.3 at SN IV 287,12; the parallel SĀ 570 at T II 151a19 only mentions the different views, without giving the discourse's title. Polak 2011: 167, however, argues that, since DN 1 has "very little, or almost nothing to do with the real doctrines of this era", "this sutta comes from the later times (sic)." This seems to misconstrue the purpose of the discourse, which is not the provision of a survey

the views listed in this discourse appear to result from absorption experiences.[128]

It would hardly work to imagine that the wrong views described in this discourse all came into existence only after early Buddhist practitioners had discovered and then introduced absorption practice as something entirely new in the ancient Indian setting. The analysis in this discourse reads considerably more naturally if one assumes that the experiences leading to the arising of these mistaken views were already known at the time the Buddha reached awakening.[129]

---

of actually held views; see Anālayo 2009 and below p. 171. Polak 2011: 167 also sees the report of an earthquake at the end of the discourse as confirming his "suspicion of the sutta's lateness". This appears to be based on the assumption that supernatural phenomena are by default later additions to the early discourses, a position that has been repeatedly criticized in current scholarship; see, e.g., the comment by Gethin 1996: 204 that the "tendency to play down the tradition of the 'miraculous' in Buddhism and to see it as peripheral … it is hard to treat this tendency as anything but revisionist", and in more detail Anālayo 2015b and 2016e. Moreover, even if the concluding part should be the result of a later addition, it does not follow that the body of the discourse must also be late.

[128] Bodhi 1978/1992: 6 comments that "the fact that a great number [of the views in DN 1], perhaps the majority, have their source in the experience of meditative attainments has significant implications for our understanding of the genetic process behind the fabrication of views. It suffices to caution us against the hasty generalization that speculative views take rise through preference for theorization over the more arduous task of practice. As our sutta shows, many of these views make their appearance only at the end of a prolonged course of meditation … for these views the very basis of their formulation is a higher experience rather than the absence of one."

[129] As already pointed out by Rhys Davids 1899: 51 note 1 more than a century ago, "the four *Gh*ânas were regarded by the early Bud-

In fact, had the Buddha discovered absorption as such, one would be at a loss to understand why the discourses do not celebrate this discovery in a way comparable to their drawing of attention to his discovery of the four noble truths as a teaching unheard of before.

The *Brahmajāla-sutta* and its parallels show rather substantial differences in their presentation of the first part of the discourse, concerned with morality; they also have variations in their exposition of some of the different viewpoints.[130] Comparative study makes it fair to conclude that the long exposition on morality in the Pāli version, for example, is probably the outcome of a later expansion. Alongside such variations, however, the parallel versions agree closely in presenting the attainment of absorption as a source for the arising of mistaken views, namely by way of identifying such attainment as being in itself the realization of Nirvāṇa here and now.[131] Needless to

dhists as older than Buddhism"; see also de La Vallée Poussin 1928: 223.

[130] See Anālayo 2009 and 2014a.

[131] DN 1 at DN I 37,1 and its parallels DĀ 21 at T I 93b20, T 21 at T I 269c22, a Tibetan discourse parallel in Weller 1934: 58,3 (§191), a discourse quotation in the **Śāriputrābhidharma*, T 1548 at T XXVIII 660b24, and a discourse quotation in D 4094 *ju* 152a4 or Q 5595 *tu* 175a8. The same versions also attribute the arising of annihilationist views to the immaterial attainments (for Sanskrit fragments corresponding to the section on annihilationism see also Hartmann 1989: 54 and SHT X 4189, Wille 2008: 307). This does not mean, as assumed by Zafiropulo 1993: 57f, that at the time of the formation of this discourse the immaterial spheres and the four absorptions were not yet seen as related to each other. The point is only that some non-Buddhists are shown up for having mistaken the attainment of the absorptions as the final goal, leading to one particular type of wrong view, but other non-Buddhists who had

say, according to the *Brahmajāla-sutta* and its parallels these are wrong views.[132] The relevant passage in the *Dīrgha-āgama* version proceeds as follows:[133]

> When having left behind sensuality as well as evil and unwholesome states, with [directed] contemplation and [sustained] awareness, with joy and happiness born of seclusion, I attain the first absorption: this is reckoned Nirvāṇa here and now.

The *Brahmajāla-sutta* and its parallels continue in similar ways for the remaining three absorptions. As explained by Bodhi (1978/1992: 31f), this depicts "attainers of the four jhānas, who mistake the rapture, bliss and peacefulness of their attainments for the supreme good." The Buddha's assessment of such absorption attainers then takes the following form in the *Dīrgha-āgama* version:[134]

> Recluses and brahmins who declare [of the first absorption] that: 'This is reckoned Nirvāṇa here and now', [do so] conditioned by feeling, which produces craving. Craving having arisen they do not realize by themselves that they are being defiled by attachment through craving and are under the power of craving.

---

further progressed to the immaterial attainments instead took these to be the final goal, resulting in another type of wrong view.

[132] If at all, absorption could only be considered Nirvāṇa here and now "in a certain sense", *pariyāyena*, AN 9.51 at AN IV 454,9, but not "in a definite sense", *nippariyāyena*, AN 9.51 at AN IV 454,14, which requires the destruction of the influxes.

[133] DĀ 21 at T I 93b20 to 93b22.

[134] DĀ 21 at T I 93c20 to 93c22 (the passage is abbreviated in the original, which only gives the full treatment for the first of the sixty-two viewpoints).

This part of the discourse reflects what Katz (1982/1989: 150) has aptly called a "psychoanalysis of metaphysical claims". Far from being informed by doxographical concerns, the issue at stake in the *Brahmajāla* is to lay bare the psychological underpinnings of the tendency to view formation. The central intent is not to present a survey of views, held in ancient India or elsewhere, but to show how clinging to any view has its basis in craving. Bodhi (1978/1992: 9) comments that

> the primary focus … is not so much the content of the view as the underlying malady of which the addiction to speculative tenets is a symptom.

Fuller (2005: 115) argues that

> the *Brahmajāla-sutta* proposes neither a sixty-third view … nor the rejection of all views … but knowledge of the cessation of craving. This is right view.

Needless to say, such right view is not the automatic outcome of absorption attainment, as the above passage amply demonstrates. It is precisely insight into the role of craving that is missing in the case of the absorption attainers described in the *Brahmajāla-sutta* and its parallels. In this way, the *Brahmajāla-sutta* and its parallels confirm the conclusions suggested above, in that the early discourses do not seem to reckon the attainment of absorption as an experience that in itself is necessarily productive of liberating insight.

Conclusion

A perusal of arguments offered in support of the assumption that absorption attainment was held in the early Buddhist discourses to be in and of itself liberating shows these to be unconvincing and at times based on misunderstandings. Such an assumption overlooks those passages that draw attention to the inherent drawback of absorption experiences and their inability to result in a total removal of sensuality and other unwholesome conditions, unless combined with the cultivation of insight.

The related position that insight contemplation of impermanence can be practiced while immersed in an absorption relies for the most part on passages that are in themselves ambivalent and could be read in two ways. The one passage held to provide certain indications in this respect turns out on closer investigation to yield the opposite result; it shows that contemplation of the impermanence of mental factors present during an absorption would take place either when not yet having fully entered attainment or else when having just emerged from it.

The mental factor of *vitakka*, whose presence qualifies the first absorption, is probably best understood in this particular context as pointing to a directing of the mind that does not involve actual thought in the sense of reflection and reasoning. Although such directing of the mind in ordinary experience takes place when thinking or communicating, in the context of absorption the same can perform its role in a manner that does not involve conceptual thinking activity.

Seclusion is a crucial precondition for absorption attainment, reflecting the need to leave behind concern with sensuality in order to be able to experience the non-sensual types of joy and happiness that arise with deepening concentration.

A perusal of the early discourses makes it appear fairly probable that their vision of absorption was such that its full attainment is not compatible with the hearing of sound. If one hears sound, this would presumably imply that one either has momentarily emerged from absorption, or else one is overestimating a concentrated condition of the mind as already being full absorption attainment, when in actual fact it seems to fall short of corresponding to the type of profound mental unification that characterizes such attainment, at least in the early discourses.

The immaterial attainments stand in a coherent continuity with absorption attainment; both appear to be considered in the early discourses to have been known before the Buddha reached awakening.

Regarding the role and significance of absorption, it remains a fact that in later tradition these no longer carry the importance they had in the early discourses. This, I contend, would be the result of the in itself natural attempt to systematize the teachings, a topic I discussed in the previous chapter. Even the basic division of the path into morality, concentration, and wisdom can easily result in obscuring the basic interrelation of these three aspects of the gradual path, if this division is interpreted in a manner that is too literal and narrow. With the growing systematization of the teachings, it was perhaps inevitable that the interrelationship between the three basic aspects of the path to awakening was no longer as clearly in the foreground of attention as it had been in earlier times.

Tranquillity and insight are closely interrelated in the early discourses, and it is only in later tradition that these came to be seen as two distinct paths of meditative practice. An illustrative example is when the *Āneñjasappāya-sutta* and its parallels showcase the contribution the cultivation of insight can make for the development of tranquillity.[135] An example for the contribution of tranquility to insight can be seen in the *Cūḷasuññata-sutta* and its parallels, which employ the perceptions of the immaterial attainments for the sake of a gradual deepening

---

[135] See in more detail Anālayo 2012c: 195ff.

of insight into emptiness.[136] The possibility of such cross-fertilization between tranquillity and insight shows that in the early discourses these two do not function as separate paths, but rather constitute complementary dimensions of the path.

In view of the loss of recognition of the transformative potential of the absorptions in later tradition, it seems to me that modern scholars and practitioners are to some extent correct in identifying that there is a problem. But I think they miss the point as long as their criticism continues to affirm implicitly the dichotomy between tranquillity and insight. In this way, the in itself justified criticism of the demotion of the absorptions in later exegesis keeps missing the point as long as such criticism continues to be based on the same dichotomy. Once this dichotomy is set aside as the natural but unfortunately misleading result of the influence of later exegetical systematization, it seems to me the situation becomes clearer. The absorptions do indeed offer a substantial and important contribution to the path to liberation, but this contribution stands in dependent interrelation with the contribution to be made by the cultivation of liberating insight.

In sum, I would propose that the solution to the bifurcation into tranquillity and insight is not found by attributing qualities of the one to the other, but by returning to an appreciation of their complementary and interrelated role as reflected in the discourses. Neither dry insight on its own nor absorption by itself can do justice to what the early discourses have to offer in terms of meditation practice.[137] The first can become

[136] See in more detail Anālayo 2012c: 325ff and 2015c: 75ff.

[137] Regarding the limitations of dry insight, I am no longer as confident as I was in Anālayo 2003: 81f that mastery of absorption is indispensable for reaching the higher two levels of awakening. My assessment at that time was influenced in particular by MN 64 at

impoverishing, the second risks missing the main point. Instead, both are at their best when cultivated in harmonious conjunction. In short:

> There is no meditation/absorption for one without wisdom,
> There is no wisdom without meditating.
> One in whom there are meditation/absorption and wisdom,
> Is indeed close to Nirvāṇa.[138]

MN I 435,26, which does convey this sense. In the meantime, however, comparative study has brought to light that the corresponding passage in the parallel MĀ 205 at T I 779b12 differs substantially and carries no such implication; see also Anālayo 2011: 356.

[138] Dhp 372; with similarly worded parallels in the Gāndhārī *Dharmapada* 58, Brough 1962/2001:127, the Patna *Dharmapada* 62, Cone 1989: 119, and the *Udānavarga* 32.25, Bernhard 1965: 439. Counterparts preserved in Chinese, which show some variations, can be found in T 210 at T IV 572a18, T 212 at T IV 766b29, and T 213 at T IV 796c20. The noun *jhāna* in the first line could be rendered as "meditation" in general, in line with the implication of the reference to "meditating", *ajhāyato*, in the second line, or else as "absorption". Even on adopting the translation "absorption", the verse does not imply that wisdom is an intrinsic quality of absorption, but only that some degree of wisdom is a prerequisite for absorption (and that meditating in general is productive of wisdom). In fact, had absorption and wisdom been considered equivalent, the stipulation in line 3 that both are needed for progress to the final goal should not have come into being in the first place.

Brahmavihāra

Introduction

The *brahmavihāra*s seem to have shared to some degree the fate of the absorptions. Presumably under the influence of later systematizations of path accounts and the resultant bifurcation into tranquillity and insight, the *brahmavihāra*s as a set also appear to have gradually lost the importance they had in early Buddhist thought. Recent attempts at restoration of their position have in turn gone rather far in the opposite direction, alleging that the *brahmavihāra*s are forms of insight in themselves.

Before taking up the four *brahmavihāra*s in general, however, I first study *anukampā* as active compassion, evident specifically in teaching activity.[1] I explore in particular the significance of the relationship between compassion and teaching for understanding the nature of the compassion of a Buddha and an arahant. Then I turn to the *brahmavihāra*s in general, contrasting their alleged salvific function to what the early discourses indicate about the potential of cultivating these four sublime states. Finally I examine several early discourses which suggest that the *brahmavihāra*s were considered to have been a pre-Buddhist type of practice, similar to the case of the absorptions.

Compassion and Teaching

In the early discourses, active expressions of compassion (*anukampā*) usually take the form of teaching the Dharma. The same

---

[1] On *karuṇā* as the meditative quality of compassion and *anukampā* as active compassion, respectively, see Anālayo 2015c: 13. Needless to say, the two are interrelated and cultivating one strengthens the other.

discourses recognize other forms of compassion, such as when family members or those who are together in a working or a learning situation are compassionately disposed toward each other.[2] However, the contexts within which such references occur give the impression that these reflect social conceptions held in the ancient Indian setting in general. When it comes to the specific Buddhist approach to compassion, teaching activities are clearly in the forefront.

The close relationship between teaching and compassion is evident, for example, in a standard phrase that occurs regularly when the Buddha concludes a teaching, just before telling his listeners that they should engage in meditative practice of what he had taught. According to the phrase in question, with the instruction just delivered the Buddha has done for his disciples what a teacher should do "out of compassion" (*anukampā*).[3]

The same is also evident in another standard formulation used by those who request instructions from the Buddha or from one of his disciples. Such a request recurrently expresses the wish that the invitation to deliver a teaching be accepted

---

[2] See, e.g., DN 31 at DN III 189,11, which describes compassion – the term used is *anukampā* – of parents toward their children, teachers toward their students, wives toward their husbands, friends toward each other, workers toward their master, and recluses and brahmins toward those who support them (notably the relationships described do not invariably involve compassion by those who are higher in the hierarchy toward those who are lower). For a translation and study of the Chinese parallels to DN 31 see Pannasiri 1950; for Sanskrit fragments see the survey in Hartmann and Wille 2006: 3; see also Martini 2013: 52f note 104.

[3] This phrase (together with its Chinese counterpart) can be found, for example, in MN 19 at MN 118,20 and its parallel MĀ 102 at T I 590a18.

"out of compassion".[4] In this way, those who teach as well as those who request to be taught are explicitly on record as considering such teaching to be an act of compassion.

Compassion is of course not the only possible motivation behind teaching activities, something the early discourses also clearly recognize.

Several passages highlight the effect of a particular teaching in leading to conversion to the Buddhist fold or else throw into relief the donations that were given to its monastic members after a successful teaching had been delivered.

The *Aṭṭhakanāgara-sutta* and its parallels, for example, conclude by describing the offerings made to the Buddhist monastic community by a lay follower who had just received an inspiring instruction from Ānanda.[5] Another discourse even takes its title from the cloth offered by a king in gratitude for the teaching received.[6] Clearly, the material benefits that could

---

[4] An example involving Sāriputta would be SN 55.26 at SN V 380,28 and its parallel MĀ 28 at T I 458c16. This passage helps to correct a suggestion by Hamilton 1950: 146 that the compassion of disciples, in contrast to the Buddha's own compassion, was just "a means to a personal end". Instead, in the early discourses the Buddha and his disciples are shown as equally engaged in compassionate teaching activity. The same also emerges from a range of discourses with advice given to the sick and dying; see in more detail Anālayo 2016f.

[5] MN 52 at MN I 353,10 (= AN 11.17 at AN V 347,8) and its parallels MĀ 217 at T I 802c18 and T 92 at T I 916c23. Notably, the teaching given concerns paths to arahantship. This discourse is one of several cases showing that teachings on liberating insight were not withheld from lay disciples; see in more detail Anālayo 2015e: 146–154.

[6] MN 88 at MN II 116,29 and its parallel MĀ 214 at T I 799a19, an agreement that is noteworthy in view of the fact that discourses in the *Majjhima-nikāya* and the *Madhyama-āgama* regularly vary regarding their respective titles.

result from teaching were recognized among the reciters of the discourses.

Nevertheless, a discourse in the *Saṃyutta-nikāya* and its parallels qualify the giving of a teaching with the wish to gain material support as an impure way of teaching.[7] A pure way of teaching takes place when one simply wishes to benefit others, an indication as relevant in present times as it was in ancient India.

In this way, from the viewpoint of the early discourses the teachings given by the Buddha and by his arahant disciples, who by dint of their inner non-attachment would have to be reckoned as not teaching for the sake of material benefits or fame, are expressions of compassion. The same of course also holds for disciples who have not yet become arahants, as long as their teaching activities are sincerely motivated by compassion instead of the wish for mundane rewards. This in turn implies that the records of these teachings, in the way they have come down to us in the *Nikāya*s and their parallels in the *Āgama*s, can be considered as testimonies of acts of compassion.

It is particularly noteworthy that this applies in the same way to the teachings given by the Buddha himself and to those

---

[7] SN 16.3 at SN II 199,14 and its parallels SĀ 1136 at T II 300a8, SĀ[2] 111 at T II 414b27, and T 121 at T II 544c28. SN 16.3 does not give any explicit indication of the type of gifts that such a teacher may wish for. Only the commentary, Spk II 169,25, indicates that the point at stake is to get robes and other requisites. The parallels, however, explicitly refer to the wish to get robes and requisites; see SĀ 1136 at T II 300a9: 為本已當得供養衣被, 飲食, 臥具, 湯藥, SĀ[2] 111 at T II 414b28: 能多與我飲食, 衣服, 病瘦醫藥, and T 121 at T II 544c29: 施衣服, 飲食, 坐臥之具, 病緣醫藥. This reflects a recurrent pattern where details, which appear to have originally come into being as a commentary, eventually came to be part of the text on which they comment; see Anālayo 2014c: 46–50 and 2015e: 441–462.

delivered by his arahant disciples. In fact the early discourses do not mark off the Buddha's compassion as something substantially distinct from the compassion of any among his arahant disciples. The expression "great compassion" is not found in the early discourses, except for the *Ekottarika-āgama*,[8] a collection that has incorporated later elements, among them some Mahāyāna ideas.[9]

Not only do the early discourses not qualify the Buddha's compassion as "great", it also does not yet appear to have been considered the result of aeons of intentional cultivation.[10] The *Ariyapariyesanā-sutta* and its *Madhyama-āgama* parallel present the quest of the Buddha-to-be for awakening as being motivated entirely in terms of wishing to liberate himself.[11] The early discourses in general do not so much as refer to the perfections (*pāramitā*), qualities held to be required for progressing on the path to Buddhahood in later tradition. The only exception is again the *Ekottarika-āgama*.[12]

---

[8] See, e.g., EĀ 38.1 at T II 717b24: 諸佛世尊成大慈悲, 以大悲為力弘益眾生, according to which all Buddhas are endowed with *mahākaruṇā*, they benefit living beings through the power of their *mahākaruṇā*.

[9] For a survey of Mahāyāna thought in the *Ekottarika-āgama* see Anālayo 2016c: 443–471.

[10] For a study of the gradual evolution of the bodhisattva ideal see Anālayo 2010 and 2017a.

[11] MN 26 at MN I 163,18 and MĀ 204 at T I 776a27; see in more detail Anālayo 2010: 20–28. As pointed out by Wangchuk 2007: 82, "there is no canonical evidence for the theory that the main motive for the Buddha's appearance in the world was for the sake of others. This idea is found only in the post-canonical literature. The overwhelming majority of the canonical material suggests that … he was concerned with his own release."

[12] EĀ 27.5 at T II 645b4 reports instructions given by the Buddha to the bodhisattva Maitreya on the cultivation of the six *pāramitās*.

The previous Buddha Dīpaṃkara, meeting whom the future Buddha Gotama supposedly decided to embark on the path to future Buddhahood, is not mentioned in the early discourses at all. The *Ekottarika-āgama* is again the only exception.[13] Even the Pāli *Jātaka* collection does not give compassion the prominent place it should have had, if this quality was indeed from the outset considered to have been the main motivating force leading to Gotama's eventual attainment of Buddhahood.[14]

In sum, as far as the early discourses allow us to judge, the Buddha's compassion was not yet seen as the final result of a long trajectory of cultivation undertaken during past lives with the intentional aim of becoming a Buddha. Instead, his compassion appears to have been considered the result of his awakening, whereby he had forever overcome those unwholesome mental conditions that are opposed to compassion.

Even after awakening, the Buddha's compassion is not depicted as motivated by the wish to save all living beings. A

Har Dayal 1932/1978: 168 suggests that the listing of six *pāramitā*s might have evolved out of the threefold training in morality, concentration, and wisdom, which is regularly mentioned in the early texts; see also above p. 88f.

[13] EĀ 20.3 at T II 599b14 and EĀ 43.2 at T II 758b27 report Dīpaṃkara predicting Gotama's future Buddhahood. As pointed out by Nattier 2004: 230, "Dīpaṃkara's complete absence from the Pāli sutta literature makes it virtually certain that traditions concerning this buddha did not gain general currency until several centuries after Śākyamuni Buddha's death"; for a study of the Dīpaṃkara narrative(s) see Matsumura 2008, 2010, 2011, and 2012.

[14] This has already been pointed out by Schmithausen 2000: 438 note 8, who comments that "in den (meist vorbuddhistischen) Geschichten, die von den Buddhisten auf frühere Leben des historischen Buddha (als Bodhisattva) projiziert worden sind, spielt das Mitleid oft gar keine Role."

discourse in the *Aṅguttara-nikāya* and its *Saṃyukta-āgama* parallel explicitly state that the Buddha was not concerned with whether the whole world or only part of it will be able to reach liberation.[15]

Texts that reflect beginning stages in the development of the full-fledged bodhisattva ideal, such as the *Mahāvastu*, the *Aṣṭa-sāhasrikā Prajñāpāramitā* (as witnessed by its earliest Chinese translation by Lokakṣema), and the *Ugraparipṛcchā*, give the impression that the compassionate wish to save living beings was also not a central factor in the early stages of the arising of the bodhisattva ideal, the main driving force rather being the wish to become equal to the Buddha.[16] The compassionate intent to save all living beings appears to have taken a central role in the conception of the bodhisattva ideal only at a subsequent stage of development.

This development had its appeal not only in the Mahāyāna traditions, but also in the Theravāda tradition, where the aspiration to become a Buddha in the future is well attested in texts and inscriptions.[17] This in turn makes it clear that the term Hīnayāna is not applicable to the Theravāda tradition.

In fact there seems to be no evidence that a Hīnayāna tradition, school, or institution ever existed anywhere throughout

---

[15] AN 10.95 at AN V 195,8 and its parallel SĀ 965 at T II 248a10 (another parallel, SĀ² 199 at T II 447c12, is less explicit in this respect, although the basic implications seem to be the same).

[16] This has been pointed out by de La Vallée Poussin 1915: 330, Fronsdal 1998: 220, and Nattier 2003: 146.

[17] This has been noted by a range of scholars; see, e.g., Rahula 1971, Tambiah 1976: 96f, Ratnayaka 1985, Endo 1996, Samuels 1997, Skilling 2003, Harvey 2007, and Chandawimala 2008. For inscriptions in Theravāda countries that document the donor's aspiration for Buddhahood see, e.g., Luce 1969: 56, Dohanian 1977: 20–25, and Assavavirulhakarn 2010: 175.

the history of Buddhism.[18] Instead of describing an actual historical reality, the forging and deployment of the term Hīnayāna appears to be just the product of polemical strategies.

In sum, the arahants depicted in the early Buddhist texts teach out of compassion, just like the Buddha, whose compassionate activity in this respect is not yet seen as the result of an intentional cultivation of compassion over a long series of past lives.

Brahmavihāra and Awakening

In what follows I turn from compassion to the whole set of four *brahmavihāra*s, critically examining the suggestion that their cultivation originally constituted an independent path to liberation in the early discourses. An argument presented in support of this suggestion is that the *Karajakāya-sutta* shows that the practice of the *brahmavihāra*s, when undertaken as a liberation of the mind (*cetovimutti*), has an effect on one's karma.[19] Further confirmation is then sought in a *Dhamma-*

[18] Silk 2002: 367f explains that "the referent of the term 'Hīnayāna', when it occurs in Buddhist texts themselves, is never any existent institution or organization, but a rhetorical fiction … a fundamental error is thus made when we imagine references to 'Hīnayāna' in Mahāyāna literature to apply to so-called Sectarian Buddhism, much less to Early Buddhism." Skilling 2013: 76 notes that "the Hīnayāna never existed, anywhere or at any time, as an establishment or organization, as a social movement, as a self-conscious historical agent. Nor was Hīnayāna a stage or period in the development of Buddhism … the Hīnayānist was defined by Mahāyānist polemics; he was a dogmatic construction, not a social identity." For a detailed discussion see Anālayo 2016c: 473–495.

[19] Wiltshire 1990: 268 comments on AN 10.208 at AN V 300,7 that "we see here that mettā eliminates in the present body kamma

pada stanza, which states that a monastic who dwells with *mettā* and has faith in the Buddha's teaching will attain the final goal,[20] and in the *Metta-sutta*'s indication that *mettā* meditation leads beyond birth in a womb, which is taken to imply final liberation.[21]

Before turning to these passages, it would be pertinent to note briefly that early Buddhist thought recognizes various types of liberation, *vimutti*. Not all of these equal the liberation from all defilements that comes with the attainment of arahantship.[22] The meditative cultivation of the *brahmavihāra*s leads to *cetovimutti*, the experience of a "liberation of the mind". Such temporary liberation falls short of being an irreversible and supreme liberation from all defilements, for designating which the same expression "liberation of the mind" needs to be qualified as "unsurpassed", *akuppa*, or else to come in combination with the expression "liberation by wisdom", *paññāvimutti*. In other words, "liberation of the mind" on its own does not refer to a level of awakening.

Regarding the relationship to karma in the *Karajakāya-sutta* and its parallels,[23] the point of the passage in question is simply about the karma influencing the next rebirth. In other

---

which would otherwise come to fruition in a future existence"; see also Maithrimurthi 1999: 73–78.

[20] Wiltshire 1990: 269 interprets Dhp 368 to imply "that metta-vihāra leads not to anāgamin status but to nibbāna itself"; see also Maithrimurthi 1999: 69.

[21] Gombrich 2009: 87 argues in relation to Sn 152 that "it is natural to interpret 'not returning to lie in a womb' as meaning that one will have escaped altogether from the cycle of rebirth."

[22] For a more detailed survey of different types of *vimutti* see Anālayo 2012a: 282–307.

[23] For a study and translation of the parallels MĀ 15 and a discourse quotation in the *Abhidharmakośopāyika-ṭīkā* see Anālayo 2012c: 489–514 and Martini 2012.

words, the passage is about a temporary suspension of the fruition of karma only, not about its final and total eradication.[24]

The effect of cultivating the *brahmavihāra*s as a liberation of the mind finds illustration in a simile which describes a conch blower who is able to make himself heard in all directions.[25] This illustrates how the *brahmavihāra*s are to be developed as a boundless radiation in all directions, as a result of which they cannot be overruled by other more limited karma.[26]

In this simile the conch blower is not able to silence any other sound forever. This aspect of the simile is concerned only with a temporary suppression. The imagery of the conch blower does not convey that the practice of the *brahmavihāra*s overcomes all limited karma forever. It only expresses that, when one is established in a *brahmavihāra*, other more limited types of karma have no scope to remain, just as when the conch is blown, other sounds will have no scope to remain and be heard.

In relation to the *Dhammapada* stanza, I think a necessary methodological requirement when interpreting a single poetic stanza is that one adopts a "systematic" reading. A systematic reading tries to contextualize any particular passage within the whole textual corpus preserved.[27] Instead of taking a single

---

[24] For a more detailed discussion see Martini 2011 and Dhammadinnā 2012/2014.

[25] The simile can be found, e.g., in MN 99 at MN II 207,22 and its parallel MĀ 152 at T I 669c10.

[26] Ps III 450,10 (commenting on MN 99) explains the import of the simile to be that the powerful karmic effect of the *brahmavihāra* practice will be stronger than other karmas of the sensual sphere and therefore have a determining effect on the next rebirth.

[27] The term "systematic reading" is used by Park 2012: 74, who explains that "by a 'systematic' reading I mean one which provides a consistent understanding of the text, consistent not merely within

textual passage on its own and out of context, for a proper understanding of early Buddhist thought any such single passage needs to be read in conjunction with other passages that bear some relation to the matter at hand. As Bodhi (2003: 47) explains, in relation to the Pāli discourses in general,

> not only are the texts themselves composed in a clipped laconic style that mocks our thirst for conceptual completeness, but their meaning often seems to rest upon a deep underlying groundwork of interconnected ideas that is nowhere stated baldly in a way that might guide interpretation … the *nikāya*s embed the basic principles of doctrine in a multitude of short, often elusive discourses that draw upon and allude to the underlying system without explicitly spelling it out. To determine the principles one has to extract them piecemeal, by considering in juxtaposition a wide assortment of texts.

On an unsystematic reading, taking the *Dhammapada* stanza on its own, one could indeed conclude that dwelling with *mettā* and having faith in the Buddha's teaching is all that is required to reach the final goal. Here is the stanza in question:[28]

---

itself but within a wider textual context." Park 2012: 78 further comments: "I regard a 'systematic' reading as an honest effort to understand the whole context of a text or its doctrinal system, proscribing minority … from appropriating the true voice of the whole text."

[28] Dhp 368: *mettavihārī yo bhikkhu, pasanno buddhasāsane, adhigacche padaṃ santaṃ, saṅkhārūpasamaṃ sukhaṃ.* The *Mahāvastu*, Senart 1897: 421,18, has a closely similar stanza, which is followed by three stanzas that differ only inasmuch as they take up the other three *brahmavihāra*s for a similar treatment. A parallel in *Udānavarga* 32.21, Bernhard 1965: 437, comes in the company of two

A monastic who dwells with *mettā*
And has faith in the Buddha's teaching,
Will reach the place of peace,
The happiness of the stilling of formations.

Yet, on adopting such an unsystematic reading in relation to another closely similar *Dhammapada* stanza, one would have to conclude that being delighted and having faith in the Buddha's teaching is all that is required to reach the final goal. Here is the other stanza in question:[29]

A monastic who is full of delight
And has faith in the Buddha's teaching,
Will reach the place of peace,
The happiness of the stilling of formations.

This *Dhammapada* stanza differs from the previously translated stanza only inasmuch as, instead of referring to dwelling with *mettā*, it stipulates being full of delight. On following the same

---

similar stanzas which revolve around the same *brahmavihāra* and having faith in the Buddha, differing in the results they depict for such practice. Thus *Udānavarga* 32.22, for example, indicates that such a monastic will not regress and draws close to Nirvāṇa, *abhavyaḥ parihāṇāya, nirvāṇayaiva so 'ntike.* A parallel in the Gāndhārī *Dharmapada* 70, Brough 1962/2001: 128, also comes together with a similar stanza, Gāndhārī *Dharmapada* 69, which indicates that the otherwise similarly described monastic in this way shakes off evil, *duṇadi pavaka dharma*. A parallel in the Patna *Dharmapada* 59, Cone 1989: 119, continues after four *pada*s similar to Dhp 368 with *dṛṣṭe va dhamme nibbāṇaṃ, yogacchemaṃ anuttaraṃ*, thereby confirming that the preceding concerns full awakening (although Roth 1980: 102 reckons this part as rather belonging to the next stanza).

[29] Dhp 381: *pāmojjabahulo bhikkhu, pasanno buddhasāsane, adhigacche padaṃ santaṃ, saṅkhārūpasamaṃ sukhaṃ.*

mode of interpretation adopted for the earlier stanza, it would result that even *brahmavihāra* practice is not needed. All that is required to reach the final goal in early Buddhist thought would be delight and faith, nothing else. This is hardly convincing.

This example perhaps suffices to show that an unsystematic reading of such stanzas fails to make sense. A proper interpretation of these verses requires an appreciation of the fact that they are not meant to provide exhaustive accounts of all that is required to reach the final goal. They only highlight in a poetic manner factors that contribute to the goal. In fact three Chinese parallels to the *Dhammapada* verse on a monastic who dwells with *mettā* explicitly mention the need for tranquillity *and* insight.[30]

The present case is similar to a point I made in the last chapter in relation to the standard descriptions of the four absorptions. In view of the drive toward comprehensiveness in later exegetical tradition, it is perhaps understandable that one expects to find the same in the early discourses, but this expectation is bound to be misleading. A single stanza in the *Dhammapada* simply cannot cover all that is required for progress on the path to awakening.

Turning to the *Metta-sutta*, of which no parallel is known, the indication that *mettā* meditation leads beyond birth in a womb is not a reference to final liberation brought about by such means only. Instead, the verse in question mentions several qualities that in combination lead beyond birth in a womb, including being "endowed with vision", *dassanena*

[30] T 210 at T IV 572a11 and T 212 at T IV 764c27: 比丘為慈, 愛敬佛教, 深入止觀, 滅行乃安, and the similarly formulated T 213 at T IV 796b18: 苾芻為慈愍, 愛敬於佛教, 深入妙止觀, 滅穢行乃安.

sampanno, which seems to be an implicit reference to having reached at least stream-entry,[31] and furthermore "having removed greed for sensual pleasures", *kāmesu vineyya gedhaṃ*.[32] Now the vision gained with stream-entry and the removal of greed for sensual pleasures would on their own suffice to go beyond birth in a womb, independent of any cultivation of the *brahmavihāra*s.[33] This goes to show that this verse also does not provide unequivocal support for the hypothesis that the *brahmavihāra*s were considered in early Buddhist thought to be in themselves capable of leading to the final goal.

Another relevant passage can be found in the report in the *Dhānañjāni-sutta* and its parallel that Sāriputta taught the *brahmavihāra*s to a brahmin who was on his deathbed. The parallel versions agree that the Buddha afterwards told Sāriputta that the brahmin could have been led to a realization higher than just rebirth in the Brahmā world.[34] This is clearly not the final goal of early Buddhist practice.

The same perspective also holds for the *Tevijja-sutta*, where the Buddha himself teaches the *brahmavihāra*s to two brahmins, in reply to being requested to explain the path to Brahmā.

---

[31] See Pj I 251,17. This also provides a background for the reference to the phrase *yan taṃ santaṃ padaṃ abhisamecca*, translated by Bodhi 2017 (forthcoming) as "having made the breakthrough to that peaceful state".

[32] Sn 152.

[33] In fact Maithrimurthi 1999: 66f argues for this line to be a later addition, as according to his assessment the *Metta-sutta* would offer better support for the supposedly salvific function of *mettā* without Sn 152: "wenn man nun davon ausgeht, daß dieses Sūtra … ursprünglich … mit dem Vers 151 endete, so würde das bedeuten, daß wir es hier mit einem alten Heilsweg zu tun haben."

[34] MN 97 at MN II 195,32 and its parallel MĀ 27 at T I 458b21; see in more detail Anālayo 2011: 570f.

In contrast to the Pāli version, parallels preserved in Chinese translation and Sanskrit fragments respectively report that at the end of the discourse the two brahmins attained stream-entry.[35]

Although in the Chinese and Sanskrit parallels they attain stream-entry at the end of the exposition, neither these two versions nor the Pāli discourse give any indication that they actually engaged in *brahmavihāra* practice. Instead, what leads to their attainment in the two parallels, in line with numerous other such attainments reported in other discourses, appears to have been the detailed explanations given by the Buddha on what constitutes the path to Brahmā, of which the description of *brahmavihāra* practice forms only the culminating point. Crucial here would have been the insightful explanation by the Buddha that the path to Brahmā requires that one become like Brahmā. This is what most of the discussion is about, namely contrasting Brahmā to brahmins in various respects and then showing that a monastic who practices the *brahmavihāra*s is similar to Brahmā in all these respects. This straightforward indication of the need to cultivate oneself in a way that accords with the goal of one's aspiration would have changed the understanding of the two young brahmins on how to reach Brahmā and thus triggered their insight.

Moreover, the final part of this exposition in all versions affirms that one who practices *brahmavihāra* will be reborn in the Brahmā world.[36] As in the case of the *Dhānañjāni-sutta* and its parallel, rebirth in the Brahmā world is certainly not

---

[35] DĀ 26 at T I 107a12 and folio 450v7 of the *Vāsiṣṭha-sūtra*; DN 13 at DN I 252,25 only mentions their taking of refuge. For a comparative study and translation of DĀ 26 see Anālayo 2015a.

[36] DN 13 at DN I 252,15, folio 450v6 of the *Vāsiṣṭha-sūtra*, and DĀ 26 at T I 107a10.

the final goal of early Buddhist soteriology. Thus the affirmation of the potential of the *brahmavihāra*s in the *Tevijja-sutta* and its parallels to lead to such elevated rebirth at the same time implies that they fall short of fulfilling the final goal of freedom from rebirth.

In sum, it seems to me that the various passages surveyed do not support the assumption that the *brahmavihāra*s were recognized in early Buddhist thought as an independent path to final liberation.[37] This notion appears just as unconvincing as the hypothesis that the absorptions constituted an independent path to the final goal.

The Potential of *brahmavihāra* Meditation

Although I think that the *brahmavihāra*s did not constitute an independent path to full liberation in early Buddhist thought, with this I certainly do not intend to take the position that *brahmavihāra* meditation does not have a rather substantial contribution to offer for progressing toward the final goal. This is in fact the theme in three of the passages just discussed.

The *Metta-sutta* does present the practice of *mettā* as capable of leading beyond birth in a womb, *if* such practice is undertaken by a virtuous one who is endowed with vision.[38] This

[37] In reply to the suggestion by Gombrich 2009: 83 that "joining *brahma* at death is a metaphor for the nirvana which follows the death of an *arahant*", Gethin 2012: 2 notes that "if, as Gombrich claims, the teaching that 'love and compassion can be salvific for the person who cultivates those feelings to the highest pitch' was such a crucial part of what the Buddha taught (p. 195), it remains something of a puzzle that he should have chosen to reveal this principally to brahmin outsiders, and in terms that were obscure to his own followers."

[38] It is not correct that the description given in Sn 149 of having a protective attitude toward others similar to that of a mother toward her

appears to be pointing to the contribution *mettā* is able to offer in particular for progress from stream-entry to non-return.

That dwelling in *mettā* can make a substantial contribution to progress to liberation is indubitably implicit in the *Dhammapada* stanza mentioned above. The *Karajakāya-sutta* and its *Madhyama-āgama* parallel confirm that a noble disciple's practice of the *brahmavihāras* is particularly relevant for the attainment of non-return.[39]

The apparent potential of *mettā* in this respect would be related to the fetters to be overcome during progress from stream-entry to non-return, which are sensual desire and ill will. These are attenuated with once-return and removed for good with non-return. Discourses in the *Aṅguttara-nikāya* and their *Saṃyukta-āgama* parallels additionally indicate that pro-

---

only son "is how one may achieve enlightenment", as assumed by Walters 2012: 162. A proper appreciation of the *Metta-sutta* needs to take into account the indications which Sn 152 itself provides on how cultivation of *mettā* can lead to going beyond rebirth in a womb (which holds independently of whether one interprets *abhisamecca* in Sn 143 to indicate the task still ahead or the already accomplished attainment of stream-entry). Thus when Crosby 2008: 38 concludes that "*mettā*, according to this text, is salvific", then this is correct only as long as such cultivation is undertaken by a virtuous person and based on the vision attained with stream-entry, leading via the removal of sensuality to non-return. The stanza does not present *mettā* as leading to realization all by itself, without being combined with these other aspects of the path. As in fact noted by Gombrich 2009: 87, "the poem does not clearly state that kindness *alone* will produce salvific results."

[39] AN 10.208 at AN V 300,12 states that a noble disciple, *ariyasāvaka*, who develops the *brahmavihāras* in this way, will progress to non-return, an indication found similarly in MĀ 15 at T I 438a22; on the slightly differing phrasing in the Tibetan version, which nevertheless also speaks of a noble disciple, see Martini 2012: 68f note 58.

gress from stream-entry to non-return requires fulfilling the training in concentration.[40]

Thus progress from stream-entry to non-return would require in particular overcoming sensual desire and ill will as well as fulfilling the training in concentration. These could indeed be accomplished with the help of *mettā*. The cultivation of *mettā* as a liberation of the mind is one of the possible options for fulfilling the training in concentration. The experience of inner happiness during deep concentration then has the potential to divest sensual pleasures of their former attraction. Because such deep concentration is developed with the help of *mettā*, this at the same time also diminishes anger, since *mettā* by its very nature reduces the tendency to react with anger, although in itself this is not sufficient to remove the tendency to anger completely.

The transformative potential of *mettā* finds confirmation in contemporary studies in the field of psychological research, which have brought to light various beneficial aspects of its practice.[41] Studies have shown that the cultivation of *mettā* has the potential to reduce anger and psychological distress,[42] as well as the negative symptoms of schizophrenia,[43] and to increase positive emotions and pro-social behavior.[44]

Of further significance is the finding that only brief exposure to *mettā* meditation can at times have an aversive effect, if the person in question is already in a negative mood.[45] This gives

---

[40] AN 3.85 at AN I 232,12 and AN 3.86 at AN I 233,22 with their parallels SĀ 820 at T II 210c1 and SĀ 821 at T II 210c27.

[41] For a survey see Hofmann et al. 2011 and Alba 2013.

[42] Carson et al. 2005.

[43] Johnson et al. 2009 and Johnson et al. 2011.

[44] Fredrickson et al. 2008 and Hutcherson et al. 2008.

[45] In a study of *mettā* as a buffer for social stress, Law 2011 found that exposure to very brief sessions of *mettā* can actually have negative

the impression that a key element for actualizing the potential of *mettā* and the other *brahmavihāra*s is that these are cultivated in a sustained manner, ideally as a liberation of the mind, and based on a firm moral foundation, so as to actualize their full potential.

In sum, there can be little doubt that to engage in the practice of *mettā* or any of the other *brahmavihāra*s can offer substantial support for progress on the path to liberation, even though such cultivation does not constitute a path to awakening in and of itself. In this respect, the *brahmavihāra*s appear to have fared similarly to the absorptions, in that in both cases the attempt to recover the respective potential seems to have gone overboard.

Pre-Buddhist *brahmavihāra* Practice

Another aspect similar to the case of the absorptions is that the early Buddhist texts consider the practice of the *brahmavihāra*s to have been a pre-Buddhist form of practice. This stands in contrast to the development of liberating insight, which the same texts consider the specific discovery of a Buddha.

The *brahmavihāra*s as ancient practices come up, for instance, in a description of a past life of the Buddha as a wheel-turning king in the *Mahāsudassana-sutta*, which in agreement

---

effects for those who are in a bad mood. Law 2011: 112 explains that "engaging in LKM [*mettā*] may bring attention to whatever feelings the participant is having in the moment. If the participant enters into a LKM session in a negative mood (or not in a positive mood), these negative (or non-positive) feelings would become more salient during the meditation. While these negative (or non-positive) feelings may dissipate in a longer meditation session, they may actually become accentuated in the short run in a brief meditation session."

with parallels preserved in Chinese and Sanskrit reports that he engaged in *brahmavihāra* meditation.[46] This implies that the practice of the *brahmavihāra* was not something the Buddha discovered only during his last lifetime.

A discourse in the *Aṅguttara-nikāya*, with parallels preserved in Chinese and Tibetan translation, relates that in ancient times a brahmin teacher instructed his disciples in the path to rebirth in the Brahmā world, himself cultivating the practice of *mettā* or else of the four *brahmavihāra*s in such a manner that he was reborn in a higher heavenly sphere than his disciples.[47] The three versions agree that the Buddha concludes his narration of these past events by qualifying the *mettā* or *brahmavihāra* practice taught at that time as inferior and not leading to awakening. This stands in contrast to the path he teaches now, which does lead to final liberation.

These few selected examples show that in the early discourses the cultivation of the *brahmavihāra*s features as something known long before the advent of the Buddha and as falling short of leading to awakening on its own, which the same discourses regularly relate to the cultivation of insight.

---

[46] DN 17 at DN II 186,28, Waldschmidt 1951: 350,15 (§34.156) and Matsumura 1988: 42,8, DĀ 2 at T I 23c25, T 5 at T I 171a11, T 6 at T I 186b25, and MĀ 68 at T I 518a4. For another past life in which he renounced the throne to cultivate the *brahmavihāra*s see MN 83 at MN II 77,28 and one of its parallels, EĀ 50.4 at T II 808b15; for a comparative study of MN 83 in the light of all its parallels see Anālayo 2011: 466–474.

[47] AN 7.62 at AN IV 104,21 and MĀ 8 at T I 429c10 indicate that the ancient teacher engaged more intensively in the practice of *mettā*, whereas a discourse quotation preserved in Tibetan, Dietz 2007: 98,24, at this point just speaks of cultivating the second *jhāna*, but earlier refers to all four *brahmavihāra*s being cultivated by the disciples of this teacher.

That contemporaries of the Buddha were familiar with the practice of the *brahmavihāra*s emerges also from a discourse in the *Saṃyutta-nikāya* and its parallels in Sanskrit fragments and Chinese translation, where non-Buddhist practitioners challenge Buddhist monastics to point out a difference between the instructions on cultivating the *brahmavihāra*s given by those practitioners and those given by the Buddha.[48] This difference, highlighted in these discourses, is precisely the yoking of the *brahmavihāra*s to liberating insight.

Conclusion

The early discourses present the Buddha and his arahant disciples as similarly engaged in teaching out of compassion. At this stage in the development of Buddhist thought, the Buddha's compassion does not yet seem to be considered the outcome of aeons of intentional practice, but rather as a result of his attainment of awakening and consequent removal of all possible obstructions to compassion from his mind.

A perusal of relevant passages among the early discourses gives the impression that the *brahmavihāra*s were not considered as a salvific form of meditation practice on their own. At the same time, however, these sources do accord considerable potential to *brahmavihāra* practice, in particular in leading from stream-entry to non-return by way of offering assistance

---

[48] SN 46.54 at SN V 115,26 and its parallels SHT IX 2051 V, Bechert and Wille 2004: 69, and SĀ 743 at T II 197b23. Gethin 1992/2001: 181 comments that in this and other discourses that provide a contrast between the contemporary practitioners and the Buddha's approach "the point in all this would seem to be not that the Buddha teaches new or original meditation subjects, but that he is unsurpassed in defining the finer points of technique and relating these to progress towards the final goal"; see also Martini 2011: 160f.

to the task of overcoming the two fetters of sensual desire and ill will.

The *brahmavihāra*s are comparable in this respect to the absorptions, which also do not seem to have been envisaged in early Buddhist thought as productive of insight in themselves. Another shared characteristic of the absorptions and the *brahmavihāra*s is that the early discourses appear to consider these as a pre-Buddhist type of practices. This stands in contrast to insight into the four noble truths, which the same discourses deem to be a discovery of the Buddha. This further confirms that to attribute the liberating function associated with insight into the four noble truths to the *brahmavihāra*s does not reflect the position in the early discourses particularly well.

Nevertheless, the cultivation of the *brahmavihāra*s, just as of the absorptions, can offer a substantial support for the type of meditation practice whose sustained undertaking has the potential to lead to the final goal, liberation from all bondage, Nirvāṇa.

Constantly meditating,
Always making a firm effort,
Such wise ones experience Nirvāṇa,
The supreme security from bondage.[49]

---

[49] Dhp 23; this has a similarly worded parallel in the Patna *Dharmapada* 16, Cone 1989: 108, and a parallel in the *Udānavarga* 4.3, Bernhard 1965: 126, which differs in relation to the first line, as it speaks of being constantly "heedful" rather than "meditating" constantly. Counterparts preserved in Chinese, which show some variations, can be found in T 210 at T IV 562b25, T 212 at T IV 637b27, and T 213 at T IV 779a5.

Conclusion

I sincerely hope the four chapters of this book have been able to provide information relevant for practitioners and scholars alike. Alongside the individual points made, in a more general sense I also hope to have been able to bring home the need to adopt the appropriate methodology when studying the early discourses. Just as in a court case or when working on statistics one would want to collect all the data and evidence available, when studying early Buddhist thought one similarly needs to take all of the relevant material into account.

In the case of any particular Pāli passage, I contend that its adequate understanding requires a "systematic" reading, in the sense of taking into account all other passages that have a potential bearing on the topic at hand, rather than ignoring what does not conform to one's personal predilections or adopting the strategy of just dismissing it as late.

For those who wish to distinguish between earlier and later strata among the early discourses, a consultation of the extant parallel versions is in my view an indispensable requirement. Comparative study can show what the common core is among various versions of a text and what the differences are between them, thereby providing clear evidence as a basis for identification of what is early and what is later. This is to my mind an approach definitely preferable over the potentially rather subjective procedure of applying distinctions of relative earliness and lateness in line with one's personal preferences.

From a practical perspective, one among the various points that perhaps have emerged from the preceding pages is that mindfulness is a mental quality that enhances memory, without being identical with it. Such mindfulness can coexist with the intentional use of concepts and evaluations, without being confined to conceptual activity, as it can also take the form of bare awareness. This can function as an integral aspect of the path to liberation as long as such awareness is informed by a previously established foundation in insight into impermanence.

Whereas mindfulness of breathing in sixteen steps appears to be a practice geared particularly to formal sitting in seclusion, for facing the challenge of everyday situations mindfulness of the body, in the sense of a proprioceptive type of awareness, falls into place. The type of embodied mindfulness cultivated in this way comes as part of a variety of perspectives on the body in early Buddhist meditation theory, ranging from insight into its lack of inherent beauty to the thrill of embodied joy and happiness during absorption.

This underlying continuity in what at first sight appear to be different positions holds for the gradual path in general. The interrelatedness of the various dimensions of this path can easily be lost out of sight with theoretical descriptions, which have the inevitable drawback that they can only describe one after the other what in actual practice is undertaken in conjunction and in various combinations, according to what circumstances demand.

This inevitable drawback of theoretical descriptions seems to have led to a loss of recognition of the intrinsically collaborative nature of tranquillity and insight, until eventually with some modern scholars these come to be seen as two competing and incompatible accounts of the path to liberation.

Yet, not only the path to liberation but even the very moment of liberation itself combines both. The realization of Nirvāṇa at the moment of awakening is at the same time a profoundly concentrated experience and an equally profoundly liberating insight, whose implications can be conveyed to others with the help of the scheme of four truths, apparently borrowed from ancient Indian medical diagnosis.

Neither absorption nor the *brahmavihāra*s appear to have been considered in early Buddhist thought as in and of themselves productive of liberating insight. Nor does it seem convincing to assume that insight into impermanence could be practiced while in an absorption attainment of the type described in the early discourses, which suggest a deeply unified mental state in which neither thought nor hearing takes place.

Just as the absorptions, so too the *brahmavihāra*s seem to have been considered pre-Buddhist practices by the early generations of the Buddha's followers, at least as far as the early discourses allow us to judge.

The four topics covered in this book – the implications of mindfulness, the path to liberation, the nature of absorption attainment, and the significance of compassion and the *brahmavihāra*s – exemplify the profundity of the teachings on meditation practice available in the early texts and their intrinsically complementary nature.

By way of concluding this study, I can probably do no better than return to the acrobat simile, whose Pāli version I quoted in the introduction. In order to complement the Pāli version, in line with the methodological requirement I mentioned above, here is the relevant part from the Chinese *Āgama* parallel.[1]

> [How does protecting oneself protect others]? Becoming familiar with one's own mind, developing it, protecting it

[1] SĀ 619 at T II 173b14 to 173b18.

accordingly, and attaining realization; this is called 'protecting oneself protects others.'

How does protecting others protect oneself? By the gift of fearlessness, the gift of non-violation, the gift of harmlessness, by having a mind of *mettā* and compassion for others; this is called 'protecting others protects oneself.'

For this reason, monastics, you should train yourself like this: 'Protecting myself I will develop the four *satipaṭṭhānas*, protecting others I will develop the four *satipaṭṭhānas*.'

Abbreviations

Abhidh-k	*Abhidharmakośabhāṣya*
Abhidh-s	*Abhidhammattha-saṅgaha*
AN	*Aṅguttara-nikāya*
Be	Burmese edition
Ce	Ceylonese edition
D	Derge edition
DĀ	*Dīrgha-āgama* (T 1)
Dhp	*Dhammapada*
Dhs	*Dhammasaṅgaṇī*
DN	*Dīgha-nikāya*
EĀ	*Ekottarika-āgama* (T 125)
EĀ2	*Ekottarika-āgama* (T 150A)
Ee	PTS edition
MĀ	*Madhyama-āgama* (T 26)
MN	*Majjhima-nikāya*
Mp	*Manorathapūraṇī*
Pj	*Paramatthajotikā*
Ps	*Papañcasūdanī*
PTS	Pali Text Society
Q	Peking edition
SĀ	*Saṃyukta-āgama* (T 99)
SĀ2	*Saṃyukta-āgama* (T 100)
SĀ3	*Saṃyukta-āgama* (T 101)
Se	Siamese edition
SHT	Sanskrithandschriften aus den Turfanfunden
SN	*Saṃyutta-nikāya*
Sn	*Sutta-nipāta*
Sp	*Samantapāsādikā*

Spk	*Sāratthappakāsinī*
T	Taishō edition (CBETA)
Vin	*Vinaya*
Vism	*Visuddhimagga*
⟨⟩	emendation
[]	supplementation

References

Agrawala, Prithvi K. 1983: *Mithuna, The Male-Female Symbol in Indian Art and Thought*, Dehli: Munshiram Manoharlal.

Akanuma, Chizen 1929/1990: *The Comparative Catalogue of Chinese Āgamas & Pāli Nikāyas*, Delhi: Sri Satguru.

Alba, Beatrice 2013: "Loving-kindness Meditation: A Field Study", *Contemporary Buddhism*, 14.2: 187–203.

Allon, Mark 1997: *Style and Function: A Study of the Dominant Stylistic Features of the Prose Portions of Pāli Canonical Sutta Texts and Their Mnemonic Function*, Tokyo: International Institute for Buddhist Studies.

Alsdorf, Ludwig 1965: *Les études Jaina, état présent et tâches futures*, Paris: Collège de France.

Anālayo 2003: *Satipaṭṭhāna, The Direct Path to Realization*, Birmingham: Windhorse Publications.

— 2006a: "Mindfulness in the Pāli Nikāyas", in *Buddhist Thought and Applied Psychological Research*, K. Nauriyal (ed.), 229–249, London: Routledge Curzon.

— 2006b: "Santuṭṭhi", in *Encyclopaedia of Buddhism*, W.G. Weeraratne (ed.), 7.4: 755–756, Sri Lanka: Department of Buddhist Affairs.

— 2007: "Oral Dimensions of Pāli Discourses: Pericopes, Other Mnemonic Techniques, and the Oral Performance Context", *Canadian Journal of Buddhist Studies*, 3: 5–33 (reprinted in 2017b).

— 2008: "Uttarimanussadhamma", in *Encyclopaedia of Buddhism*, W.G. Weeraratne (ed.), 8.2: 462–465, Sri Lanka: Department of Buddhist Affairs.

— 2009: "Views and the Tathāgata – A Comparative Study and Translation of the Brahmajāla in the Chinese Dīrgha-āgama", in *Buddhist and Pali Studies in Honour of the Venerable Professor Kakkapalliye Anuruddha*, K.L. Dhammajoti et al. (ed.), 183–234, Hong Kong: Centre of Buddhist Studies, University of Hong Kong (reprinted in 2017b).
— 2010: *The Genesis of the Bodhisattva Ideal*, Hamburg: Hamburg University Press.
— 2011: *A Comparative Study of the Majjhima-nikāya*, Taiwan: Dharma Drum Publishing Corporation.
— 2012a: *Excursions into the Thought-world of the Pāli Discourses*, Washington: Pariyatti Editions.
— 2012b: "The Historical Value of the Pāli Discourses", *Indo-Iranian Journal*, 55: 223–253 (reprinted in 2017b).
— 2012c: *Madhyama-āgama Studies*, Taipei: Dharma Drum Publishing Corporation.
— 2013a: "Mindfulness in Early Buddhism", *Journal of the Centre for Buddhist Studies, Sri Lanka*, 11: 147–174.
— 2013b: *Perspectives on Satipaṭṭhāna*, Cambridge: Windhorse Publications.
— 2014a: "The Brahmajāla and the Early Buddhist Oral Tradition", *Annual Report of the International Research Institute for Advanced Buddhology at Soka University*, 17: 41–59 (reprinted in 2017b).
— 2014b: "The Buddha's Last Meditation in the Dīrgha-āgama", *Indian International Journal of Buddhist Studies*, 15: 1–43 (reprinted in 2017b).
— 2014c: *The Dawn of Abhidharma*, Hamburg: Hamburg University Press.
— 2014d: "Exploring Satipaṭṭhāna in Study and Practice", *Canadian Journal of Buddhist Studies*, 10: 73–95.

— 2014e: "The First Absorption (Dhyāna) in Early Indian Buddhism – A Study of Source Material from the Madhyama-āgama", in *Cultural Histories of Meditation*, H. Eifring (ed.), 69–90, Oslo: Hermes Academic Publishing.
— 2014f: "The Mass Suicide of Monks in Discourse and Vinaya Literature" (with an addendum by Richard Gombrich), *Journal of the Oxford Centre for Buddhist Studies*, 7: 11–55.
— 2014g: "Perspectives on the Body in Early Buddhist Meditation", in *Buddhist Meditative Traditions: Their Origin and Development*, Chuang Kuo-pin (ed.), 21–49, Taipei: Shin Wen Feng Print.
— 2014h: "Three Chinese Dīrgha-āgama Discourses Without Parallels", in *Research on the Dīrgha-āgama*, Dhammadinnā (ed.), 1–55, Taipei: Dharma Drum Publishing Corporation (reprinted in 2017b).
— 2015a: "Brahmavihāra and Awakening, A Study of the Dīrgha-āgama Parallel to the Tevijja-sutta", *Asian Literature and Translation: A Journal of Religion and Culture*, 3.4: 1–27 (reprinted in 2017b).
— 2015b: "The Buddha's Fire Miracles", *Journal of the Oxford Centre for Buddhist Studies*, 9: 9–42 (reprinted in 2017b).
— 2015c: *Compassion and Emptiness in Early Buddhist Meditation*, Cambridge: Windhorse Publications.
— 2015d: "Compassion in the Āgamas and Nikāyas", *Dharma Drum Journal of Buddhist Studies*, 16: 1–30.
— 2015e: *Saṃyukta-āgama Studies*, Taipei: Dharma Drum Publishing Corporation.
— 2015f: "The Sixteen Steps of Mindfulness of Breathing in Three Vinayas", *Anveṣaṇā*, 10–25.
— 2015g: "Understanding and Practicing the Satipaṭṭhāna-sutta", in *Buddhist Foundations of Mindfulness*, E. Shonin et al. (ed.), 71–88, Cham: Springer.

— 2015h: "Understanding and Practicing the Ānāpānasati-sutta", in *Buddhist Foundations of Mindfulness*, E. Shonin et al. (ed.), 55–69, Cham: Springer.
— 2016a: "A Brief Criticism of the 'Two Paths to Liberation' Theory", *Journal of the Oxford Centre for Buddhist Studies*, 11: 38–51.
— 2016b: "Early Buddhist Mindfulness and Memory, the Body, and Pain", *Mindfulness*, 7: 1271–1280.
— 2016c: *Ekottarika-āgama Studies*, Taipei: Dharma Drum Publishing Corporation.
— 2016d: "The Gradual Path of Training in the Dīrgha-āgama, From Sense-restraint to Imperturbability", *Indian International Journal of Buddhist Studies*, 17: 1–24 (reprinted in 2017b).
— 2016e: "Levitation in Early Buddhist Discourse", *Journal of the Oxford Centre for Buddhist Studies*, 10: 11–26 (reprinted in 2017b).
— 2016f: *Mindfully Facing Disease and Death, Compassionate Advice from Early Buddhist Texts*, Cambridge: Windhorse Publications.
— 2016g: "The Second Absorption in Early Buddhist Discourse", in *Buddhist Meditative Traditions: Dialogue and Comparison*, Chuang Kuo-pin (ed.), 25–58, Taiwan: Dharma Drum Publishing Corporation.
— 2016h: "On the Supposedly Liberating Function of the First Absorption", *Buddhist Studies Review*, 33.1/2: 267–276.
— 2017a: *Buddhapada and the Bodhisattva Path*, Bochum: Projekt Verlag.
— 2017b: *Dīrgha-āgama Studies*, Taipei: Dharma Drum Publishing Corporation.

— 2017c: *A Meditator's Life of the Buddha, Based on the Early Discourses*, Cambridge: Windhorse Publications (forthcoming).
— 2017d: "The School Affiliation of the Madhyama-āgama", in *Research on the Madhyama-āgama*, Dhammadinnā (ed.), 55–76, Taipei: Dharma Drum Publishing Corporation.
Ānandajoti Bhikkhu 2016: *Paccavekkhaṇā, The Reflections*, http://www.ancient-buddhist-texts.net/Texts-and-Translations/Short-Pieces/Reflections.pdf
Arbel, Keren 2015: "The Liberative Role of Jhānic Joy (pīti) and Pleasure (sukha) in the Early Buddhist Path to Awakening", *Buddhist Studies Review*, 32.2: 179–205.
Assavavirulhakarn, Prapod 2010: *The Ascendancy of Theravāda Buddhism in Southeast Asia*, Chiang Mai: Silkworm Books.
Baer, Ruth A. 2011: "Measuring Mindfulness", *Contemporary Buddhism*, 12.1: 241–261.
Banerjea, Jitendra Nath 1930: "The 'Webbed Fingers' of Buddha", *Indian Historical Quarterly*, 6.4: 717–727.
— 1931a: "Uṣṇīṣaśiraskatā in the Early Buddha Images of India", *Indian Historical Quarterly*, 7.3: 499–514.
— 1931b: "The 'Webbed Fingers' of Buddha", *Indian Historical Quarterly*, 7.3: 654–656.
Bareau, André 1963 (vol. 1): *Recherches sur la biographie du Buddha dans les Sūtrapiṭaka et le Vinayapiṭaka anciens: de la quête de l'éveil à la conversion de Śāriputra et de Maudgalyāyana*, Paris: École Française d'Extrême-Orient.
— 1966: "L'origine du Dīrgha-āgama traduit en chinois par Buddhayaśas", in *Essays Offered to G.H. Luce by His Colleagues and Friends in Honour of His Seventy-fifth Birthday*, B. Shin et al. (ed.), 49–58, Ascona: Artibus Asiae.

Barua, Benimadhab 1921/1981: *A History of Pre-Buddhistic Indian Philosophy*, Delhi: Motilal Banarsidass.
Batchelor, Stephen 2015: *After Buddhism, Rethinking the Dharma for a Secular Age*, New Haven: Yale University Press.
Bateson, H. 1909: "Body (Buddhist)", in *Encyclopædia of Religion and Ethics*, J. Hastings (ed.), 2: 758–760, Edinburgh: T. & T. Clark.
Bautze-Picron, Claudine 2010: "The Lady under the Tree, A Visual Pattern from Māyā to Tārā and Avalokiteśvara", in *The Birth of the Buddha, Proceedings of the Seminar Held in Lumbini, Nepal, October 2004*, C. Cueppers et al. (ed.), 193–237, Lumbini: Lumbini International Research Institute.
Bechert, Heinz and K. Wille 1989: *Sanskrithandschriften aus den Turfanfunden, Teil 6*, Stuttgart: Franz Steiner.
— 2004: *Sanskrithandschriften aus den Turfanfunden, Teil 9*, Wiesbaden: Franz Steiner.
Bendall, Cecil 1902/1970: *Çikshāsamuccaya: A Compendium of Buddhistic Teaching Compiled by Çāntideva, Chiefly from Earlier Mahāyāna-Sūtras*, Osnabrück: Biblio Verlag.
Bergonzi, Mauro 1980: "Osservazioni su samatha e vipassanā nel buddhismo Theravāda", *Rivista degli Studi Orientali*, 54: 143–170 and 327–357.
Bernhard, Franz 1965 (vol. 1): *Udānavarga*, Göttingen: Vandenhoeck & Ruprecht.
Bevalkar, Shripad Krishna 1954: *The Śāntiparvan [Part III: Mokṣadharma, A] Being the Twelfth Book of the Mahābhārata, The Great Epic of India*, Poona: Bhandarkar Oriental Research Institute.
Bhagwat, N.K. 1946: "Did the Buddha Kill the Child in Man (Bhūṇa)?", in *B.C. Law Volume, Part 2*, R. Bhandarkar et al.

(ed.), 61–75, Poona: Bhandarkar Oriental Research Institute.

Bishop, Scott R., M. Lau, S. Shapiro, L. Carlson, N.D. Anderson, J. Carmody, Z.V. Segal, S. Abbey, M. Speca, D. Velting, and G. Devins 2004: "Mindfulness: A Proposed Operational Definition", *Clinical Psychology: Science and Practice*, 11.3: 230–241.

Black, Brian 2011: "Ambaṭṭha and Śvetaketu: Literary Connections between the Upaniṣads and Early Buddhist Narratives", *Journal of the American Academy of Religion*, 79.1: 136–161.

Bodhi, Bhikkhu 1978/1992: *The All-embracing Net of Views, The Brahmajāla Sutta and Its Commentaries, Translated from the Pali*, Kandy: Buddhist Publication Society.

— 1993: *A Comprehensive Manual of Abhidhamma, The Abhidhammattha Sangaha of Ācariya Anuruddha*, Kandy: Buddhist Publication Society.

— 2000: *The Connected Discourses of the Buddha, A New Translation of the Saṃyutta Nikāya*, Boston: Wisdom Publications.

— 2003: "Musīla and Nārada Revisited: Seeking the Key to Interpretation", in *Approaching the Dhamma, Buddhist Texts and Practice in South and Southeast Asia*, A.M. Blackburn and J. Samuels (ed.), 47–68, Seattle: Pariyatti Editions.

— 2007: "The Susīma-sutta and the Wisdom-liberated Arahant", *Journal of the Pali Text Society*, 29: 50–74.

— 2009: "Susīma's Conversation with the Buddha: A Second Study of the Susīma-sutta", *Journal of the Pali Text Society*, 30: 33–80.

— 2011: "What Does Mindfulness Really Mean? A Canonical Perspective", *Contemporary Buddhism*, 12.1: 19–39.

— 2012: *The Numerical Discourses of the Buddha, A Translation of the Aṅguttara Nikāya*, Boston: Wisdom Publications.
— 2017: *The Suttanipāta, A Collection of Ancient Buddhist Texts, Translated from the Pāli Together with its Commentary Paramatthajotikā II, 'The Elucidator of the Supreme Meaning', and Excerpts from the Niddesa,* Boston: Wisdom Publications (forthcoming).
Bollée, Willem B. 2005: "Physical Aspects of Some Mahāpuruṣas, Descent, Foetality and Birth", *Wiener Zeitschrift für die Kunde Südasiens*, 49: 5–34.
Brahm, Ajahn 2006: *Mindfulness, Bliss, and Beyond, A Meditator's Handbook*, Boston: Wisdom Publications.
Bronkhorst, Johannes 1985: "Dharma and Abhidharma", *Bulletin of the School of Oriental and African Studies*, 48: 305–320.
— 1993/2000: *The Two Traditions of Meditation in Ancient India*, Delhi: Motilal Banarsidass.
— 2007: *Greater Magadha, Studies in the Culture of Early India*, Leiden: Brill.
— 2009: *Buddhist Teaching in India*, Boston: Wisdom Publications.
Brough, John 1962/2001: *The Gāndhārī Dharmapada, Edited with an Introduction and Commentary*, Delhi: Motilal Banarsidass.
Brown, Kirk Warren, R.M. Ryan, R.J. Goodman, and Anālayo 2016: "Mindfulness Enhances Episodic Memory Performance, Evidence from a Multimethod Investigation", *PLoS ONE*, 11.4: e0153309.
Bucknell, Roderick S. 1984: "The Buddhist Path to Liberation: An Analysis of the Listing of Stages", *Journal of the International Association of Buddhist Studies*, 7.2: 7–40.

— 1993: "Reinterpreting the jhānas", *Journal of the International Association of Buddhist Studies*, 16.2: 375–409.

— 2010: "Taking Account of the Indic Source-text", in *Translating Buddhist Chinese, Problems and Prospects*, K. Meisig (ed.), 45–52, Wiesbaden: Harrassowitz.

Burnouf, Eugène 1852/1925: "Appendice n° VIII, sur les trente-deux signes caractéristiques d'un grand homme", in *Le Lotus de la Bonne Loi, traduit du sanscrit, accompagné d'un commentaire et de vingt et un mémoires relatifs au buddhisme*, 553–583, Paris: Librairie Orientale et Américaine.

Buswell, R.E. Jr. and R.M. Gimello 1992/1994: "Introduction", in *Paths to Liberation, The Mārga and Its Transformations in Buddhist Thought*, R.E. Buswell Jr. and R.M. Gimello (ed.), 1–36, Delhi: Motilal Banarsidass.

Carrithers, Michael 1983: *The Buddha*, Oxford: Oxford University Press.

Carson, James W., F.J. Keefe, T.R. Lynch, K.M. Carson, V. Goli, A.M. Fras, and S.R. Thorp 2005: "Loving-kindness Meditation for Chronic Low Back Pain", *Journal of Holistic Nursing*, 23.3: 287–304.

Catherine, Shaila 2008: *Focused and Fearless, A Meditator's Guide to States of Deep Joy, Calm, and Clarity*, Boston: Wisdom Publications.

Chandawimala, Rangama 2008: "Bodhisattva Practice in Sri Lankan Buddhism with Special Reference to the Abhayagiri Fraternity", *Indian International Journal of Buddhist Studies*, 9: 23–43.

Charpentier, Jarl 1922: *The Uttarādhyayanasūtra, Being the First Mūlasūtra of the Śvetāmbara Jains, Edited with an Introduction, Critical Notes and a Commentary*, Uppsala: Appelbergs Boktryckeri Aktiebolag.

Chung Jin-il 2014: "Puṇya-sūtra of the Ekottarikāgama in Comparison with the Fu-jing of the Chinese Madhyamāgama", *Critical Review for Buddhist Studies*, 16: 9–33.

— 2017: "Śrutānṛśamsa-sūtra of the Dīrgha-āgama in Comparison with the Wende-jing 聞德經 of the Madhyama-āgama", in *Research on the Madhyama-āgama*, Dhammadinnā (ed.), 113–146, Taipei: Dharma Drum Publishing Corporation.

Chung Jin-il and T. Fukita 2011: *A Survey of the Sanskrit Fragments Corresponding to the Chinese Madhyamāgama, Including References to Sanskrit Parallels, Citations, Numerical Categories of Doctrinal Concepts, and Stock Phrases*, Tokyo: Sankibo.

Cicuzza, Claudio 2011: *A Mirror Reflecting the Entire World, The Pāli Buddhapādamaṅgala or 'Auspicious Signs on the Buddha's Feet', Critical Edition with English Translation*, Bangkok/Lumbini: Fragile Palm Leaves Foundation, Lumbini International Research Institute.

Clough, S. Bradley 2012: *Early Indian and Theravāda Buddhism, Soteriological Controversy and Diversity*, New York: Cambria Press.

Collett, Alice and Anālayo 2014: "Bhikkhave and bhikkhu as Gender-inclusive Terminology in Early Buddhist Texts", *Journal of Buddhist Ethics*, 21: 760–797.

Collins, Steven 1997: "The Body in Theravāda Buddhist Monasticism", in *Religion and the Body*, S. Coakley (ed.), 185–204, Cambridge: Cambridge University Press.

Cone, Margaret 1989: "Patna Dharmapada", *Journal of the Pali Text Society*, 13: 101–217.

Conze, Edward 1956: *Buddhist Meditation*, London: George Allen and Unwin.

Coomaraswamy, Ananda K. 1928: "The Buddha's cūḍā, Hair, uṣṇīṣa, and Crown", *Journal of the Royal Asiatic Society*, 815–841.

Cousins, L.S. 1984: "Samatha-yāna and vipassanā-yāna", in *Buddhist Studies in Honour of Hammalava Saddhātissa*, G. Dhammapāla et al. (ed), 56–68, Nugegoda: University of Jayewardenapura.

— 1992: "Vitakka/vitarka and vicāra, Stages of samādhi in Buddhism and Yoga", *Indo-Iranian Journal*, 35: 137–157.

— 1996: "Good or Skilful? Kusala in Canon and Commentary", *Journal of Buddhist Ethics*, 3: 136–164.

— 2009: "Scholar Monks and Meditator Monks Revisited", in *Destroying Māra Forever: Buddhist Ethics Essays in Honor of Damien Keown*, J. Powers et al. (ed.), 31–46, New York: Snow Lion.

Cox, Collett 1992/1993: "Mindfulness and Memory: The Scope of smṛti from Early Buddhism to the Sarvāstivādin Abhidharma", in *In the Mirror of Memory, Reflections on Mindfulness and Remembrance in Indian and Tibetan Buddhism*, J. Gyatso (ed.), 67–108, Delhi: Sri Satguru.

— 1992/1994: "Attainment through Abandonment: The Sarvāstivāda Path of Removing Defilements", in *Paths to Liberation, The Mārga and Its Transformations in Buddhist Thought*, R.E. Buswell Jr. and R.M. Gimello (ed.), 63–105, Delhi: Motilal Banarsidass.

Crangle, Edward Fitzpatrick 1994: *The Origin and Development of Early Indian Contemplative Practices*, Wiesbaden: Harrassowitz.

Crosby, Kate 2008: "Gendered Symbols in Theravada Buddhism: Missed Positives in the Representation of the Female", *Hsuan Chuang Journal of Buddhist Studies*, 9: 31–47.

de La Vallée Poussin, Louis 1915: "Mahāvastu", in *Encyclopædia of Religion and Ethics*, J. Hastings (ed.), 8: 328–330, Edinburgh: T. & T. Clark.

— 1923/1971 (vol. 1), 1926/1971 (vol. 2), 1924/1971 (vol. 3), 1925/1980a (vol. 4), 1925/1980b (vol. 5), 1931/1980 (vol. 6): *L'Abhidharmakośa de Vasubandhu, traduction et annotations*, É. Lamotte (ed.), Bruxelles: Institut Belge des Hautes Études Chinoises.
— 1928: "Agnosticism (Buddhist)", in *Encyclopedia of Religion and Ethics*, J. Hastings (ed.), 1: 220–225, New York: Charles Scribner's Sons.
— 1929: "Extase et spéculation (dhyāna et prajñā)", in *Indian Studies in Honor of Charles Rockwell Lanman*, 135–136, Cambridge: Harvard University Press.
— 1936/1937: "Musīla et Nārada: le chemin du nirvāṇa", *Mélanges Chinois et Bouddhiques*, 5: 189–222.
Deleanu, Florin 1992: "Mindfulness of Breathing in the Dhyāna Sūtras", in *Transactions of the International Conference of Orientalists in Japan, no. 37*, 42–57, Tokyo: Institute of Eastern Culture.
Demiéville, Paul 1951: "À propos du concile de Vaiśālī", *T'oung Pao*, 40: 239–296.
Dessein, Bart 2016: "On Uttering and Hearing Sound When in the First Trance Stage: Theravāda, Sarvāstivāda and Mahāsāṃghika Viewpoints", in *Buddhist Meditative Traditions: Dialogue and Comparison*, Chuang Kuo-pin (ed.), 59–77, Taiwan: Dharma Drum Publishing Corporation.
Dhammadinnā 2012/2014: "Semantics of Wholesomeness: Purification of Intention and the Soteriological Function of the Immeasurables (appamāṇas) in Early Buddhist Thought", in *Buddhist Meditative Traditions: Their Origin and Development*, Chuang Kuo-pin (ed.), 51–129, Taipei: Shin Wen Feng Print.
Dhammajoti, Bhikkhu K.L 2008: "The Sixteen-mode Mindfulness of Breathing", *Journal of the Centre for Buddhist Studies, Sri Lanka*, 6: 251–288.

— 2009: "The aśubhā Meditation in the Sarvāstivāda", *Journal of the Centre for Buddhist Studies, Sri Lanka*, 7: 248–295.

Dietz, Siglinde 2006: "Fragments Containing Lists of the 32 mahāpuruṣalakṣaṇas", in *Jaina-Itihāsa-Ratna, Festschrift für Gustav Roth zum 90. Geburtstag*, U. Hüsken et al. (ed.), 153–162, Marburg: Indica et Tibetica.

— 2007: "The Saptasūryodayasūtra", in *Indica et Tibetica 65, Festschrift für Michael Hahn zum 65. Geburtstag von Freunden und Schülern überreicht*, K. Klaus and J.-U. Hartmann (ed.), 93–112, Wien: Arbeitskreis für tibetische und buddhistische Studien, Universität Wien.

DiSimone, Charles 2016: *Faith in the Teacher: The Prāsādika and Prāsādanīya Sūtras from the (Mūla-)Sarvāstivāda Dīrghāgama Manuscript, A Synoptic Critical Edition, Translation, and Textual Analysis*, PhD thesis, München: Ludwig-Maximilians-Universität.

Dissanayake, Wimal 1993: "Self and Body in Theravada Buddhism, A Tropological Analysis of the 'Dhammapada'", in *Self as Body in Asian Theory and Practice*, T.P. Kasulis et al. (ed.), 123–145, Albany: State University of New York Press.

Ditrich, Tamara 2016: "Interpretations of the Terms ajjhattaṃ and bahiddhā, From the Pali Nikāyas to the Abhidhamma", in *Text, History, and Philosophy, Abhidharma across Buddhist Scholastic Traditions*, B. Dessein and W. Teng (ed.), 108–145, Leiden: Brill.

Dohanian, Diran Kavork 1977: *The Mahāyāna Buddhist Sculpture of Ceylon*, New York: Garland Publishing.

Dudukovic, Nicole M., S. DuBrow, and A.D. Wagner 2009: "Attention During Memory Retrieval Enhances Future Remembering", *Memory & Cognition*, 37.7: 953–961.

Dunne, John 2011: "Toward an Understanding of Non-dual Mindfulness", *Contemporary Buddhism*, 12.1: 71–88.

Egge, James R. 2003: "Interpretative Strategies for Seeing the Body of the Buddha", in *Constituting Communities: Theravāda Buddhism and the Religious Cultures of South and Southeast Asia*, J.C. Holt et al. (ed.), 189–208, Albany: State University of New York Press.

Eimer, Helmut 1976: *Skizzen des Erlösungsweges in buddhistischen Begriffsreihen*, Bonn: Religionswissenschaftliches Seminar der Universität Bonn.

Eliade, Mircea 1958: *Yoga: Immortality and Freedom*, W.R. Trask (trsl.), London: Routledge and Kegan Paul.

Endo Toshiichi 1996: "Bodhisattas in the Pāli Commentaries", *Bukkyō Kenkyū*, 25: 65–92.

Enomoto Fumio 1986: "On the Formation of the Original Texts of the Chinese Āgamas", *Buddhist Studies Review*, 3: 19–30.

Falk, Maryla 1939/2004: *Il mito psicologico nell'India antica*, Milano: Adelphi Edizioni.

Faure, Bernard 1998: *The Red Thread, Buddhist Approaches to Sexuality*, Princeton: Princeton University Press.

Fischer, Klaus 1979: *Erotik und Askese in Kult und Kunst der Inder*, Köln: DuMont.

— 1980: "Hidden Symbolism in Stūpa-Railing Reliefs: Coincidentia Oppositorum of Māra and Kāma", in *The Stūpa, Its Religious, Historical and Architectural Significance*, A.L. Dallapiccola et al. (ed.), 90–99, Wiesbaden: Franz Steiner.

Foucher, Alfred 1918 (vol. 2): *L'art gréco-bouddhique du Gandhâra, étude sur les origines de l'influence classique dans l'art bouddhique de l'Inde et de l'Extrême-Orient*, Paris: Ernest Leroux.

Franke, Otto 1917: "Die Buddhalehre in ihrer erreichbarältesten Gestalt (im Dīghanikāya)", *Zeitschrift der Deutschen Morgenländischen Gesellschaft*, 71: 50–98.

Fredrickson, Barbara L., M.A. Cohn, K.A. Coffey, J. Pek, and S.M. Finkel 2008: "Open Hearts Build Lives: Positive Emotions, Induced Through Loving-kindness Meditation, Build Consequential Personal Resources", *Journal of Personality and Social Psychology*, 95.5: 1045–1062.

Freiberger, Oliver 2000: *Der Orden in der Lehre, Zur religiösen Deutung des Saṅgha im frühen Buddhismus*, Wiesbaden: Harrassowitz.

Fronsdal, Egil 1998: *The Dawn of the Bodhisattva Path, Studies in a Religious Ideal of Ancient Indian Buddhists with Particular Emphasis on the Earliest Extant Perfection of Wisdom Sutra*, PhD thesis, Stanford University.

Fuller, Paul 2005: *The Notion of diṭṭhi in Theravāda Buddhism, The Point of View*, London: Curzon.

Gangajot, Kaur 2016: "Buddhist Meditation: A Brief Examination of samatha and vipassanā in Theravāda Tradition", *Indian International Journal of Buddhist Studies*, 17: 147–165.

Gethin, Rupert 1992/2001: *The Buddhist Path to Awakening: A Study of the Bodhi-Pakkhiyā Dhammā, Second Edition*, Leiden: Brill.

— 1996: "The Resurrection and Buddhism", in *Resurrection Reconsidered*, G. d'Costa (ed.), 201–216, Oxford: Oneworld.

— 1997: "Wrong View (micchā-diṭṭhi) and Right View (sammā-diṭṭhi) in the Theravāda Abhidhamma", in *Recent Researches in Buddhist Studies, Essays in Honour of Professor Y. Karunadasa*, K.L. Dhammajoti et al. (ed.), 211–229, Colombo: Y. Karunadasa Felicitation Committee.

— 2007: "What's in a Repetition? On Counting the suttas of the Saṃyutta-nikāya", *Journal of the Pali Text Society*, 29: 365–387.
— 2011: "On Some Definitions of Mindfulness", *Contemporary Buddhism*, 12.1: 263–279.
— 2012: [Review of Gombrich 2009], *H-Buddhism, H-Net Reviews*, http://www.h-net.org/reviews/showpdf.php?id=31586
— 2014: "Keeping the Buddha's Rules, The View from the Sūtra Piṭaka", in *Buddhism and Law, An Introduction*, R.R. French and M.A. Nathan (ed.), 63–77, New York: Cambridge University Press.
Gimello, Robert M. 1978: "Mysticism and Meditation", in *Mysticism and Philosophical Analysis*, S.T. Katz (ed.), 170–199, London: Sheldon Press.
Giustarini, Giuliano 2011: "The Truth of the Body: The Liberating Role of Physical (and Mental) Boundaries in asubhabhāvanā", *Thai International Journal of Buddhist Studies*, 2: 96–124.
Gnoli, Raniero 1977 (vol. 1) and 1978 (vol. 2): *The Gilgit Manuscript of the Saṅghabhedavastu, Being the 17th and Last Section of the Vinaya of the Mūlasarvāstivādin*, Roma: Istituto Italiano per il Medio ed Estremo Oriente.
Gombrich, Richard 1984: "Notes on the Brahminical Background to Buddhist Ethics", in *Buddhist Studies in Honor of Hammalava Saddhatissa*, Dhammapāla et al. (ed.), 91–102, Sri Lanka: University of Jayewardenepura.
— 1996: *How Buddhism Began, The Conditioned Genesis of the Early Teachings*, London: Athlone.
— 2009: *What the Buddha Thought*, London: Equinox.
Gómez, Luis O. 1999: "Seeing, Touching, Counting, Accounting, sāṃkhya as Formal Thought and Intuition", *Asiatische Studien*, 53.3: 693–711.

Govinda, Lama Anagarika 1961/1991: *The Psychological Attitude of Early Buddhist Philosophy and Its Systematic Representation According to Abhidhamma Tradition*, Delhi: Motilal Banarsidass.

Greene, Eric Mathew 2006: *Of Bones and Buddhas, Contemplation of the Corpse and Its Connection to Meditations on Purity as Evidenced by 5th Century Chinese Meditation Manuals*, MA thesis, Berkeley: University of California.

Griffiths, Paul 1981: "Concentration or Insight: The Problematic of Theravāda Buddhist Meditation-theory", *Journal of the American Academy of Religion*, 49.4: 605–624.

— 1983: "Buddhist jhāna: A Form-critical Study", *Religion*, 13: 55–68.

Guang Xing 2005: *The Concept of the Buddha, Its Evolution from Early Buddhism to the trikāya Theory*, London: Routledge Curzon.

Gunaratana, Henepola 1985/1996: *The Path of Serenity and Insight, An Explanation of the Buddhist jhānas*, Delhi: Motilal Banarsidass.

— 2007: "Should We Come Out of jhāna to Practice vipassanā?", in *Buddhist Studies in Honour of Venerable Kirindigalle Dhammaratana*, S. Ratnayaka (ed.), 41–74, Colombo: Felicitation Committee.

Hamilton, Clarence H. 1950: "The Idea of Compassion in Mahāyāna Buddhism", *Journal of the American Oriental Society*, 70.3: 145–151.

Hamilton, Sue 1995: "From the Buddha to Buddhaghosa, Changing Attitudes towards the Human Body in Theravāda Buddhism", in *Religious Reflections on the Human Body*, J.M. Law (ed.), 46–63, Bloomington: Indiana University Press.

Har Dayal 1932/1978: *The Bodhisattva Doctrine in Buddhist Sanskrit Literature*, Delhi: Motilal Banarsidass.

Harris, Elizabeth J. 2012: "Sleeping Next to My Coffin: Representations of the Body in Theravāda Buddhism", *Buddhist Studies Review*, 29.1: 105–120.

Hartmann, Jens-Uwe 1989: "Fragmente aus dem Dīrghāgama der Sarvāstivādins", in *Sanskrit-Texte aus dem Buddhistischen Kanon: Neuentdeckungen und Neueditionen*, 37–67, Göttingen: Vandenhoeck & Ruprecht.

Hartmann, Jens-Uwe and K. Wille 2006: "A Version of the Śikhālakasūtra/Siṅgālovādasutta", in *Buddhist Manuscripts, (Manuscripts in the Schøyen Collection)*, J. Braarvig (ed.), 3: 1–6, Oslo: Hermes.

— 2014: "The Manuscript of the Dīrghāgama and the Private Collection in Virginia", in *From Birch Bark to Digital Data: Recent Advances in Buddhist Manuscript Research*, P. Harrison and J.-U. Hartmann (ed.), 137–155, Wien: Verlag der Österreichischen Akademie der Wissenschaften.

Hartranft, Chip 2011: "Did the Buddha Teach satipaṭṭhāna?", *Insight Journal*, 35: 4–10.

Harvey, Peter 2007: "Bodhisattva Career in the Theravāda", in *Encyclopedia of Buddhism*, D. Keown et al. (ed.), 83–87, London: Routledge.

— 2009: "The Approach to Knowledge and Truth in the Theravāda Record of the Discourses of the Buddha", in *Buddhist Philosophy, Essential Readings*, W. Edelglass and J.L. Garfield (ed.), 175–184, Oxford: Oxford University Press.

— 2015: "Mindfulness in Theravāda samatha and vipassanā Meditations, and in Secular Mindfulness", in *Buddhist Foundations of Mindfulness*, E. Shonin et al. (ed.), 115–137, Cham: Springer.

Hayashima Kyosho 1958: "Asubhānupassanā in Buddhist Meditation", *Indogaku Bukkyōgaku Kenkyū*, 7.1: 374–365.

Heiler, Friedrich 1922: *Die Buddhistische Versenkung, Eine Religionsgeschichtliche Untersuchung*, München: Ernst Reinhardt.

Hirakawa Akira 1987: "Buddhist Literature: Survey of Texts", in *The Encyclopedia of Religion*, M. Eliade (ed.), 2: 509–529, New York: Macmillan.

— 1997: *Buddhist Chinese–Sanskrit Dictionary*, Tokyo: Reiyukai.

Hofmann, Stefan G., P. Grossman, and D.E. Hinton 2011: "Loving-kindness and Compassion Meditation: Potential for Psychological Interventions", *Clinical Psychology Review*, 31.7: 1126–1132.

Horner, I.B. 1946: "Gotama and the Other Sects", *Journal of the American Oriental Society*, 66: 283–289.

Hutcherson, Cendri A., E.M. Seppala, and J.J. Gross 2008: "Loving-kindness Meditation Increases Social Connectedness", *Emotion*, 8.5: 720–724.

Hu-von Hinüber, Haiyan 1994: *Das Poṣadhavastu, Vorschriften für die buddhistische Beichtfeier im Vinaya der Mūlasarvāstivādins*, Reinbek: Wezler.

Ireland, John D. 1998: "Jhāna and samādhi", *Buddhist Studies Review*, 15.2: 193–204.

Johnson, David P., D.L. Penn, B.L. Fredrickson, A.M. Kring, P.S. Meyer, L.I. Catalino, and M. Brantley 2011: "A Pilot Study of Loving Kindness Meditation for the Negative Symptoms of Schizophrenia", *Schizophrenia Research*, 129: 137–140.

Johnson, David P., D.L. Penn, B.L. Fredrickson, P.S. Meyer, A.M. Kring, and M. Brantley 2009: "Loving-kindness Meditation to Enhance Recovery from Negative Symptoms of Schizophrenia", *Journal of Clinical Psychology*, 65.5: 499–509.

Kabat-Zinn, Jon 2011: "Some Reflections on the Origins of MBSR, Skillful Means, and the Trouble with Maps", *Contemporary Buddhism*, 12.1: 281–306.

Kajiyama Yūichi 1972: "Body, the", in *Encyclopaedia of Buddhism*, G.P. Malalasekera (ed.), 3.2: 255–262, Sri Lanka: Department of Buddhist Affairs.

Katz, Nathan 1982/1989: *Buddhist Images of Human Perfection, The Arahant of the Sutta Piṭaka Compared with the Bodhisattva and the Mahāsiddha*, Delhi: Motilal Banarsidass.

Keown, Damien 1992/2001: *The Nature of Buddhist Ethics*, New York: Palgrave.

Kerr, Catherine E., M.D. Sacchet, S.W. Lazar, C.I. Moore, and S.R. Jones 2013: "Mindfulness Starts with the Body: Somatosensory Attention and Top-down Modulation of Cortical Alpha Rhythms in Mindfulness Meditation", *Frontiers in Human Neuroscience*, 7.12: 1–15.

Khantipālo Bhikkhu 1980: *Bag of Bones, A Miscellany on the Body*, Kandy: Buddhist Publication Society (online PDF version).

King, Winston L. 1980/1992: *Theravāda Meditation: The Buddhist Transformation of Yoga*, Delhi: Motilal Banarsidass.

Kramrisch, S. 1935: "Emblems of the Universal Being", *Journal of the Indian Society of Oriental Art*, 3: 148–165.

Krishan, Y. 1966: "The Hair on the Buddha's Head and uṣṇīṣa", *East and West*, 16.3/4: 275–290.

Kuan Tse-Fu 2007: "Annotated Translation of the Chinese Version of the Kāyagatāsati Sutta", *Indian International Journal of Buddhist Studies*, 8: 175–194.

— 2008: *Mindfulness in Early Buddhism, New Approaches Through Psychology and Textual Analysis of Pali, Chinese and Sanskrit Sources*, London: Routledge.

— 2015: "Mindfulness in Similes in Early Buddhist Literature", in *Buddhist Foundations of Mindfulness*, E. Shonin et al. (ed.), 267–285, Cham: Springer.

Law, Rita W. 2011: *An Analogue Study of Loving-kindness Meditation as a Buffer against Social Stress*, PhD thesis, University of Arizona.

Liú Zhen 2010: *Dhyānāni tapaś ca*, 禅定与苦修, Shanghai: 古籍出版社.

Lü Cheng 1963: "Āgama", in *Encyclopaedia of Buddhism*, G.P. Malalasekera (ed.), 1.2: 241–244, Sri Lanka: Department of Buddhist Affairs.

Luce, G.H. 1969 (vol. 1): *Old Burma – Early Pagán*, New York: J.J. Augustin.

MacQueen, Graeme 1988: *A Study of the Śrāmaṇyaphala-Sūtra*, Wiesbaden: Harrassowitz.

Maithrimurthi, Mudagamuwe 1999: *Wohlwollen, Mitleid, Freude und Gleichmut, Eine ideengeschichtliche Untersuchung der vier apramāṇas in der buddhistischen Ethik und Spiritualität von den Anfängen bis hin zum frühen Yogācāra*, Stuttgart: Franz Steiner.

Martini, Giuliana 2011: "Meditative Dynamics of the Early Buddhist appamāṇas", *Canadian Journal of Buddhist Studies*, 7: 137–180.

— 2012: "The 'Discourse on Accumulated Actions' in Śamathadeva's Abhidharmakośopāyikā", *Indian International Journal of Buddhist Studies*, 13: 49–79.

— 2013: "Bodhisattva Texts, Ideologies and Rituals in Khotan in the Fifth and Sixth Centuries", in *Buddhism among the Iranian Peoples of Central Asia*, M. De Chiara et al. (ed.), 11–67, Wien: Österreichische Akademie der Wissenschaften.

Matilal, Bimal Krishna 1980: "Ignorance of Misconception? A Note on Avidyā in Buddhism", in *Buddhist Studies in*

Honour of Walpola Rahula, S. Balasooriya et al. (ed.), 154–164, London: Fraser.

Matsumura Hisashi 1988: *The Mahāsudarśanāvadāna and the Mahāsudarśanasūtra*, Delhi: Sri Satguru.

Matsumura Junko 2008: "The Sumedhakathā in Pāli Literature: Summation of Theravāda-tradition Versions and Proof of Linkage to the Northern Textual Tradition", *Journal of Indian and Buddhist Studies*, 56.3: 1086–1094.

— 2010: "The Sumedhakathā in Pāli Literature and Its Relation to the Northern Buddhist Textual Tradition", *Journal of the International College for Postgraduate Buddhist Studies*, 14: 101–133.

— 2011: "An Independent sūtra on the Dīpaṃkara Prophecy", *Journal of the International College for Postgraduate Buddhist Studies*, 15: 81–141.

— 2012: "The Formation and Development of the Dīpaṃkara Prophecy Story", *Journal of Indian and Buddhist Studies*, 60.3: 80–89.

Mayeda Egaku 1985: "Japanese Studies on the Schools of the Chinese Āgamas", in *Zur Schulzugehörigkeit von Werken der Hīnayāna-Literatur, Erster Teil*, H. Bechert (ed.), 1: 94–103, Göttingen: Vandenhoeck & Ruprecht.

Meisig, Konrad 1987: *Das Śrāmaṇyaphala-sūtra: Synoptische Übersetzung und Glossar der chinesischen Fassungen verglichen mit dem Sanskrit und Pāli*, Wiesbaden: Harrassowitz.

— 1990: "Meditation (Dhyâna) in der ältesten buddhistischen Lehre", in *Ihr Alle Seid aber Brüder, Festschrift für A. Th. Khoury zum 60. Geburtstag*, L. Hagemann et al. (ed.), 541–554, Würzburg: Echter.

— 1993: "On the Archetype of the Ambāṣṭasūtra", *Wiener Zeitschrift für die Kunde Südasiens, Supplementband*, 229–237.

Melzer, Gudrun 2006: *Ein Abschnitt aus dem Dīrghāgama*, PhD thesis, Ludwig-Maximilians-Universität.

Monier-Williams, M. 1889/1995: *Buddhism in Its Connexion with Brahmanism and Hinduism, and in Its Contrast with Christianity*, Delhi: Munshiram Manoharlal.

— 1899/1999: *A Sanskrit-English Dictionary, Etymologically and Philologically Arranged, with Special Reference to Cognate Indo-European Languages*, Delhi: Motilal Banarsidass.

Mrozik, Susanne 2002: "The Value of Human Differences: South Asian Buddhist Contributions Toward an Embodied Virtue Theory", *Journal of Buddhist Ethics*, 9: 1–33.

— 2007: *Virtuous Bodies: The Physical Dimension of Morality in Buddhist Ethics*, New York: Oxford University Press.

Nakanishi Maiko and O. von Hinüber 2014: *Kanaganahalli Inscriptions, Supplement to the Annual Report of the International Research Institute for Advanced Buddhology at Soka University for the Academic Year 2013*, Tokyo: International Research Institute for Advanced Buddhology, Soka University.

Ñāṇamoli, Bhikkhu 1975/1991: *The Path of Purification (Visuddhimagga) by Bhadantācariya Buddhaghosa*, Kandy: Buddhist Publication Society.

— 1995/2005: *The Middle Length Discourses of the Buddha, A Translation of the Majjhima Nikāya*, Bhikkhu Bodhi (ed.), Boston: Wisdom Publications.

Ñāṇaponika Thera 1949/1985: *Abhidhamma Studies, Researches in Buddhist Psychology*, Kandy: Buddhist Publication Society.

— 1968/1986: *The Power of Mindfulness, An Inquiry into the Scope of Bare Attention and the Principal Sources of Its Strength*, Kandy: Buddhist Publication Society.

Nattier, Jan 2003: *A Few Good Men, The Bodhisattva Path According to The Inquiry of Ugra (Ugraparipṛcchā)*, Honolulu: University of Hawai'i Press.
— 2004: "Dīpaṃkara", in *Encyclopedia of Buddhism*, R.E. Buswell (ed.), 1: 230, New York: Macmillan.
Nitta Tomomichi 2008: "The Significance of the Thirty-two Lakkhaṇas of a Buddha", *Journal of Indian and Buddhist Studies*, 56.3: 1095–1101.
Norman, K.R. 2004: "On Translating the Suttanipāta", *Buddhist Studies Review*, 21.1: 69–84.
Nyanatiloka Mahāthera 1907/1984 (vol. 3): *Die Lehrreden des Buddha aus der Angereihten Sammlung*, Nyanaponika (ed.), Freiburg: Aurum Verlag.
Oberlies, Thomas 2003: "Ein bibliographischer Überblick über die kanonischen Texte der Śrāvakayāna-Schulen des Buddhismus (ausgenommen der des Mahāvihāra-Theravāda)", *Wiener Zeitschrift für die Kunde Südasiens*, 47: 37–84.
Olendski, Andrew 2011: "The Construction of Mindfulness", *Contemporary Buddhism*, 12.1: 55–70.
Olivelle, Patrick 2002: "Deconstruction of the Body in Indian Asceticism", in *Asceticism*, V.L. Wimbush and R. Valantasis (ed.), 188–210, New York: Oxford University Press.
Ospina, M.B., K. Bond, M. Karkaneh, L. Tjosvold, B. Vandermeer, Y. Liang, L. Bialy, N. Hooton, N. Buscemi, D.M. Dryden, and T.P. Klassen 2007: *Meditation Practices for Health: State of the Research. Evidence Report/Technology Assessment No. 155*, AHRQ Publication No. 07-E010. Rockville: Agency for Healthcare Research and Quality.
Pande, Govind Chandra 1957: *Studies in the Origins of Buddhism*, Allahabad: University of Allahabad, Department of Ancient History.

Pannasiri, Bhadanta 1950: "Sigālovāda-Sutta", *Visva-Bharati Annals*, 3: 150–228.

Park, Jungnok 2012: *How Buddhism Acquired a Soul on the Way to China*, Sheffield: Equinox.

Pāsādika, Bhikkhu 2009: "Āḷāra/Ārāḍa Kālāma et al. and some Disputed Points", in *Buddhist and Pali Studies in Honour of the Venerable Professor Kakkapalliye Anuruddha*, K.L. Dhammajoti and Y. Karunadasa (ed.), 89–96, Hong Kong: Centre of Buddhist Studies, University of Hong Kong.

Pitzer-Reyl, Renate 1984: *Die Frau im Frühen Buddhismus*, Berlin: Verlag von Dietrich Reimer.

Polak, Grzegorz 2011: *Reexamining jhāna: Towards a Critical Reconstruction of Early Buddhist Soteriology*, Lublin: Wydawnictwo UMCS.

— 2016: "How Was Liberating Insight Related to the Development of the Four jhānas in Early Buddhism? A New Perspective through an Interdisciplinary Approach", *Journal of the Oxford Centre for Buddhist Studies*, 10: 85–112.

Poonacha, K.P. 2011: *Excavations at Kanaganahalli (Sannati), Taluk Chitapur, Dist. Gulbarga, Karnataka*, New Delhi: Archaeological Survey of India.

Powers, John 2009: *A Bull of a Man, Images of Masculinity, Sex, and the Body in Indian Buddhism*, Cambridge: Harvard University Press.

Pradhan, Pralhad 1967: *Abhidharmakośabhāṣya of Vasubandhu*, Patna: K.P. Jayaswal Research Institute.

Quagliotti, Anna Maria 1998: *Buddhapadas, An Essay on the Representations of the Footprints of the Buddha with a Descriptive Catalogue of the Indian Specimens from the 2nd century B.C. to the 4th century A.D.*, Kamakura: Institute of the Silk Road Studies.

Radich, Michael David 2007: *The Somatics of Liberation: Ideas about Embodiment in Buddhism from Its Origins to the Fifth Century C.E.*, PhD thesis, Harvard University.

Rahula, Walpola 1971: "L'idéal du bodhisattva dans le Theravāda et le Mahāyāna", *Journal Asiatique*, 259: 63–70.

Ramers, Peter 1996: *Die 'drei Kapitel über die Sittlichkeit im Śrāmaṇyaphala-sūtra', Die Fassungen des Dīghanikāya und Saṃghabhedavastu, verglichen mit dem Tibetischen und Mongolischen*, PhD thesis, Rheinische Friedrich-Wilhelms-Universität.

Ratnayaka, Shanta 1985: "The Bodhisattva Ideal of the Theravāda", *Journal of the International Association of Buddhist Studies*, 8.2: 85–110.

Regnier, Rita H. 1997: "Les mains du Buddha dans la légende et dans l'iconographie de l'Inde ancienne", in *Recent Researches in Buddhist Studies, Essays in Honour of Professor Y. Karunadasa*, K.L. Dhammajoti et al. (ed.), 567–592, Colombo: Y. Karunadasa Felicitation Committee.

Rhys Davids, T.W. 1899 (vol. 1): *Dialogues of the Buddha, Translated from the Pāli of the Dīgha Nikāya*, London: Oxford University Press.

Rosenstreich, Eyal 2016: "Mindfulness and False-memories: The Impact of Mindfulness Practices on the DRM Paradigm", *The Journal of Psychology*, 150.1: 58–71.

Roth Gustav 1980: "Text of the Patna Dharmapada", in "Particular Features of the Language of the Ārya-Mahāsāṃghika-Lokottaravādins and Their Importance for Early Buddhist Tradition", in *The Language of the Earliest Buddhist Tradition*, H. Bechert (ed.), 93–135, Göttingen: Vandenhoeck & Ruprecht.

Saksena, Baburam 1936: "Pāli bhūnaha", *Bulletin of the School of Oriental and African Studies*, 8: 713–714.

Salomon, R. 2007: "Recent Discoveries of Early Buddhist Manuscripts and Their Implications for the History of Buddhist Texts and Canons", in *Between the Empires: Society in India 300 BCE to 400 CE*, P. Olivelle (ed.), 349–382, New York: Oxford University Press.

Samtani, N.H. 1971: *The Arthaviniścaya-sūtra & Its Commentary (Nibandhana), (Written by Bhikṣu Vīryaśrīdatta of Śrī-Nālandāvihāra), Critically Edited and Annotated for the First Time with Introduction and Several Indices*, Patna: K.P. Jayaswal Research Institute.

Samuels, Jeffrey 1997: "The Bodhisattva Ideal in Theravāda Buddhist Theory and Practice, A Reevaluation of the Bodhisattva-śrāvaka Opposition", *Philosophy East and West*, 47.3: 399–415 (reprinted 2013 in *The Bodhisattva Ideal, Essays on the Emergence of Mahāyāna*, Bhikkhu Nyanatusita (ed.), 31–50, Kandy: Buddhist Publication Society).

Sastri, K.A. Nilakanta 1940: "Cakravartin", *New Indian Antiquary*, 3: 307–321.

Schlingloff, Dieter 1964: *Ein buddhistisches Yogalehrbuch*, Berlin: Akademie Verlag.

— 1981: "Erzählung und Bild: Die Darstellungsformen von Handlungsabläufen in der europäischen und indischen Kunst", *Beiträge zur Allgemeinen und Vergleichenden Archäologie*, 3: 87–213.

Schmidt, Stefan 2011: "Mindfulness in East and West – Is It the Same?", in *Neuroscience, Consciousness and Spirituality*, H. Walach et al. (ed.), 23–38, Dordrecht: Springer.

Schmithausen, Lambert 1981: "On Some Aspects of Descriptions or Theories of 'Liberating Insight' and 'Enlightenment' in Early Buddhism", in *Studien zum Jainismus und Buddhismus, Gedenkschrift für Ludwig Alsdorf*, K. Bruh and A. Wezler. (ed.), 199–250, Wiesbaden: Franz Steiner.

— 1987: "Beiträge zur Schulzugehörigkeit und Textgeschichte kanonischer und postkanonischer buddhistischer Materialien", in *Zur Schulzugehörigkeit von Werken der Hīnayāna-Literatur, Zweiter Teil*, H. Bechert (ed.), 2: 304–403, Göttingen: Vandenhoeck & Ruprecht.

— 2000: "Mitleid und Leerheit, Zu Spiritualität und Heilsziel des Mahāyāna", in *Der Buddhismus als Anfrage an christliche Theologie und Philosophie*, A. Bsteh (ed.), 437–455, Mödling: St. Gabriel.

— 2012: "Achtsamkeit 'innen', 'außen' und 'innen wie außen'", in *Achtsamkeit, Ein buddhistisches Konzept erobert die Wissenschaft, mit einem Beitrag S.H. des Dalai Lama*, M. Zimmerman, C. Spitz, and S. Schmidt (ed.), 291–303, Bern: Hans Huber Verlag.

— 2013: "Kuśala and akuśala, Reconsidering the Original Meaning of a Basic Pair of Terms of Buddhist Spirituality and Ethics and Its Development up to Early Yogācāra", in *The Foundation for Yoga Practitioners, The Buddhist Yogācārabhūmi Treatise and Its Adaptation in India, East Asia, and Tibet*, U.T. Kragh (ed.), 440–495, Cambridge: Harvard University Press.

Schopen, Gregory 1985: "Two Problems in the History of Indian Buddhism, The Layman/Monk Distinction and the Doctrines of the Transference of Merit", *Studien zur Indologie und Iranistik*, 10: 9–47.

Senart, Émile 1882: *Essai sur la légende du Buddha, son caractère et ses origines*, Paris: Ernest Leroux.

— 1890 (vol. 2) and 1897 (vol. 3): *Le Mahāvastu, texte sanscrit publié pour la première fois et accompagné d'introductions et d'un commentaire*, Paris: Imprimerie Nationale.

— 1900: "Bouddhisme et yoga", *Revue de l'Histoire des Religions*, 42: 345–364.

Sferra, Francesco 2008: "Appendix: Kośagatavastiguhyatā", in *South Asian Archaeology 1999, Proceedings of the Fifteenth International Conference of the European Association of South Asian Archaeologists held at the Universiteit Leiden, 5–9 July, 1999*, E.M. Raven (ed.), 9–13, Groningen: Egbert Forstein.

— 2011: "Tecniche di composizione del canone Pāli, trasmissione e construzione del sapere nel buddhismo Theravāda", in *L'insegnamento delle technai nelle culture antiche, Atti del Convegno Ercolano, 23–24 marzo 2009*, A. Roselli and R. Velardi (ed.), 95–107, Pisa: Fabrizio Serra.

Shah, Umakant P. 1987: *Jaina-Rūpa-Maṇḍana (Jaina Iconography)*, Delhi: Abhinav Publications.

Shankman, Richard 2008: *The Experience of samādhi, An Indepth Exploration of Buddhist Meditation*, Boston: Shambala.

Shukla, Karunesha 1973 (vol. 1): *Śrāvakabhūmi of Ācārya Asaṅga*, Patna: K.P. Jayaswal Research Institute.

Shulman, Eviatar 2010: "Mindful Wisdom, The Sati-paṭṭhānasutta on Mindfulness, Memory and Liberation", *History of Religions*, 49.4: 393–420.

— 2014: *Rethinking the Buddha, Early Buddhist Philosophy as Meditative Perception*, Cambridge University Press.

Silk, Jonathan A. 2002: "What, if Anything, Is Mahāyāna Buddhism? Problems of Definitions and Classifications", *Numen*, 49: 355–405.

Silverlock, Blair 2009: *An Edition, Translation and Study of the Bodha-sūtra from the Manuscript of the Gilgit Dīrghāgama of the (Mūla-)Sarvāstivādins*, BA thesis, University of Sydney.

Skilling, Peter 1981: "Uddaka Rāmaputta and Rāma", *Pāli Buddhist Review*, 6: 99–104.

— 1992: "Symbols on the Body, Feet, and Hands of a Buddha, Part I – Lists", *The Journal of the Siam Society*, 80.2: 67–79.

— 1993: "Theravādin Literature in Tibetan Translation", *Journal of the Pali Text Society*, 19: 69–201.

— 1994 (vol. 1): *Mahāsūtras: Great Discourses of the Buddha*, Oxford: Pali Text Society.

— 1996: "Symbols on the Body, Feet, and Hands of a Buddha, Part II – Short Lists", *The Journal of the Siam Society*, 84.1: 5–28.

— 2003: "Three Types of Bodhisatta in Theravādin Tradition, A Bibliographical Excursion", in *Buddhist and Indian Studies in Honour of Professor Sodo Mori*, 91–102, Hamamatsu: Kokusai Bukkyoto Kyokai.

— 2013: "Vaidalya, Mahāyāna, and Bodhisatva in India: An Essay towards Historical Understanding", in *The Bodhisattva Ideal, Essays on the Emergence of Mahāyāna*, Bhikkhu Nyanatusita (ed.), 69–162, Kandy: Buddhist Publication Society.

Somaratne, G.A. 1998: *The Saṃyuttanikāya of the Suttapiṭaka, Volume I, the Sagāthavagga*, Oxford: Pali Text Society.

— 2003: "The Sutta Pericope of 'the Cessation' and Its Interpretation", *Journal of the Centre for Buddhist Studies, Sri Lanka*, 1: 207–228.

— 2006: "Saññāvedayitanirodha", in *Encyclopaedia of Buddhism*, W.G. Weeraratne (ed.), 7.4: 742–750, Sri Lanka: Department of Buddhist Affairs.

Soothill, William Edward and L. Hodous 1937/2000: *A Dictionary of Chinese Buddhist Terms, with Sanskrit and English Equivalents and a Sanskrit-Pali Index*, Delhi: Motilal Banarsidass.

Śrāvakabhūmi Study Group 1998: *Śrāvakabhūmi, Revised Sanskrit Text and Japanese Translation, the First Chapter*, Tokyo: Sankibo.

Stache-Rosen, Valentina 1968: *Dogmatische Begriffsreihen im älteren Buddhismus II; Das Saṅgītisūtra und sein Kommentar Saṅgītiparyāya*, Berlin: Akademie Verlag

Strong, John S. 2001: *The Buddha, A Short Biography*, Oxford: Oneworld.

Stuart, Daniel M. 2013: *Thinking about Cessation: The Pṛṣṭhapālasūtra of the Dīrghāgama in Context*, Wien: Arbeitskreis für Tibetische und Buddhistische Studien, Universität Wien.

Stuart-Fox, Martin 1989: "Jhāna and Buddhist Scholasticism", *Journal of the International Association of Buddhist Studies*, 12.2: 79–110.

Stutterheim, W.F. 1929: "Le jālalakṣaṇa de l'image du Bouddha", *Acta Orientalia*, 7: 232–237.

Sujato, Bhikkhu 2001: *A Swift Pair of Messengers*, Penang: Inward Path.

— 2005: *A History of Mindfulness, How Insight Worsted Tranquility in the Satipatthana sutta*, Taipei: Corporate Body of the Buddha Educational Foundation.

Swearer, Donald K. 1972: "Two Types of Saving Knowledge in the Pāli suttas", *Philosophy East and West*, 22.4: 355–371.

Syinchen Shi 2010: *Issues in śamatha and vipaśyanā: A Comparative Study of Buddhist Meditation*, PhD thesis, University of the West.

Tambiah, S.J. 1976: *World Conqueror and World Renouncer, A Study of Buddhism and Polity in Thailand Against a Historical Background*, Cambridge: Cambridge University Press.

Ṭhānissaro, Bhikkhu 2012: *Right Mindfulness, Memory & Ardency on the Buddhist Path*, California: Metta Forest Monastery.

Tournier, Vincent 2012: "The Mahāvastu and the Vinayapiṭaka of the Mahāsāṃghika-Lokottaravādins", *Annual Report of the International Research Institute for Advanced Buddhology at Soka University*, 15: 87–104.

van Lohuizen-de Leeuw, Johanna Engelberta 1995: *The 'Scythian' Period, An Approach to the History, Art, Epigraphy and Palaeography of Northern India From the 1st Century B.C. to the 3rd Century A.D.*, Delhi: Munshiram Manoharlal.

van Oosterwijk, R.C. 2012: *Doctrinal Backgrounds of Vipassanā-meditation, Insight in Current Methods and According to Canonical Sources*, Groningen: Barkhuis.

van Vugt, Marieke K. 2015: "Cognitive Benefits of Mindfulness Meditation", in *Handbook of Mindfulness: Theory, Research, and Practice*, K.W. Brown, J.D. Creswell, and R.M. Ryan (ed.), 190–207, New York: Guilford.

Vetter, Tilmann 1988: *The Ideas and Meditative Practices of Early Buddhism*, Leiden: Brill.

— 2000: *The 'Khandha Passages' in the Vinayapiṭaka and the Four Main Nikāyas*, Wien: Österreichische Akademie der Wissenschaften.

von Rospatt, Alexander 1995: *The Buddhist Doctrine of Momentariness: A Survey of the Origins and Early Phase of This Doctrine up to Vasubandhu*, Stuttgart: Franz Steiner Verlag.

von Simson, Georg 1965: *Zur Diktion einiger Lehrtexte des buddhistischen Sanskritkanons*, München: J. Kitzinger.

Waddell, L.A. 1914/1915: "Buddha's Diadem or 'uṣṇīṣa', Its Origin, Nature and Functions, A Study of Buddhist Origins", *Ostasiatische Zeitschrift, Beiträge zur Kenntnis der Kultur und Kunst des Fernen Ostens*, 3: 131–168.

Waldschmidt, Ernst 1930: "Die Entwicklungsgeschichte des Buddhabildes in Indien", *Ostasiatische Zeitschrift*, 6.6: 265–277.

— 1950 (vol. 1) and 1951 (vol. 2): *Das Mahāparinirvāṇasūtra, Text in Sanskrit und tibetisch, verglichen mit dem Pāli nebst einer Übersetzung der chinesischen Entsprechung im Vinaya der Mūlasarvāstivādins, auf Grund von Turfan-Handschriften herausgegeben und bearbeitet*, Berlin: Akademie Verlag.

— 1980: "Central Asian sūtra Fragments and Their Relation to the Chinese Āgamas", in *The Language of the Earliest Buddhist Tradition*, H. Bechert (ed.), 136–174, Göttingen: Vandenhoeck & Ruprecht.

Waldschmidt Ernst, W. Clawiter, and L. Sander-Holzmann 1968: *Sanskrithandschriften aus den Turfanfunden Teil II*, Wiesbaden: Franz Steiner.

Walters, William H. 2012: "New Light on Enlightenment: A Convergence of Recent Scholarship and Emerging Neuroscience?", *Journal of the Oxford Centre for Buddhist Studies*, 3: 157–176.

Wangchuk, Dorji 2007: *The Resolve to Become a Buddha, A Study of the bodhicitta Concept in Indo-Tibetan Buddhism*, Tokyo: International Institute for Buddhist Studies.

Wayman, Alex 1961: *Analysis of the Śrāvakabhūmi Manuscript*, Berkeley: University of California Press.

Weber, Claudia 1994: *Wesen und Eigenschaften des Buddha in der Tradition des Hīnayāna Buddhismus*, Wiesbaden: Harrassowitz.

Weeratunge, S. 2004: "The Use of Word-repetition in Pāli Canonical Texts – A Brief Study of Its Historical Background", *Journal of the Centre for Buddhist Studies, Sri Lanka*, 2: 135–143.

Weller, Friedrich 1934: *Brahmajālasūtra, tibetischer und mongolischer Text*, Leipzig: Harrassowitz.

Wille, Klaus 2008: *Sanskrithandschriften aus den Turfanfunden, Teil 10*, Stuttgart: Franz Steiner.

Willemen, Charles 2008: "Kumārajīva's 'Explanatory Discourse' about Abhidharmic Literature", *Journal of the International College for Postgraduate Buddhist Studies*, 12: 37–83.

Wilson, Liz 2004: "Body, Perspectives on the", in *Encyclopedia of Buddhism*, R.E. Buswell (ed.), 1: 63–66, New York: Macmillan.

Wiltshire, Martin G. 1990: *Ascetic Figures Before and In Early Buddhism, The Emergence of Gautama as the Buddha*, Berlin: Mouton de Gruyter.

Wimalaratana, Bellanwilla 1994 (?): *Concept of Great Man (Mahāpurisa) in Buddhist Literature and Iconography*, Singapore: Buddhist Research Society.

Wüst, Walther 1928: "Das Leibesproblem in der buddhistische Pālilyrik", *Zeitschrift für Buddhismus und verwandte Gebiete*, 8: 62–85.

Wynne, Alexander 2002: "An Interpretation of 'Released on Both Sides' (ubhato-bhāga-vimutti), and the Ramifications for the Study of Early Buddhism", *Buddhist Studies Review*, 19.1: 31–40.

— 2007: *The Origin of Buddhist Meditation*, London: Routledge.

Yamabe Nobuyoshi 1999: *The Sūtra on the Ocean-like Samādhi of the Visualization of the Buddha: The Interfusion of the Chinese and Indian Cultures in Central Asia as Re-*

flected in a Fifth Century Apocryphal Sūtra, PhD thesis, Yale University.

Zafiropulo, Ghiorgo 1993: *L'illumination du Buddha, de la quête à l'annonce de l'éveil, essais de chronologie relative et de stratigraphie textuelle*, Innsbruck: Institut für Sprachwissenschaft der Universität Innsbruck.

Zin, Monika 2003: "The uṣṇīsa as a Physical Characteristic of the Buddha's Relatives and Successors", *Silk Road Art and Archaeology*, 9: 107–129.

Index

B

C

I

J

K

L

M

N

P

R

S

About the Barre Center for Buddhist Studies

The Barre Center for Buddhist Studies is a non-profit educational organization dedicated to exploring Buddhist thought and practice as a living tradition, faithful to its origins, yet adaptable to the current world. The Center, located in Barre, Massachusetts, offers residential and online courses combining study, discussion, and meditation for the purpose of deepening personal practice while building and supporting communities of like-minded practitioners. Our programming is rooted in the classical Buddhist tradition of the earliest teachings and practices, but calls for dialogue with other schools of Buddhism and with other academic fields—and with each other. All courses support both silent meditation practice and critical, dialogical investigation of the teachings.

BCBS was founded in 1991 by teachers at Insight Meditation Society (IMS), including Joseph Goldstein and Sharon Salzberg, and is connected to both IMS and the Forest Refuge by trails through the woods.

BCBS is committed to cultivating a community that reflects the diversity of our society and our world. We seek to promote the inclusion, equity and participation of people of diverse identities so that all may feel welcome, safe, and respected within this community. Find out more about our mission, our programs, and sign up for our free monthly e-newsletter at www.bcbsdharma.org.

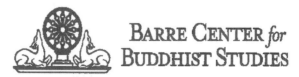

41797753R00151

Made in the USA
Middletown, DE
24 March 2017